TRANSCULTURATION

THE CULTURAL FACTOR IN TRANSLATION AND OTHER COMMUNICATION TASKS

R. DANIEL SHAW

William Carey Library

PASADENA, CALIFORNIA

Published by
William Carey Library
Post Office Box 40129
1705 North Sierra Bonita Avenue
Pasadena, California 91104

ISBN 0-87808-216-6
LC# 88-071335

Cover disign by Mary Lou Totten
Type preparation by Dataprose, Seattle, Washington

Printed in the United States of America

To my wife, Karen,
and my three sons,
Rick, Rob and Ryan

Together we shared the experiences
that make this book possible.

Edited By
Leilani Leaño
and
Stephen Niyang

CONTENTS

PART I
Toward Discovering Culture

PART II
Toward Appreciating Culture

PART III
Toward Transculturation

FOREWORD

During the past thirty years, great strides have been made in the theory of linguistics. They have tremendously affected the theory and practice of translation. A translator was once simply a person who knew two languages and somehow managed to take a text in one of those languages and produce a text in the other. The results were sometimes good, but often not so good. As scholars became interested in the application of linguistic theories to the translation process, a whole new field developed—a field which is just now being taken seriously in college and university programs.

Translation is not only a formal linguistic matter; it is intimately related to everyday life and culture, into the total worldview of the people who speak the source and receptor languages. From the beginning of his work on translation theory, Nida stressed the cultural aspects of translation. Similarly, Beekman and Callow have discussed the impact of the source language and the receptor language cultures on the decisions to be made by the translator in choosing lexical equivalents in the translation. In my own recent book on translation, I devote a chapter to the communication situation, including the cultural context. The importance of the relationship between anthropology and translation has been acknowledged by those working in translation theory throughout the development of the theory.

However, Dr. Shaw, in this book, has shown us many ways in which we can bring the work of the two disciplines together. He points out the importance of worldview studies as part of the translation task. These studies are not to be confined to studies of the receptor language culture, but must also include the source language culture and the cultures of translators themselves. Translation is taking a message given in one culture and language and expressing it in such a way that it will be the same message in another language and culture. Dr. Shaw helps the reader to see this clearly by the use of many illustrations presented along with his discussion.

I am convinced that this book will force us all to give more attention to the relationship between anthropology and translation. It will open areas of research that will in the end affect both disciplines in positive ways, because it has identified the matters on which research is needed. One of my hopes is that it will inspire anthropologists to study, not just receptor language cultures, but to aid in understanding the Biblical cultures of both Old and New Testaments even as Dr. Shaw is suggesting here.

The emphasis of the book is on the application of anthropological methods to the task of translation. It will be of great interest to all teachers and students of translation. Similarly, missionaries, pastors, and all who need to understand and appreciate the context into which the Scriptures were presented and must "translate" them into another reality (whatever that may be) will find the principles developed in this book very useful. Dr. Shaw is to be applauded for this excellent presentation, a framework useful in relating future research on cultural matters to the translation task. It is also an encouragement for us all to look more carefully at the importance of anthropological issues in relation to the Word. It serves as a foundation for ongoing research in this newly developing field.

Mildred L. Larson
International Translation Coordinator
Summer Institute of Linguistics
Dallas, December 1986

PREFACE

This book is an attempt to apply anthropological insight to communication principles. Its purpose is to help communicators who are not anthropologists present the gospel (including translated Scripture) effectively within a specific culture. This material is designed to (1) create a greater appreciation for the cultural context into which the source text was communicated, and (2) transfer that understanding so that modern receptors can appreciate the meaning of the text and apply it to their own cultural context. Therefore, I seek to develop a *transcultural methodology* that will ensure better communication, more understandable translations. Transculturation is to the cultural aspects of communication what translation to the linguistic aspects of our discipline. This then is a resource book, a guide for discovering the cultural factors that affect the communication process.

Many of the ideas, techniques, and processes presented in this book come out of extensive field experience as a Bible translator with the Samo, a small people group in the Western Province of Papua New Guinea. In my role as an international anthropology consultant with the Summer Institute of Linguistics (SIL), I have had numerous opportunities to assist translators struggling with cultural issues. These experiences are reflected in many of the suggestions made throughout the book. I express my appreciation to the many translators and students who have raised the issues and sought answers with me. All have contributed substantially to this book.

The publication costs for this book were made available by the Tyndale House Foundation. Their interaction with Living Bibles International and its translation potential around the world provide an admirable example of the interdependence encouraged in chapter 17. Their assistance in this project is gratefully acknowledged.

As with any project of this sort, there are many who have made a substantial contribution. My wife, Karen has spent countless hours listening to me as well as reading through the manuscript. Fran Popovich, my research assistant and SIL colleague, painstakingly looked up references, read the manuscript, and made valuable suggestions as did my teaching assistants Brian Bailey, Jennifer Dilliha and Arden Sanders. Dulcie Grant, my secretary at the School of World Mission, did much of the typing, while Georgia Grimes, a student, translator and friend, did the detail work necessary to produce the manuscript. Two graduate students and translators, Leilani Leaño (Philippines) and Stephen Niyang (Nigeria), edited the material to ensure acceptability to an international audience as well as expatriates seeking to apply these concepts to cross-cultural interaction. They reflect the increasing internationalization of our discipline. Finally, I thank Millie Larson for her contribution, both to this book and to the discipline we share.

R.D.S.
Pasadena
November 1987

INTRODUCTION

BIBLE TRANSLATION: A TRANSCULTURAL EXPERIENCE

Mary is poring over a stack of books, exegeting Ephesians chapter 6. Reflecting on sermons she has heard, she knows the focus here is on the "whole armor of God". The armor is necessary to fight the spiritual battle. In the midst of this deliberation a commotion outside distracts her. People are shouting as a lifeless body is carried into the village. Amid wailing and tears of grief Mary is told that the woman has just been killed by marauding spirits while working in her garden. Can this be true? Can there be actual spirits that would physically destroy a living human being? Surely the woman simply had a heart attack. Mary mumbles something about the comfort of the believer and the grieving relatives take the body to the house. Shocked by what she has seen and heard, Mary returns to her books to examine the exegesis and ponder the reality of these people who so need God's Word. Could this passage be dealing with something more than spiritual warfare in the heavens and apply to people in life and death relationships between themselves and their world?

This hypothetical translator[1] is experiencing the reality of a cultural clash: the clash between the perspective of her own unquestioned culture and that held by the people she so desperately wants to reach with the gospel. For Mary, the spirits are but mere representations of a spiritual force that God relates to; there is no direct human involvement because, to her knowledge, she has never encountered spirits personally. Her experience does not prepare her for what she has seen. To the mourners, the spirit world is a reality they must deal with on a daily basis and this death is further evidence of that reality. How will the translator handle Eph. 6? How will the recipients interpret the passage? If they are to receive God's Word as He intended, Mary must understand three things: (1) what the Apostle Paul meant as he penned this well-known passage—including his cultural perspective and that of the Ephesians, (2) Mary's own predisposed

1

cultural bias, and (3) the perspecive of the people for whom Mary is translating.

Three cultures are interacting here: (1) the New Testament Greco-Roman culture, (2) the translator's culture and (3) the receptor culture. This cultural mix sets up what, throughout this book, is called the *communication or translation context*. Each component in this context needs to be clearly understood by all who desire to engage in communicating the gospel with a minimum amount of cultural skewing. Translation is the effective repackaging of the original meaning in a form necessary to ensure the same meaning is communicated with more or less the same impact for those who now receive it for the first time (Nida & Reyburn 1982:32). Thus translation includes the necessity for incorporating cultural context, i.e. *transculturation* is part of the communication process.

How people receive God's message will depend, to a large extent, on how well the communicator understands the source cultural forms and meanings and how well those are presented within the cultural context of the receptors. A successful transfer of meaning depends largely on how well communicators understand their own worldview with respect to both the source and receptor. Bible translators must consciously attempt to communicate the original message without the trappings of their own cultural bias. Of course, when the translator is from the receptor culture, the translation context is simplified.

Bible translators have long been aware of the linguistic component in the translation process. Study of the original languages and the importance of speaking and understanding the linguistic structure of the receptor language have been hallmarks of successful translation (Beekman 1965). It has always been clear that translations must speak correctly in order to be properly understood. The part culture plays in bringing understanding of original meaning into the new cultural situation has not been understood as well. Without question, just as a translation must talk right it must also act right in order for people to understand the message (Loewen 1971, Headland 1974).

Recall Mary's trauma as she attempted to rationalize her own perspective about spiritual forces with that of a people who obviously believe these forces strongly affect daily life. What, in fact, was the Apostle saying in his original context? How did the Ephesians understand the spirit world? What would they have understood Paul to mean when they heard/read this letter for the first time? Could that understanding be similar to the perception of the people who are mourning their relative's death? Might not this spiritual warfare be a factor in the human response to Christ who made all things seen and unseen (Col. 1:16)? Correctly translated, this passage could give hope to the mourners who need to know that God is stronger than marauding spirits. This message of hope could be the key that unlocks the hearts of these people for Christ. It could give them renewed hope of salvation from their immediate fears and an understanding of themselves in relation to a loving God who has provided a way of escape that can give them eternal life. Cultural understanding is the key to God's Word clearly communicating its intended meaning so receptors not only understand the message, but act upon it to end their search for salvation. Only then can they come into the light of the glorious gospel, not "just listening to His word, [but] putting it into practice" (Jas. 1:22).[2]

AN OVERVIEW OF THE BOOK

The book opens with a discussion of a Biblical approach to culture that sets the tone for what follows. This is more than an apologetic; it establishes the context out of which the concepts and principles presented can be discussed.

The book is divided into three major sections: (1) discovering the cultural sub-systems that affect every context, (2) appreciating the cultural contexts that give meaning to each society reflected in the communication process, and (3) developing a transcultural approach in order to communicate effectively.

Toward Discovering Culture

The sub-systems that pertain to any culture are dealt with in five short chapters. The world does not need another anthropology text book, even from a Christian perspective; many already exist (Grunlan and Mayers 1979, Hiebert 1985, Nida 1954, etc.). The focus here is on the culture concept and its impact upon communicating the gospel in general and Bible translation in particular. By developing the 'three cultures model' and relating that to an understanding of communication principles and the cultural sub-systems, a theoretical perspective is developed which can help all communicators apply basic anthropological techniques to their minisitry. How is culture reflected in the original autographs and their translation? What must communicators know about their own cultures in order to eliminate cultural bias as much as possible? How can translators study culture so that relevance is communicated in the translated 'word' without jeopardizing the 'truth' of the original? These are the concerns of this book; developing a cultural sensitivity which will affect the meaning of the message, whatever form of communication is used.

One objective of this book is to encourage readers to develop an attitude of putting receptors first and carefully considering the source with respect to the intended meaning of the message. This approach encourages cross-cultural witnesses to consider their own cultural values as they develop an understanding of the source and the receptor contexts. Mono-cultural communicators must carefully consider the source context and apply it to their own. It is this total awareness of interacting cultural presuppositions that forms the concept behind this book, not anthropological principles as such. However, anthropology provides the vehicle for understanding the complexities of the total communication/translation context.[3]

These chapters are followed by a discussion of culture as a system, a worldview that integrates all aspects such that change in one area will affect all other parts of the system. This is not a new idea but a very important one for communicators whose work, it is hoped, will effect a change of allegiance in the receptors.

Toward Appreciating Culture

This section relates the principles of Section I to each of the three societies that make up the translation context: Biblical societies, receptor societies and the translator's own society (when that is different). Each represents a cultural system: ideas, values, behavior and patterns, that reflect different meanings or worldviews. It is not intended that this book detail the Hebrew or the Greco-Roman cultures. Much has been written on these cultures that is well documented (Bailey 1983, Booth 1933, de Vaux 1961, Edersheim 1976, Meeks 1983, Rogerson 1979, and Wilson 1977, to name only a few). The intent here is to acknowledge the effect of culture on the meaning the original authors intended, and the futility of communicating Biblical principles without appreciating the context into which those principles were originally set. If communicators are outsiders to the receptor context it is necessary to have a wide sphere of common experience in that culture (Dye 1980: 81ff). Without making this effort, they are at the mercy of their assistants' understanding of a passage (including the linguistic and cultural implications) and can never be sure what is really being communicated.

Finally, a keen sense of cultural self-awareness is critical to successful communication both cross-culturally and mono-culturally. As translators know and understand their own window on reality, they can consciously make adjustments and predict trouble spots that will demand special care. Such cultural awareness can have a dramatic effect on the translation process as well as the results.

Toward Transculturation

Applying the culture concept to exegesis, translation, and the communication of the gospel is an essential conclusion to the progressive development of the book. These principles assist the communicator in applying a cultural awareness to the entire translation process. So much of what has been shrouded in the mist of implied information is cultural in nature. Much of the imagery of figures of speech is culturally-based. Even the linguistic structure of a language may, as Pike has suggested, be better understood if cultural factors are applied (Pike 1967). Effective communication takes place when made relevant to people's assumptions, within their conceptual framework. The translator's awareness of these concepts and the possible effects of Scripture upon them can ensure a much more dynamic translation (Shaw and Kraft 1983). That translation, in turn, should fit into the life of the church, become a tool for evangelism and the foundation for Christian growth.

THE NEXT STEP

In light of international developments and the changing political scene around the world, a nagging question surfaces. If culture is so important to the communication task, and the perspective of the translator has such an effect on the communicated meaning of the message, could it be that expatriate translators are not the best primary translators?[4] The corollary follows; if expatriates should not be primary translators, who can, or will? If nationals should be the primary translators how should they be trained and what effect might such a change in methodology have upon the world-wide strategy of missions? Such questions are increasingly being asked (especially by people of the so-called third world) and demand an answer. Wherever possible, expatriates should encourage national translators and ensure they receive the necessary training to understand the Biblical background and communicate the Scriptures within a context meaningful to their own people. This book attempts to serve as a bridge in that process. It is designed for use by both expatriates seeking to discover another culture and for mono-cultural communicators seeking to make Scripture relevant to their own people.

This does not imply that expatriate translators are no longer needed or are a burden to the national church. Rather their job, like that of missionaries in general, has changed to one of training, consulting, and encouraging nationals as they do the job; providing a technical expertise otherwise unavailable. In those areas where levels of education are insufficient to warrant local translation projects, outsiders can begin work with the intention of preparing local translators to take over as they are able. This is a significant departure from the more traditional approach, but once the primary translator is a member of the receptor group, one cultural link is removed. Having made this shift, the emphasis can be placed on providing the Biblical, cultural and translation principles necessary to help nationals communicate the message in their own context. National translators, no matter how well trained, still need Biblical materials as well as the fellowship of expatriate specialists. We need to all work together as a body for the glory of our Lord.

This book is an attempt to take Scripture seriously, under-stand the cultural implications of God's communication to human beings in all contexts, and apply that to the effective communica-tion of the Good News, whatever form it takes. These cultural concerns relate directly to understanding Biblical meaning and they demand an integration of anthropology and Biblical study in a new way—understanding the context of the text. This leads to a new methodology—a transcultural approach to the communica-tion task. The goal is people in every language and culture who can appreciate and know God and the reality of His love within their own frame of reference: transculturation. To that end this book is written.

Notes

1. All references to translators reflect the focus of this book. Most of the principles, however, relate to the much broader arena of communica-tion of the gospel. Thus 'translator' is used almost synonymously with 'communicator' in the hope that readers will apply the concepts to their specific ministry. The basic principles necessary for Bible translation are broadly relevant for all forms of cross-cultural inter-

action, and it is hoped that this book will be read and utilized by that broader audience. With the growing internationalization of missions, people working outside of their National context are herein referred to as 'expatriates'. However, the problems of nationals working cross-culturally within their national cultural region and expatriates coming from outside that context are very similar and are not distinguished in this book. Where necessary, 'expatriate' and 'national' communicators are contrasted and the specific differences pointed out. The focus is on the impact of culture upon understanding the Biblical message and how to turn that into the gospel communicating the eternal Word in human forms: linguistic and cultural.

2. All Scripture quotes used in this book are taken from the United Bible Society's *Good News Bible* unless otherwise indicated. *Today's English Version* (TEV), as it is known world-wide, is intended for an international audience and is widely used throughout the world today. In keeping with this international perspective, the version is used here.

3. Many of the details of cultural relationship to communication and, especially Bible translation, are very much in the developmental phase. This is a new field and much research is currently in progress. This means, however, that readers should seek for ways to implement the concepts in their particular ministry. The focus is on discovering what people do and say not on a particular anthropological theory or argument. More advanced readers may find this approach unsophisticated anthropologically, but it should assist missionaries and translators in discovering the Biblical cultures and the meanings people attach to their own cultural forms. These will often be very different from each other. Yet understanding these forms and their meanings is essential to the communication of the message we bring, for without them the message has no meaning at all. This book is an attempt to integrate cultural studies, translation theory and the communication process. It is an attempt to develop a network of interaction within which approaches for communicating the gospel can be developed.

4. As detailed in chapter 17, there are a wide range of translation programs in existence in the world today. Traditional programs in which an expatriate translator learns the language and culture of a people group and then works closely with individuals of that group to produce a translation are still the most common type and represent what most people in the 'Western' church think of when discussing Bible translation. As presented in chapter 12 these individuals minister at an E_3 level and represent the greatest communicational distance. Nationals who communicate with people of their own or similar cultural background may serve as mother-tongue-translators (E_1 level communication) or other-tongue-translators working with people in their own country (E_2 level communication). See chapter 12 for details of these definitions.

CHAPTER ONE
A Biblical Perspective of Culture

THE CREATION AND CULTURE

Before the world was created, the Word already existed; he was with God, and he was the same as God. From the very beginning the Word was with God. Through him God made all things; not one thing in all creation was made without him. The Word was the source of life, and this life brought light to mankind (Jn. 1:1-4).

God made all things through His Word. The Word is the source of all life as well as everything including the entire universe. As a Bible translator, I like to think of the creation as the first translation. God spoke and things happened—the world came into being. That which resulted from God's words is a manifestation of what God meant as He spoke (Gen 1:3ff). The light, land, living beings and all else reflected the substance of God's word; His word had meaning and the substance of that meaning tells us something about the creator. The words were conceived in God's mind and are communicated to us through the creation which human beings, affected by culture, perceive in a wide variety of ways. God created the human perceptive apparatus, but the way people perceive the reality of the world around them (REALITY with a capitol "R" from God's view) varies greatly from society to society (reality with a small "r" from a human perspective).

Social scientists seek to understand people and observe their behavior patterns. By formulating questions they strive to understand what is important in order to appreciate the meaning of observed behavior in a particular context. Similarly, we can observe what God did and through this general revelation come to appreciate His work. Through special revelation the specific acts of a God who cares about His creation and all that is in it are made known to us. Thus God's meaning to people with a

9

particular cultural perspective is available to them through the
creation (Rom. 1:18-20). However, their understanding of that
meaning, translated to them through what they can perceive, is
highly variable and requires the rest of Scripture—a dynamic
reason for the world-wide Bible translation explosion taking place
today. People need to understand the way God provided for a
restored relationship with Himself as well as how human beings
should interact with others. Scripture reveals this dynamic of
relationship to God through Jesus Christ: the Word made flesh.

Human beings are the crown of all creation. God views them
as having infinite worth and dignity in every aspect of their
created being. And they were given dominion over all the rest of
creation:

> What is man, that you think of him; mere man, that you care for
> him? Yet you made him inferior only to yourself; you crowned
> him with glory and honor. You appointed him ruler over
> everything you made; you placed him over all creation: sheep
> and cattle, and the wild animals too; the birds and the fish and
> the creatures in the seas (Ps. 8:4-8).

The creation narrative describes people as being created in
the *image of God*. At creation humans were endowed with
supremely unique attributes. The image of God in humanity
"indicates, first, a purpose of God for man, and, second, a quality
of man's existence" (Cairns 1953:52). This must not be miscon-
strued as an essential being in and of the human self, but rather
pointing beyond mere human attributes to a living, dynamic
relationship between the creator and the creature—the source and
the receptor. Thus the real being of humanity does not consist in
a sum of attributes, but in a relationship.

Perhaps this is reflected in human relationships which are
epitomized in the interaction patterns between kin in small scale,
face-to-face societies. The social sciences have adequately demonstrated that personhood can exist only as individuals interact with
other individuals in a social context. For this we were created, not
only for interpersonal relationships with other human beings as
important as they may be, but also for personal interaction with a
creating God who made us in His own image (Gen. 3:8,9).

The Law that God gave to Moses, focused on this whole area
of relationship. The first four commandments emphasized the
God-human relationship: who God is, worship only the true God,
do not abuse the relationship and worship regularly. Commandments 5 - 10 deal with relationships on the human level: honor

parents, commit no murder, adultery or theft, tell no lies, and desire not what others have (Ex. 20:1-17). Throughout the world, we see these considerations prominent in cultural ideals, codes of ethics, and emphases on smooth interpersonal relationships. But how they are manifested in specific behavior patterns is a product of cultural variation. Christ himself summed up the law with respect to these two sets of relationship: Godward and toward other human beings.

> Love the Lord your God with all your heart, with all your soul, and with all your mind [vertical relationship]. This is the greatest and the most important commandment. The second most important commandment is like it: love your neighbor as you love yourself [horizontal relationship]. The whole Law of Moses and the teachings of the prophets depend on these two commandments (Mt. 22:37-40).

By creating people, God, in effect, created culture, a product of being human. Each society has rules that control behavior and allow people to organize interaction with their world: physically, socially, and spiritually. The *cultural diversity* we find in the world is a beautiful expression of the way God created humanity with a propensity for variety. The linguistic scramble at Babel was itself a creative act which insured a dispersion of cultural and linguistic manifestations throughout the world God had made (Gen. 11:1-9). Humanity was also created with a free will, the ability to make choices. This resulted in a rejection of the first cultural rules given by God. God's rules were a set of guidelines with cause-and-effect results: to eat of the fruit would result in death, spiritual and physical, as well as the human misery associated with it. Choice not only relates to disobedience, but to accepting God's provision for right relationships, for restoration of fellowship to God through right choices—a relationship with Christ as Lord. A focus on *the image of God* conveys a capacity for ethical behavior among human beings (Murphy-O'Conner 1982:48ff).

THE IMPACT OF SIN

Because of sin, at the fall, human beings lost their real identity and purpose (communication with the Creator and dominion over the creation). The world was thrown into chaos and God's intention for the creation was thwarted and His relationship with people changed. A radical reversal in human nature occurred. A nature originally oriented toward God was turned away from Him. Uprightness of heart, originally derived from God, was no longer innate to human nature. The image of God in human beings diminished (though the potential for actualization was present). People were no longer able to realize the potential God intended for them.

Through sin, humanity dethroned the Creator and enthroned the creation as an object of worship. Thus the created powers and authorities (the manifestations of God's intended meaning) took His place. Rather than exercising dominion over the creation as intended, the seen and the unseen took control of human fears (Rom. 1:25). These beliefs confuse and frustrate much of humanity today, creating the great religious systems of the world: people seeking to find God rather than recognizing God's search for them and acknowledging the true God, the creator and Lord of the universe (Gen. 3:9, Rev. 3:20, 21).

CHRIST AND CULTURE

As a result of sin, which God had anticipated, He put His plan into effect. Only an individual who had a pre-fall relationship with God, one who truly lived in His image, could restore the potential humanity had lost. The Apostle Paul puts it like this:

> Even before the world was made, God had already chosen us to be his through our union with Christ, so that we would be holy and without fault before him . . . In all his wisdom and insight God did what he had purposed, and made known to us the secret plan he had already decided to complete by means of Christ. This plan, which God will complete when the time is right, is to bring all creation together, everything in heaven and on earth, with Christ as head (Eph. 1:4, 9, 10).

In describing how God accomplished this, the Apostle demonstrates the relationship between the creation, including humanity, and the process of restoring it to its created/intended purpose:

> Christ is the visible likeness of the invisible God. He is the first-born Son, superior to all created things. For through him God created everything in heaven and on earth, the seen and the unseen things, including spiritual powers, lords, rulers, and authorities. God created the whole universe through him and for him. Christ existed before all things, and in union with him all things have their proper place [this is the relationship between Christ and the creation including the powers human-

kind fears]. He is the head of his body, the church; he is the source of the body's life. He is the first-born Son, who was raised from death, in order that he alone might have the first place in all things. For it was by God's own decision that the Son has in himself the full nature of God. Through the Son, then, God decided to bring the whole universe back to himself. God made peace through his Son's death on the cross and so brought back to himself all things, both on earth and in heaven (Col.1:15-20).

The focus here is on the relationship between Christ and the restored creation: the condition God intended from the beginning. In a sense Christ was the person God intended Adam to be. Christ is the image and glory of God, and through him creation and salvation are related:

> . . . in Christ we see what God intended men to be when he set about making them in his own image. At the same time, of course, Christ as the image of God also reveals God to us. Hence, the phrase 'image of God', when applied to Christ, has a divine and human reference. In order to see God, we look to Christ. We must also look to Christ to see man as God intended him to be. Jesus is the whole, complete person men seek to be. In him we see man stripped of the sin which disfigures and scars him; we see man in his real identity . . . [Christ] is the head of a new humanity, a new creation. To any man who belongs to this new creation . . . Christ mediates the true image and glory of God (Strelan 1977:72).

The Apostle Paul, recognizing this truth, contrasts Adam and Christ in Romans 5:12-19 and Philippians 2:6-8. Adam's descendents are urged to have the same attitude as Christ in order that they may obtain what their ancestor lost and thereby reestablish the relationship to God that He created them for in the first place (Figure 1:1). This contrast demonstrates the differences in the nature of a creating, sinless God and the nature of created, sinful human beings. In order to restore the image of God, humanity must accept God's provision by giving allegiance to Christ and thereby gaining life and holiness (Rom. 5:21).

FIGURE 1:1

Adam and Christ Contrasted in Action and Consequence

ADAM	CHRIST
The reign of death (broken relationship)	The reign of life (restored relationship)
ACTION: Effected by one man	Effected by one man
One Act of Disobedience	One Act of Obedience
RESULT: Judgment on all people	Salvation for all people
DEATH	LIFE

This is not to say that individuals accepting Christ as Lord of their lives never again sin, or exercise their fallen human nature. Rather, by restoration of a relationship with God, people accept a new lifestyle which fulfills the purpose of God in their lives (Rom. 6:20-23). Thus they become the people God created them to be within the bounds of their own context. That context is both a cultural and ideological one, and understanding it demands a study of all its aspects, noting the interaction between beliefs and values and their observable cultural manifestations.

THE INCARNATIONAL MODEL

God chose not to remain separate from culture, above it, without being involved.[1] Rather He chose, through Christ, to become thoroughly involved: to be above it (as God), but to work in and through it (as a human being). Hence, throughout Scripture, we see a heavy emphasis on God's becoming involved in human affairs. Abraham, Isaac and Jacob all talked with God. The Scriptures themselves are a record of God's Spirit communicating

infinite truth in finite forms. The manifestations of God throughout human history clearly demonstrate that people cannot perceive God or His perspective outside of human experience, a
people's language and culture.

Christ was the epitome of this incarnational style of communication. He entered into a human context; he became a Jew. He
made himself vulnerable (an incredible risk) in order to win
respect and establish credibility. He walked and talked. He
interacted on a personal level with people. He laughed and cried.
He was a friend as well as an enemy. He was a total person,
completely human, a revelation of God.[2]

As Jesus interacted in his world, he was full of surprises. His
disciples never knew what to expect next. This *discovery principle*
was central to his communication of truth. People needed to
discover truth on their own rather than being told. He did not go
around telling everyone he was God in human form. He asked his
disciples who they thought he was, and when Peter answered
correctly, he specifically forbade them to tell others, because the
time was not right (Mk. 8:29, 30). Even John the Baptist was
confused and sent a delegation to learn the truth. Jesus' response
was to encourage them to return and speak of what they had
experienced—demonstrations of divine revelation (Mt. 11:2-6).
Pilate asked him who he was, and Jesus asked a question
designed to challenge the governor to discovery (Jn. 18:34); Pilate
flunked the test (Jn. 18:38). Jesus was usually appropriate to the
cultural standards and when not he demonstrated where culture
was wrong (as when he interacted with prostitutes and taxcollec-
tors, people considered marginal by the cultural watchdogs—Mt.
11:16-19, Lk. 19:7ff, etc.). Jesus had no predigested answers. Rather,
he forced people to work through their experience with him and
thereby discover truth, for example, the rich young ruler (Mt.
19:16-23) and the woman at the well (Jn. 4:5-30).

This approach to human interaction provides both an example and a message for communicating God's truth in the world
today. Each culture has general knowledge based on creation and
their own culturally determined restraints. If we can find the key
to revealing truth in that context, using a redemptive or cultural
analogy, then we can proceed to assist people in discovering the
whole counsel of God, help them discover the truth about Him
within their context (Olson 1978, Richardson 1974). What did
Christ have to say about their interests and needs? How would he
have related had he come to them? Those who represent him

today become the incarnation for those with whom they interact. They, as we shall see, are the translation and continue—for the people of that culture—what Christ began so long ago (Kraft 1979:276-290).

THE APOSTLE PAUL ON COMMUNICATION STRATEGY

I am a free man, nobody's slave, but I make myself everybody's slave in order to win as many people as possible. While working with the Jews, I live like a Jew in order to win them; and even though I myself am not subject to the Law of Moses, I live as though I were when working with those who are, in order to win them. In the same way, when working with Gentiles, I live like a Gentile, outside the Jewish Law, in order to win Gentiles. This does not mean that I don't obey God's law; I am really under Christ's law. Among the weak in faith I become weak like one of them, in order to win them. So I become all things to all men, that I may save some of them by whatever means are possible. All this I do for the gospel's sake, in order to share in its blessings (I Cor. 9:19-23).

Here the Apostle to the Gentiles develops his communicational philosophy and answers his critics. At first glance this appears to be very relativistic, discounting Jewishness when with the Gentiles and vice versa. He even goes so far as to say he attempts to be all things to all people. But what does this do for the absolutes of the gospel which God so clearly spells out through Scripture? How are these absolutes reflected in the various cultural contexts of Paul's day? That appears to be just his point. In any context, communicators must first establish relevance and be recognized as a belonger "when with the Jews/Gentiles/weak I live as one of them"). The individual wishing to present God's absolutes, must first earn the right to do so, and then, communicating out of a knowledge of that situation, present the absolutes in such a way that they will be recognized as meaningful for those who hear the gospel message ("though I myself am not subject, I live as those who are in order to win them"). Paul is very positive here, wishing to communicate to Jews and Gentiles, weak and strong, the wonderful truths about "R" reality. But he knew he could not do it without understanding the "r" reality of the specific cultural context (Hiebert 1986). This is not moral relativism, but an application of cultural understanding to the effective communication of God's truth. It is cultural relevance, not *cultural relativism* (Nida 1954:52).

Paul lived his life in order to give credibility to his message. He did everything possible to establish the authenticity of the gospel by being credible himself. In the synagogues he established himself as a Jew and when given the opportunity to speak did so using their communication styles—recounting the history of their forefathers, Abraham, Isaac and Jacob. He established the lineage of Christ and demonstrated how he was indeed the promised Messiah (see Acts 13:16-41, 17:2-4). When with Gentiles, on the other hand, Paul knew that the Jewish style would not communicate effectively so, having done his homework, he spoke to them in the philosophical terms with which they were familiar —in order to win them (Acts 17:22-31). This matter of relevance was central to Paul's methodology as we note over and over again both in the accounts of his ministry throughout the book of Acts, and his personal accounting of these incidents in his own writings (Rom. 2:12-15, I Cor. 7:17-24, 9:19-22, 10:23-33).

The gospel message is a call to life, to apply truth to all that people do and say (Col. 3:16,17). Paul knew that people only understand the message to the extent that they can apply it to their lives; they must identify with it in terms of who they are and what they do in a specific cultural setting. This is the *incarnational model* (Prost 1986). Paul understood well what Christ was saying as He communicated His incarnation so that people "might have life—life in all its fullness" (Jn. 10:10).

Paul understood *receptor-oriented communication* and developed his message to meet the needs of his audience. This is not relativism; it is effective communication designed to bring people face to face with truth and force a decision based on the relevance of the message. Throughout the accounts in Acts, Paul's message was received by some and rejected by others. Those who received, applied the message to effect changes in their lives and thereby became more fulfilled members of the society. Those who rejected, subsequently made life very difficult for Paul, forcing him to move on. However, those who remained, established churches and turned their world upside down (Acts 17:6, 7). What a testimony; people understood Paul's message and applied it to living their lives!

Paul, himself, applied these principles to his own life. As a missionary home on furlough, he went to the temple to take a vow and worship. This got him in trouble with those who concluded he had desecrated the temple by bringing in Gentiles. There were also those who felt Paul's actions were inconsistent with what he had been preaching. (Acts 21:27-36). Clearly, they did not recognize the need for cultural relevance. Christianity, as Paul lived and preached it, cuts across all cultures and can be applied to any context in which human beings live. As Christ came to fulfill people's lives, so those who are fulfilled will become better members of their culture; striving to live up to its ideals, a lifestyle that may be difficult for people to achieve. In this way unbelievers notice a difference and seek to learn about the change. This provides an ideal opportunity for relevant communication of the gospel: witnessing to the hope that is within them (I Pet. 3:15).

With this model of relevance in mind, we see God as the source and humanity as the receptor of communication. God had to act totally within the human field of experience in order to be understood. That experience lies entirely within the realm of language and culture, and more specifically *the* language and culture of a people group He sought to reach. For them to understand the divine communication, it had to be transmitted within the context of their particular experience. This led to countless culture-specific injunctions and commands through the whole of Scripture. However, as Kraft (1979:139-143) points out, frequency is important. The greater the supracultural concern, the more often an item or concept will be presented in a variety of ways. The individual occurrences of various issues such as the braiding of women's hair, or the length of hair worn by males vis-à-vis females, are probably culture specific (I Cor. 11:13-16, I Tim. 2:9, and I Pet. 3:3). They are mentioned not as general principles upon which to base our understanding of God and His relationship to culture (if they are, we deliberately violate God's law moment by moment on the basis of culture), but as an indication of God's great concern that people of all cultures live up to their cultural distinctives. The violation of such injunctions would infringe upon specific cultural expectations and reduce an individual's effectiveness in communicating the true gospel message (which transcends these cultural issues) in that context.[3]

Perhaps this contributes to the length of the Canon. God's message to humanity takes the form of many stories and incidents (case studies) in many different linguistic and cultural forms. It is the blending of these many cases which ultimately combine to reveal the truth about God, His relationship to human beings, and how that relationship (broken when Adam and Eve sinned) can be restored through faith. The message of these countless incidents adds up to the supracultural message (the absolutes) of God's revelation to His creation, including people living within the context of a wide variety of languages and cultures.

Jesus Christ and the Apostle Paul understood the difference between cross-cultural and mono-cultural communication. They both understood the need for presenting the message with respect to the needs of an audience. Paul's broad education and wide travels made him an excellent communicator both in verbal and literary forms. As the apostle to the Gentiles he was aware of the problems, as well as possible benefits, of colonialism, acculturation, and culture change. The first century world was alive with excitement and cultural variety, and in this context the message of Jesus Christ needed to be presented in a relevant way. As modern communicators of the gospel, Bible translators and others involved in missions should also be aware of these principles and attempt to convey an attitude of concern and care.

In missions today we bring these principles of communication from the first century world and place them over the 20th century situation. We then relate them to insights from the social sciences to present a model that helps us understand the complexities of the communication process of which Bible translation is a part. This is the missiological task (Glasser and McGavran 1983). The combined cultural and theological study necessary to appreciate humanity in its social and conceptual context is the study of *missiology*. It developed in recent years through the work of scholars deeply concerned about the 'human condition' and how Christianity relates to it (Hesselgrave 1978, Stott 1979 and Winter 1981). We will draw on many of these principles during the course of this book and point them out as it is appropriate.

The variety of social contexts among the people groups of the world today creates the need for a book such as this. Here we seek to grapple with these cultural factors. Language is a cultural universal, the means by which culture is organized and transmitted. Without it, human cultures would be impossible. Language, on the other hand, would be largely nonsense were it not for the significant cultural contexts in which it is realized and from which it derives meaning. While language is critical and cannot be minimized, the focus throughout this book is on culture: discovering it, making it work for the communicator and applying it to the total task of communicating the gospel.

Culture, then, dramatically affects our understanding of God's message. It also affects how the message is transmitted. We call this process *translation:* insuring that others understand and relate the meaning of the message to their specific context. In this sense, every communicator, every pastor, every evangelical witness is a translator: one who brings into a specific context what God has communicated to all of humanity.

Paul concludes the passage in I Cor. 9 by saying: "all this I do for the gospel's sake in order to share in its blessings." His apparent relativism is part of the gospel message working in the hearts of the hearers as well as what that message does for the messengers: building them up in the faith, conforming them to the image of God so they might share in the blessings. This great truth rings throughout Scripture—the Word, manifest at creation, is the source of a restored relationship with God made known to all people in the person of Jesus Christ (Jn. 1:1). This is the challenge of Bible Translation, making Him known to the peoples of the world.

Suggested Reading

Gill, Jerry. *On Knowing God.* Westminster Press, 1984

Gilliland, Dean. *Pauline Theology and Mission Practice.* Baker, 1984

Kraft, Charles. *Christianity in Culture.* Orbis, 1979

Notes

1. See Kraft (1979:103-120) for an excellent review of theological positions of God in relation to culture.
2. See Kraft (1979 Part IV:169-260) for an extended discussion on the dynamics of revelation.
3. For a good discussion of absolutes and cultural relativism see Pike (1979:139-145).

PART I

TOWARD DISCOVERING CULTURE

The theory upon which this section draws comes directly from cultural anthropology. Anthropologists have long discussed cultural sub-systems which appear to be universal. People of every culture, regardless of where they live or what they believe, must deal with each of these cultural factors in order to maintain their livelihood and exist as a community. Each culture, however, deals with these common concerns in different ways. Of importance to the structure of this book is to note the ways in which cultures in Biblical times dealt with the same issues which are of concern to cultures in today's world. While human commonality greatly assists communicators, the differences effected by time and distance between Biblical cultures and modern receptors must be explained if people are to understand the Scriptures as God intended.

Tools for discovering these cultural factors are the subject of this section. The sub-systems form the organization of the chapters and, indeed, structure the material throughout the book. They are more than hypothetical concerns. They are the factors upon which all cultural systems are built and thus relate in a dynamic way to all aspects of communicating the Gospel across cultural boundaries.

CHAPTER TWO
An Approach to Culture

Anthropology has made a vital contribution to the study of translation, missions, and cross-cultural communication. Many of the methods and principles used by anthropologists can provide an understanding of the source and receptor cultures with which communicators must deal, not to mention providing a perspective on their own cultures in relation to these.

Cross-cultural interaction is extremely common in our modern world—so common, in fact, that it is not considered very important to take other cultures into account because there has been so much contact. After delivering a lecture at an Indonesian University some years ago I sat down while a faculty member gave a brief summary in Indonesian. During the reception that followed, my 'interpreter' asked why I disapproved of his comments. I was mystified. I had not understood a word, yet he was asking why I did not like what he said. A friend eventually straightened the problem out: I had sat with my legs crossed, pointing my foot at the podium the entire time he was speaking— highly impolite in his culture. I quickly apologized, pleading ignorance, but the damage was done; I had shamed the one who made my presentation clear to the audience—a cultural blunder of the worst order.

Understanding culture does make a difference! The problem is that expatriates go into new situations unaware of the rules, the little things that may upset people or cast a shadow on developing and continuing relationships. Fortunately, people around the world tend to be forgiving of outsiders in the early stages of interaction. This provides a period of adjustment and learning while developing trust relationships. Take advantage of this grace period to eliminate behavioral forms from your culture that may be considered offensive because of the very different meanings they convey. Cultural behavior is largely a matter of habit, and in

23

the early stages of cross-cultural experience, learning new habits is essential to eventual success. But so much is happening around the newly-arrived outsider that the risk of overload is high and culture stress inevitable (S. Dye 1974, 1982).

Utilizing anthropological concepts and methods can greatly assist anyone in a cross-cultural situation. This is one reason for the rise of missiology as a recognized discipline—a conscious combination of social science theory and method and the passion of fulfilling the great commission. Knowing how to recognize and organize cultural activity can assist in focusing attention and help to reduce stress for an outsider. Applying these principles to what one intuitively knows is the challenge for an inside communicator.

CULTURE DEFINED

Broadly speaking, anthropologists tend to group cultural behavior into five categories or cultural sub-systems.

Economics - A system for utilizing the environment
and deriving a living.

Ideology - A system of beliefs and observances relating to
origins, present conditions, and the future.

Kinship - A system of interpersonal relationships.

Social Structure - A system of group interaction.

Political Organization - A system of internal and external
controls and regulations.

Before we can relate these cultural factors to the communication process in the chapters that follow, we must define and clarify our approach to culture.

Definitions of culture are almost as numerous as anthropologists. Harris sums them up: "The culture concept comes down to behavior patterns associated with particular groups of people, that is to 'customs', or to a people's 'way of life' " (Harris 1968:16). This traditional definition focuses on culture as 'patterned' and 'shared' (Benedict 1934, Kluckhohn 1965). It encourages a researcher to discover the products of the system a people subscribe to. What is this culture made of? What are all its parts? Organize and codify these and we will understand the culture which made or devised them. This is a very subjective, external way of perceiving culture, and though useful, particularly in the early stages of investigation, does not help us "grasp the native's point of view" (Malinowski 1922:25).

A definition which more accurately reflects that objective comes from Spradley: "Culture is the acquired knowledge that people use to interpret experience and generate behavior" (Spradley 1980:6). Here, rather than viewing culture as a list of what people have and do, the focus is on knowledge—what people within a society need "to know or believe in order to operate in a manner acceptable to its members" (Goodenough 1957:167). This cognitive definition forces us to consider the shared symbols that enable people to give form and meaning to their specific experiences (Geertz 1973). Pike draws on this distinction when discussing "language in relation to a unified theory of the structure of human behavior" (Pike 1967).

PERSPECTIVE IMPORTANT

Language and culture each contribute to our understanding of the other. Both are essential to appreciate the acquired knowledge necessary to act and speak appropriately within a specific context. This is why it is essential to study all the languages and cultures involved in a translation venture. There must be appreciation for the cultural context from which the source was communicated in order to make it relevant within the context of the receptor. It is similarly essential that translators have a command of the receptor language and are able to use it in data collection, questioning, and analysis of both linguistic and cultural materials. Furthermore, translators should also appreciate the affect their own language and culture (if different) has on the entire process. This is the only way to avoid the accusations of a Chinese friend who maintains that the Chinese were restricted in their understanding of Biblical truth by the cultural perspective of the Western translators, as well meaning as they were. The Chinese were not able to appreciate the relational emphasis of the Hebrew language as well as its picturesque style until they produced their own translations.

An appreciation for perspective is why the incarnation is so crucial: God became thoroughly immersed in a culture in order to adequately relate the divine message to humanity. Jesus Christ grew up in the Jewish sub-culture of the Galilean town of

Nazareth, assimilating all that was necessary for a knowledgeable member of that community. He acted and spoke right in that context and, in fact, did it so well that all were amazed, and he gained a wide reputation (Lk. 2:47,52).[1] Similarly, all communicators must become thoroughly involved with the receptor language and culture in order to effectively translate the message of the source so as to avoid distortion caused by differences in language or culture. The translation must *talk right* and *act right* for the message to have meaning.

Culture, then, can be viewed as a system of communicative knowledge: all that we must know in order to communicate the source message. So long as communicators remain external to the system, classifying the parts from another perspective, they remain bound to Harris's definition. It is only as dynamic interaction takes place and the system becomes a cognitive part of our communication experience that we break through the cultural barrier to new horizons of knowledge—knowledge that can allow for a new incarnation within a context where it has never been before. The translation of Scripture becomes a new thing as it takes shape in a linguistic and cultural system (Pike 1979:95). People conceive of God and His revelation in ways not previously possible because their knowledge is different than any other cultural grouping (Kraft 1979:66-77). It is little wonder that John was awed by what he saw and heard around the throne (Rev. 7:9).

Etic and Emic

This ability to translate experience from one language and culture into another is possible because of common cultural principles which come from being human. Pike makes this very clear in his discussion of 'etic' and 'emic'. The etic concept, though derived from a linguistic principle (all the sounds made by the human vocal apparatus and available to any language) applies to culture as well. These are the general concepts upon which human cultures are based. The emic principle, on the other hand, focuses on the cultural manifestations of these concepts (the specific concepts and behavior patterns a given culture chooses to extract from the general pool and uses to organize its culture). This is analogous to sounds and their ordering to produce the speech flow of a specific language. In Pike's view, the generalizations must come out of a wide knowledge of cultural specifics—the theories of *culture* should be constructed from an understanding of many specific *cultures*. Etic and emic are but two views of the same data: general with respect to all other cultures and specific with respect to the principles of one culture (Pike 1967:37-41).

This is quite different from Harris's discussion of the concept. He sees etics as patterns of behavior and emics as what goes on in people's heads (Fisher and Werner 1978:198-201). Carried to its logical conclusion Harris's perspective leads to an understanding of culture which makes the anthropologist the final authority, not the culture bearers. A researcher's final determination of what is "patterned and shared" may be analytically correct (emic), but the people may not recognize it because it does not relate to their conceptual framework. Analytically correct but cognitively incorrect is all too often the final "emic analysis" of anthropological or linguistic investigation.

For example, when analyzing the Samo language, my wife and I had to make a technical decision that we knew would affect the outcome. We made a choice which seemed parsimonious and elegant. Based on this decision we produced an alphabet and taught several Samo to read and write. However, there were many 'hard' words which complicated learning for the new readers. An analysis of the problem determined that all the difficult spots related to our linguistic decision. When we re-analyzed the data and changed the alphabet to reflect an equally valid solution, the difficulties disappeared and people learned to read and write much more quickly (Shaw and Shaw 1977). They did not respond to the linguistic validity of our first solution—it was not emic for them.

Surface Structure and Deep Structure

Surface structure relates to most cultural manifestations, characterized by the products and activities represented by the broad cultural sub-systems. Anything that can be viewed and described by an outsider is, by its very nature, part of the surface structure. It is what people make and do and others can see and describe; this leads to Harris's definition of culture.

The deep structure, on the other hand, holds the meaning of those surface manifestations. The meanings of the various cultural forms are also held in common by the members of a society and are often more implicit than explicit. Meaning, however, is that aspect of the structure which embodies the essential concerns and assumptions of a people.

In the previous example of Samo orthography, the deep structure implied by the surface level alphabet had great significance for the Samo, though they could not articulate it. They intuitively reacted to the alphabet thereby demonstrating much deeper levels of meaning. We must not, however, equate emic with deep structure or etic with surface structure. The etic-emic distinction relates to understanding from different vantage points (from outside a culture vs. within), while the surface-deep structure contrast relates meaning to behavioral patterns within a cultural system. It establishes what people need to know in order to act right.

Communicators should be concerned with reality from a people's perspective and the meanings, both explicit and implicit, which they attach to it. What does reality mean to those who hold to another worldview? What is the local view of a particular activity and why, i.e. what does it mean to them? Our communication, including the translations we produce, must reflect a people's perspective in order to have relevance. In order to communicate effectively, God always begins by relating to a cultural reality as expressed in the way people "live and move and exist" (Acts 17:28). Since God does this, how much more should we who follow His example? This is not to say that Scripture does not reflect another reality—God's. But He introduces that through the cultural forms and meanings people understand—incarnation.

A COMMUNICATION MODEL

The Source, Message, Receptor (S.M.R.) communication model presented by Nida and Taber (1969:22, 23) and adapted by M. Kraft (1978) focuses on the importance of experience. When the field of experience (Figure 2:1) is the same, i.e. shared within a cultural context, the potential for receptors receiving the message intended by the source is fairly high. However, receptors decode the message, not on the basis of what the source intends, but rather with respect to their own field of experience. Thus the broader the field of shared experience, the greater the likelihood receptors will understand the message as the source intended (Figure 2:2).

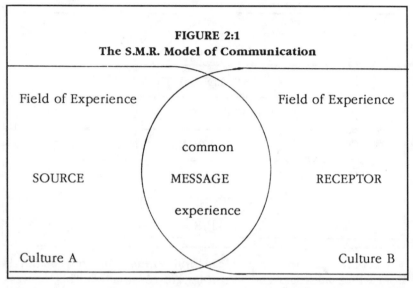

FIGURE 2:1
The S.M.R. Model of Communication

Field of Experience   Field of Experience

common

SOURCE   MESSAGE   RECEPTOR

experience

Culture A   Culture B

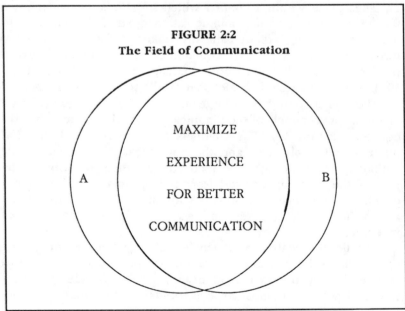

FIGURE 2:2
The Field of Communication

MAXIMIZE

EXPERIENCE

A   FOR BETTER   B

COMMUNICATION

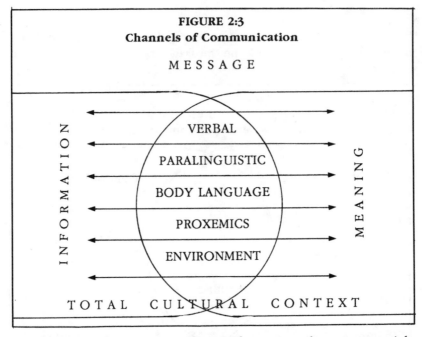

FIGURE 2:3
Channels of Communication

MESSAGE

INFORMATION — VERBAL / PARALINGUISTIC / BODY LANGUAGE / PROXEMICS / ENVIRONMENT — MEANING

TOTAL   CULTURAL   CONTEXT

People seek to communicate *information,* the raw materials from which *messages* and *meanings* are constructed. This, however, takes place within a *context* which structures the communication. Thus in a specific communication event, information, context, and meaning are dynamically linked. Information is structured into a message and communicated within a context to produce signals that a receptor transforms into meaning (Kraft 1983:115). As suggested by McLuhan, Hall, and others, the messenger (i.e. the medium) is in large measure the message. Thus the medium or channel of communication is also crucial to this equation (Figure 2:3). The channels of communication that Hall discusses all apply here and the non-verbal is as crucial as the verbal (if not more so). The total context, then, contributes that part of the meaning derived from the information of a specific event. That information is largely cultural; something happened at a specific time and place and way and specific people were involved.

Within the matrix of a single culture, there are countless opportunities for miscommunication. Despite shared experience people do not always communicate so as to be clearly understood. However, in most aspects of daily life, where common knowledge is assumed, effective communication is an expected result. When this common shared experience is lost in a cross-cultural interaction, communication is much less effective. When interactants are from different cultures, their respective fields of experience vary. This reduces the commonality upon which they can build a context for communication. While their humanity offers a point of contact, it takes time to build the trust, rapport, and understanding necessary to engage in more than casual conversation.

This matter of cultural diversity is of central importance if the Scriptures are to be understood. Minimally, there is the culture of the Hebrew society of Old Testament times (within which there is great diversity, as will be discussed in chapter 9), the Greco-Roman culture of the New Testament period (which was by no means uniform), and the great variety of receptor cultures found in the world today. Add to this the growing group of cultures from which translators come and the cultural complexities of a translation project take on enormous proportions. At least three cultures (representing the Source, the Receptor and the Messenger) present a complex cultural matrix that must be untangled for the Scriptural message to be effectively communicated.[2] This matrix is the *translation context* that forms the theoretical foundation of this book.

Within this complex of cultural interaction, there is yet another factor affecting the entire communication process: God. As a holy, absolute, supracultural being, He desires to communicate to finite, culture-bound humanity. Incarnation takes place whenever God communicates (in whatever form) to human beings. Historically, He did so within the linguistic and cultural context of those with whom He interacted; God had to use forms people already knew. Christ's incarnation is the epitome of the principle which continues to apply to our day as we seek to embody God's message for modern people.

THE THREE CULTURES MODEL

Anthropologists have long recognized a wide variety of culture types ranging from bands of wandering nomads to modern city dwellers. In surveying this literature Dye (1980:310-331) has detailed an analytical model for appreciating cultural diversity. This model maintains that all cultures can be categorized within three archetypical cultural types: dependent, face-to-face, kinship cultures (sometimes called tribal); intra-dependent, peasant cultures; and inter-dependent, industrial cultures. Drawing on the work of Service (1962) and others, Dye focuses on the levels of socio-economic adaptation to establish the three types, where they are located, and what they mean to those who live within them.

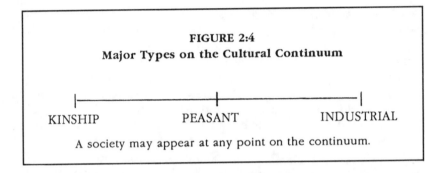

FIGURE 2:4
Major Types on the Cultural Continuum

KINSHIP   PEASANT   INDUSTRIAL

A society may appear at any point on the continuum.

Obviously there is a variety of cultures within the range of each major category. However, the theory maintains that societies falling within each range must seek to solve similar types of problems. Thus all cultures of the industrial type must solve problems of development such as urbanization, crime, congestion, lonliness, pollution, and rapid change. Unless these concerns are dealt with and individual needs met, the society may not survive.

Knowing something of the character of each of these three broad culture types, communicators entering a different culture can develop some expectations about the circumstances under which they may be working. They can research similar contexts that have been studied in order to develop an empathy and attitude for learning even before they arrive.

Expatriates who anticipate involvement with people living in kinship societies will know they must place high value on developing relationships with the local kin group and may need to join that group in order to gain acceptance.

Individuals who become immersed in a peasant culture will need to be aware of the specialized roles and perhaps predetermine which role they will adopt in order to develop relationships that will most benefit their communication. They can be sure they should not adopt roles associated with the elite if they seek to identify with the peasantry and vice versa. Due to the nature of hierarchical societies, it is unlikely that a single individual will successfully identify with both the peasantry and elite.

Those involved with industrial societies will need to be aware of the multitude of potential roles and not assume that those roles are the same in each culture. Though highly commercial, Americans view commercialism very differently from the Japanese, for example. With these thoughts in mind we turn now to a discussion of the key features that characterize each major culture type.

Principles of the Model

The economic base upon which each culture type depends lays the ground work for our discussion. Economics, however, can never be isolated from other cultural factors. This is why these cultural types are often referred to as 'levels of socio-economic adaptation". The social aspect establishes the nature of interpersonal relationships while the economic base identifies the primary source for deriving a living. This can be summarized as follows:

SOCIAL LEVEL	ECONOMIC BASE
Kinship/Familial Focus on group	Subsistence
Peasant/Hierarchical Focus on status	Market
Industrial/Impersonal Focus on individual	Commercial

This interplay between social and economic factors establishes many of the peculiarities of each culture type and leads to the concerns that motivate the people who live in these contexts. Thus ownership is seen as a group matter in kinship societies; what belongs to one belongs to all. In peasant societies ownership is often an indication of status with conspicuous consumption a lifestyle for the elite. Land is usually owned by the elite who dictate its use and, to some degree, the people who live upon and develop it. In industrial societies, ownership is an individual matter that is determined by personal status, whether ascribed or achieved.

While these are generalizations from which specific cases vary considerably, they provide a framework for understanding that can be a great help when interacting cross-culturally. If translators from industrial nations know the importance of group interaction in a kinship society, or the stress of family and social status in a peasant society, personal interests and concerns can be laid aside in favor of the need to develop interaction patterns that will establish credibility in the new context. Without this credibility, communication of the gospel (in whatever form) may not be meaningful because receptors have not seen meaning (from their perspective) in the life of the communicator.

The accompanying contrastive features chart (see Figure 2:7) details the basic differences between these three broad culture types and provides those who become aware of these concepts with a basic map for finding their way into a specific situation. It helps to have some idea of what to look for, what to expect. This chart is an initial tool to assist communicators moving into cross-cultural situations.

These culture types, however, should not be viewed as stages in an evolutionary process. Rather they interactively affect each other as in Figure 2:5. No culture, irrespective of its isolation and remoteness, can exist solely on its own in the modern world. Each culture is in touch with other cultures of varying types. They affect each other and this becomes a dynamic part of culture contact. The Samo have been affected by their association with the rest of Papua New Guinea through interaction with administrators, missionaries and businesses, not to mention my family and me. With schools, churches, medical facilities, roads and airstrips proliferating, they are no longer an isolated people group in the forest. They have changed as a result of contact with others.

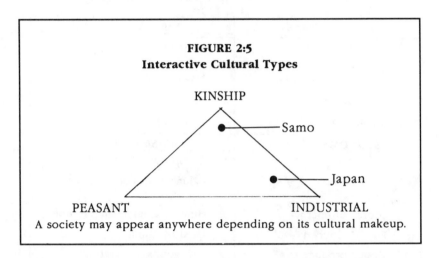

FIGURE 2:5
Interactive Cultural Types

KINSHIP

Samo

Japan

PEASANT   INDUSTRIAL

A society may appear anywhere depending on its cultural makeup.

At this point in the computer age, we need to add another culture type: Post-Industrial Culture, characterized by Naisbitt's megatrends of high technology, rapid culture change and the need for close human relationships (Naisbitt 1982). The addition of this cultural type increases the scope for interaction and the effect of change as represented in Figure 2:6.

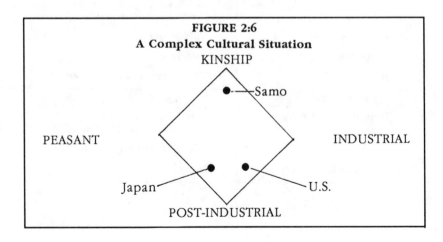

FIGURE 2:6
A Complex Cultural Situation
KINSHIP

Samo

PEASANT   INDUSTRIAL

Japan   U.S.

POST-INDUSTRIAL

FIGURE 2:7
Contrastive Features of Three Different Culture Types

BASIC CONTRASTS	KINSHIP	
1. Government	Mono-cultural independent groups	
2. Dominant institution	Clan, kin group	
3. Economic base	Gardening, hunting	
4. Occupations	Generalists	
ECONOMY	**SUBSISTENCE**	
1. Land	Group owned, shared	
2. Land value	Valuable for corporate use, available	
3. Source of energy	Human, animal, simple tools	
4. Food produced	Used by 'family'	
5. Goods produced	Few goods, generalists, for personal use	
6. Hard times	Dependent on nature and family cohesiveness	
7. Dominant economic relationships	Egalitarian	
8. Education	Informal	
9. Goal of education	Control supernatural	
10. Ideal life style	Village people	
11. Time orientation	Timeless	
12. Leisure	Varies, often considerable	
IDEOLOGY	**ANIMISM**	
1. Importance of religion	Permeates all life, no sacred/secular distinction	
2. Ancestors	Ghosts nurtured, placated	
3. Function for society	Unity	

PEASANT (with elite)	INDUSTRIAL
States. regional inter-dependence	Interdependent nations
Lord-Servant	Corporation
Farming, crafts	Industrial (agro-business)
Specialized occupations	Multiplied roles

MARKET	COMMERCIAL
Individually owned by elite	Individual, less important
Valuable to elite for use by peasants, scarce	Monetary value
Human, animal	Fuel powered machinery
Sell part, eat part	Raise for sale, buy food
Many goods, artisans for trade	Vast number of goods, laborers, for money
Dependent on nature and elite	Locally independent internationally dependent
Competitive, unequal	Commercial
Apprenticeship, special schools for elite	Extensive, formal, specialized
Maintain social structure	Technological knowledge
Idealized behavior of elite	Upper middle class
Busy, but not time oriented	Focal value on time
For elite only	Regulated and organized

ANIMISM + NATIONAL RELIGION	MANY RELIGIONS
Important, sacred/secular sometimes distinguished	Unimportant, sacred/secular sharply separated
Respected	Forgotten
Acceptance of roles in society	Obedience to law

IDEOLOGY (cont.)	ANIMISM	
4. Function for individuals	Control environment, establish individual's place	
5. Religious buildings	None, or not elaborate	
6. Religious specialists	Part time	
7. Importance of mythology	Sacred tales which validate the belief system	
SOCIAL RELATIONSHIPS	**FAMILIAL**	
1. Kinship	Everything	
2. Type of family	Extended family	
3. Marriage function	Build kinship ties, trade ties, labor force, etc.	
4. Polygamy	Functional	
5. Dominant dyads	Brother-brother, father-son	
6. Old, sick, jobless	Cared for in home	
POLITICAL ORGANIZATION	**COMMUNITY**	
1. Structure	Small independent units	
2. Internal control (law)	Negative sanctions; shame/ restitution	
3. External control (govt.)	Non-kin relations, warfare between locally defined groups	
4. Participation by Common people	Alliance/defiance, community in control, full rights	
5. Leadership	Local leaders, achieved	
6. Power of rulers	Weak	

ANIMISM & NATIONAL RELIGION	MANY RELIGIONS
Comfort, reaffirm personal worth	Sense of belonging, identification
Extensive temples sponsored by elite	Equal to other buildings
Full time, important	Full time, less important
Tales which relate to the past, thereby revealing a heritage	Fairy tales with no relevance to present (Science provides functional substitute)
HIERARCHICAL	**IMPERSONAL**
Extra means of coping	Unimportant
Varies widely	Nuclear (old, sick, excluded)
Economically helpful	Meet personal needs, basic unit of society
Recreational	Dysfunctional
Parent-child, patron-worker	Husband-wife friend-friend
Old respected, all cared for	Institutionalized
KINGDOM	**REPUBLIC**
National, regional autonomy	National and international
Shame, gossip, civil law	Civil/criminal law
Regional inter-dependence, warfare within region, interest groups, etc., religious sanctions	International politics, warfare between nations
Alien control, limited rights	Politics at all levels, citizens' control
Hereditary rules from elite	Politicians
Very great (Lords)	Power divided among many specialists

The Model Applied

Many places in the world today include an overlay of two or more culture types, necessitating a variety of interaction which can exhaust cross-cultural investigators. A knowledge of what is happening, however, can be most helpful in alleviating frustration. I recently conducted a seminar in an Asian nation and observed considerable anxiety among the participants. I listened as they discussed the cultural contexts in which they worked. These contexts were primarily kinship groups and most students were involved in close relationships with the people. At the same time, however, they were also interacting with officials who came from other parts of the nation. These officials were basically of a peasant cultural type and were concerned about the development of the people under their jurisdiction. They expressed this concern by forcing external changes which moved the people into a development cycle that made them look more like the peasantry the officials knew so well. Social classes were forming so that the indigenous population began to resemble a peasantry that performed basic tasks and provided goods for the politically elite officialdom. Translators who represented the industrial culture type, felt themselves torn by the social and political dynamics of this change situation. All three culture types were represented and each group felt it had an understanding of reality not shared by the others. Such a complex social situation introduces the need to apply the communication model with its focus on the receptor's field of experience.

Once communicators enter a specific cultural context, they can begin study by focusing on the local manifestations of general cultural principles. These etic generalities provide an initial introduction to local patterns. They can be used to discover local characteristics of each cultural sub-system and gradually determine the emic meaning of behavior patterns. This type of study demands the use of anthropological principles to understand and work within a particular setting.

A DISCOVERY PROCEDURE FOR CULTURAL AWARENESS

As expatriate communicators begin to interact with a particular group of people, they need to be aware of their own impact on the group and the changes they may bring about. At the same time they should (to the extent possible) lay aside their own cultural identity and relate to the people in order to build a trust relationship out of which they can present the gospel. Mayers (1987:5-15) addresses all of this in his concept of the prior question of trust (PQT).

Actually the PQT relates to a series of questions designed to assist communicators in discovering another culture. These are questions that help an outsider observe surface level behavior and use that information to anticipate deeper level responses as observation and questions combine to build understanding. This series of questions are:

1. What is the cultural norm?

2. Are people operating within it?

3. How is change brought about within the culture?

4. Who is responsible for changing the cultural norms?

These questions lead to an investigation of the culture, how change works and the importance of change agents. It also points to the need for an organized methodology to begin cultural research and analysis. In order to move beyond the first question, communicators must analyze the cultural sub-systems and note the meaning of behavior patterns with respect to the expectations of other individuals within the society (norms). Anthropologists have long used personal involvement along with observation techniques to develop an initial understanding of a people. Known as participant observation it is the focal point of involvement and cultural analysis.

A vital piece of equipment people bring to a study is their eyes. Field workers need to develop their observation skills and use them to the maximum. Early impressions in another culture are soon forgotten as you become accustomed to what seemed so strange or different in the beginning. Another essential piece of equipment is a sharp pencil. Once involved in observation, a good record of activities is necessary. Who was involved, what was happening, where and when did it take place and what did people say about it? In writing all this out you will raise questions about details or meanings of activities. Record these questions to ask people later.

Reflection upon the event will raise more questions the answers to which will lead to your own effective participation and discovering how participants feel, what they think and how the activities affect other sub-systems within the culture. Your outside questions will precipitate inside responses—take careful note of these. Learn who the experts are for the activity or concern in focus and ask what questions you should use with them. Now you will be getting insider questions that will encourage better inside (emic) responses thereby giving you a better idea of what is important to the people for whom these activities are part of life. Another useful technique is listening to how children ask about things they need to know. How, in turn, do parents or other teachers respond? What styles of communication do they employ in their answers? To discover meaning, then, you must add questions to observation and participation. This will result in learning more than the appropriate actions, it will incorporate the meaning of those actions for the participants. I call this process the Observation-Questioning Technique.

To gain knowledge of a people's culture, communicators need the following: (1) trust, (2) a basic ability to communicate in a language common to the people, (3) a data base of observation to draw upon, (4) selected questions based on observation that force people to reflect on their responses and, finally, (5) relate all this to effective incarnational communication with the people of that community.

With respect to points one and five, communicators should approach language and culture, and an understanding of that context out of close human interaction so that people know and trust them. The PQT helps outsiders do this. The product of their labors (a translation for example) will then relate to a local, emic perspective and bear a credibility it would otherwise not have. People will be able to identify with it and, therefore, want to use the Scriptures in order to understand what God has said. Because the translation acts and talks right, people will be drawn by the Holy Spirit to understand His message (Jn. 12:32). Only as translation comes out of this perspective with respect to both the source and the receptor will it be the gospel—*the good news*— that God intended. Only then will it impact the culture and produce changes, not because someone said so but because people respond to God's word and apply it to their own lives. It is the responsibility of the translator to ensure this incarnational approach—a holy task indeed!

Points two, three and four above, relate to the methodology. Language learning skills and use of the language in context are essential to good communication, as is the development of good learning patterns consistent with the culture. The Brewsters are well known for their language and culture learning workshops around the world, and their writings have assisted countless more in developing these skills. Combining linguistic principles with basic human concerns and interaction patterns, students begin immediately to relate within a community and establish rapport (trust) in a manner consistent with the culture to which they are adapting. This methodology combines scientific techniques with human concerns to provide an interactive model for functioning within a society. Knowing how and when to ask the right questions (in order to improve the data base you are constantly updating) is critical to effective communication of the gospel at a later stage in the contact cycle (Brewster and Brewster 1976, 1981, 1984).

This cultural approach, then, reflects an attitude which puts the receptor first, and carefully considers the source with respect to the intended meaning of the message. This approach also forces communicators to consider their own cultural values and what they mean in light of God's original communication to all human beings. In the chapters that follow, we will examine each of the cultural sub-systems and thereby develop an understanding upon which to build a base for effective communication of the gospel.

Suggested Reading

Brewster, Tom and Betty Sue. *Bonding*. Lingua House, 1982.

Hiebert, Paul. *Cultural Anthropology*. Baker, 1983. Chapts. 2 & 3.

Mayers, Marvin. *Christianity Confronts Culture*. Zondervan, 1974/1987.

Notes

1. Jesus was a Galilean; this was his own culture. He was born and raised in it. He had a distinct advantage over those who enter into cross-cultural contexts as adults. However, as outsiders we must adapt to the extent possible—apply the incarnation principle. At the very least we need to adapt to the extent that being outsiders does not obstruct effective communication of the gospel message (see chapter 12 for a full discussion of this).

2. The situation is really more complex than indicated because the original receptors were secondary receivers who could not know the circumstances, or responses, of the primary receptors. For example, the Apostle Paul was not a Roman but received God's Word and communicated with the Romans accordingly. And the Romans were a very different audience with a culture quite distinct from that of the Ephesians. Thus we are dealing with layers of culture which affect what we now call the source. Modern receptors add a multiplicity of cultural variation that astounds the mind. The cultural aspects of the translation process, than, are considerably more complex than immediately apparent.

CHAPTER THREE
Economic Factors

Economic interests captivate the world today. Hearts stop and start with the latest stock market conditions as these are affected by oil prices, political circumstances, and the latest predictions of the economic pundits. Though related, the anthropological interest in economics is on the general cultural type of the people and its effect upon how they make a living. Knowing the culture type will allow you to predict many of the basic economic concerns people must deal with: the ecology, the way they develop their environment and what they use to do it, and their process of making a living.

A people's manner of making a living is a major interest for communicators. It offers an avenue of initial entry because so much can be observed before analysis is either possible or necessary. We now turn to explore some of these economic factors and note how they affect communicating the gospel.

TOWARD DISCOVERING ECONOMIC FACTORS

The Environmental Base

Where people live has a considerable effect upon much of what they do and even how they do it. The Samo, living in the dense tropical rain forest of Papua New Guinea, use gardening practices very different from the Huli who live in the Highlands where there is less than 1/4 the rainfall. They, in turn, are very different again from peoples living on the islands.

People learn to live with their environment and how to most effectively use it to their maximum benefit. Therefore, one of the first things a communicator needs to know is something about the local environment and its effect upon the lifestyle of those who live there. Lifestyle, then, is affected by geography: climactic conditions, water ways, land availability and fertility, flora and fauna, etc. All of this affects a people's understanding of Scripture. For example, the fishing complex so much a part of Christ's interaction with the disciples may be completely unknown to a highlands people for whom the largest body of water is a rapidly flowing stream.

Simple observation can be very helpful in this initial phase. Also of importance is what people say about their environment as well as what they do with it. It may be difficult in the early stages to understand all that is said, but discovering the ecology of a region relates well to initial language learning. How a language is structured can give valuable clues as to what the people who speak that language consider important. The Eskimo have many words for snow while the Samo include locational information in 81% of all spoken sentences (Shaw and Shaw 1973). Such lexical proliferation for aspects of the environment provide a wealth of material for semantic study that will eventually lead to valuable information about the worldview reflected in the language.

While watching the Samo prepare a garden plot, I was intrigued by the way they cleared the undergrowth and planted under the forest canopy, only cutting the large trees after the crop was growing well. When I questioned them about this practice (that apparently destroyed much of the newly rooted crop) the Samo showed me the thin, leached out, top soil that could not support the new crop in torrential rains. The new plants needed protection. In fact, the amount of crop loss when the trees fall is relatively small, as reported by Schieffelin for a similar phenomena among the Kaluli in the region of Mt. Bosavi 40 miles to the east (Schieffelin 1971). This practice proved well suited for the region as a government agricultural officer discovered when he proceeded to 'assist' the Samo by teaching them to use a slash and burn method. Cutting the trees in mid-March (when rainfall of 8 inches per night is common), it was July before he could burn the trees and plant a small garden whose meager crop took literally tons of commercial fertilizer (all brought in by chartered aircraft). The Samo quietly shook their heads and went back to their time honored techniques of utilizing the rain forest environment (they try to plant in July when the rain fall is less).

Technology

Equipped with a basic understanding of the ecology, you can proceed to learn how people respond to that environment. The technology of a people relates to their material culture, the things they have and use. Depending on their socio-economic level, much of what people use may come directly from the environment.

Societies at a kinship level of socio-economic adaptation, depend primarily on a subsistence economy. They make their own tools, clothes, houses and everything in them from the materials available in the environment. Peasants depend more on imported materials, often made available by the elite. Peasants often use these raw materials to make trade items which are then sold back to the elite in the market place. This symbiotic (but unequal) relationship establishes a cultural reciprocity between the classes of a peasant society which assists all involved and maintains the system. Cultures based on a commercial system of exchange rarely depend upon the immediate environment for their material culture. The environment can be modified, materials imported, and conditions changed depending on the technological level of the society. Understanding these tools for utilizing the environment is a technological study. The more sophisticated the source from which translators take a text, or receptor cultures into which they translate, the more complex this study becomes. Extensive research is necessary when the source and receptor cultures are widely divergent, as when translating a New Testament text from the Greco-Roman pre-industrial culture type for a modern Kinship receptor living in an environment very different from Bible lands. In such cases careful research will assist in making adjustments and noting areas that need explanation.

Economic Technique

This is the study of how people use their material culture to develop their economy, i.e. how they produce food, make houses, clothes, etc. It is one thing to make a bow and arrow, quite another to use it effectively to bring home meat. In the modern world we speak of "making money". What we mean has nothing to do with how the item itself is made but how we earn or obtain money to use for the goods and services necessary to exist within a culture. The process of earning money is an economic concern just as the process of making a bow and arrow is of economic interest to my Samo brothers. Therefore, economic technique is more than just the means of procuring a living through the use of the material culture. It also relates to how the materials of the culture are procured (by making them, buying them, etc.) and the extent of technology necessary for that to happen.

Often, apparently sophisticated economic techniques are of little use in a cultural context with a different economic base. Such was the case with the use of fertilizer to make the agricultural officer's garden grow. The Samo had no money to buy the fertilizer or the training to use it. And if they were to use it they would develop a dependence for outside materials that could, in fact, not be supplied on a regular basis.

The people of Biblical times developed and utilized their economic techniques in order to make the most of their environment and what it supplied for them. Many of the peoples of the world today can identify with those conditions much better than individuals who assume an industrial economic base. The story of the Israelites journeying through the desert is a case in point. Their concerns about food and water, the durability of clothing and shoes, and their housing arrangements will be appreciated by most kinship and peasant peoples of the world. They will recognize what God did for the Israelites far more than will individuals from the industrial nations.

As communicators, we need to familiarize ourselves with the economic techniques of peoples in Biblical times. Their solutions fit their circumstances and should be understood if the translation is to reflect their concerns. What planting, harvesting and storing techniques were assumed by the writers and their audience? These issues can then be reflected in the translation in order to help people living under very different environmental conditions (or similar conditions as the case may be) relate that information to their understanding of Scripture.

Economic Process

With a basic understanding of the environment and a people's technology, we now turn to discovering the process necessary to make the system work. This focuses on the ways people interact within their economic system to maximize its effectiveness: division of labor (who does what and when?) forms of exchange, distribution of goods, etc. Are there distinct economic spheres which are the jurisdiction of certain individuals, as in the Kula ring off the tip of the island of New Guinea (Malinowski 1922:81ff)? In short, how do people develop their economy to best meet their needs?

Division of Labor. The division of labor may be based on sex, age, status, education, or any other culturally defined characteristic that establishes who does what. Knowing the criteria people bring to bear upon correct roles within the economic sphere may assist a translator in communicating Biblical truth. For example, when communicating who God is and what He does, it may be best to focus on culturally defined issues (protection, provision, sustaining, encouraging, etc.). Are male or female roles considered most prominent? Do the aged or those of high social status perform these responsibilities, or is someone else in control? In short how will the people view God when we communicate these roles with respect to those in His care? Again we note the integrated nature of culture; economics and the belief system in this case. Understanding the division of labor can help a translator assign appropriate role behavior to Biblical characters or indicate how and why they are significantly different.

Wealth. An appreciation for the concept of wealth and its distribution may also be important. The industrial concept of private property is often misunderstood by people of other culture types. In many societies wealth is measured not by how much one can accumulate, but by how much one may be able to give away. In several cultures of Papua New Guinea, giving away goods (pigs, garden produce, and ceremonial paraphernalia) is a means of building obligations which can be called on for personal benefit at a later date (Rosman & Rubel 1981). The feasts accompanying rites of passage in Old Testament times may fall into this 'give away' concept of building prestige and be understood by peoples of kinship and peasant cultures better than individuals from industrial cultures. An example would be Abraham's celebration of Isaac's weaning (Gen. 20:8).

ECONOMIC EFFECTS ON THE COMMUNICATION PROCESS

The Apostle Paul speaks of Christ as the cornerstone (Eph. 2:20 — see also other writers, I Pet. 2:5-7, Ps. 118:22). This was a reference to the building styles used at that time, when the cornerstone acted as the foundation upon which the entire structure was built. This practice found its way into present day construction in the form of an inscribed plaque indicating the date and particulars of a building project.

The Samo, living in the lowland swamps do not use cornerstones. In fact, when building, they do not use stones at all. They do, however, have corner posts which serve as the main props for the rafters to rest on. When I applied this information to the passage, I received quizzical looks from my assistants. They did not view these corner posts as critical in the same way I did. After further observation and discussion, it became evident that a crucial moment in house construction is when the ridge pole is laid across the lattice work of rafters. Though these rafters rest on beams which in turn rest on the corner posts that are firmly placed in the ground, it is the tightly secured ridge pole that gives the entire structure its rigidity and strength. It is the ridge pole, then, that the Samo consider vital to the building project. Great care is taken in securing the right kind of wood: strong but light. Just like that, Christ makes a Christian strong, says Paul to the Samo, and they understand the meaning intended far better than a lengthy explanation about cornerstones.[1]

These are critical concerns if people are going to understand the message when they first hear it. Without such considerations, Scripture may be viewed as meaningless. The above example was particularly meaningful when translating the parable of wise and foolish builders (Mt. 7:24-27). Neither rocks nor sand are familiar to the Samo in their forest environment. But the wise man tied his ridge pole on tight, and when the winds came the house stood firm. The foolish man, on the other hand, was in a hurry and did not take time to select the right materials or properly secure them. The result was a flattened house when buffeted by winds such as come in the season known as *wau* (October - January). With this, the Samo identified and understood the message of the familiar parable. The forms for communicating the message were very different from the original source, but the meaning intended by Jesus was crystal clear and the Samo are able to act on this new knowledge with respect to their consideration of Christ and His claims upon their lives (see chapters 13-15 for a discussion of cultural substitutes and idiomatic translation).

These economic considerations are central to the translation process and cross-cultural communication in general. It is essential for the communicator to be aware of environmental differences between the source and receptor cultures and make adjustments as necessary to keep the focus on the meaning of the text. If such adjustments are not made, the focus may become the strangeness of a foreign custom, building with stones, rather than on the meaning of wise living, with Christ at the center of human existence (strengthening the entire structure). With their eyes on foreign issues, receptors may well miss the real message and not see Christ at all. The translation would then be little more than a quaint story about a man who lived a long time ago in a strange and far off place: an individual who meant nothing to them and who was not worth taking the time from real-life economic considerations to understand.

Local economic considerations may also have a drastic effect on the translation process. When do people spend time obtaining a living, and where do they go? The Samo literally spend their lives at the 'grocery store': removing the starch from the sago palm in the swamps, gardening the nearby hillsides, planting, weeding, harvesting and hunting in the forest. All this economic activity takes them away from the longhouse and into their environment where they often spend several weeks at a time without coming home. This posed a problem for us while learning their language. We wanted to interact with them as much as possible so we could translate the Scriptures effectively. We, therefore, spent much time in the forest with them, following their activities and learning what was important to them. When we needed solitude, we stayed home, knowing that the village would be deserted, especially during highly productive times such as the dry season in July, and harvest time for certain crops in November and December.

These economic patterns also had an affect on who would be willing to work closely with us on a regular basis. As long as we were involved in language learning, our focus was on as wide a population as possible, but when we started translating, we selected several individuals we felt could help us most. The problem was that they were also key individuals in the society. They needed to be involved in economic activity in order that the entire group might benefit. As a result, we set up a team with a rotation system that allowed sufficient time to fulfill social and economic responsibilities. At the same time they also assisted their people by providing *spiritual food* through the translation. This worked well, but demanded a sensitivity to their system and how to work within it. We often scheduled times away from the region to coincide with periods when they needed to concentrate on subsistence activities. This ensured that we did not place undue pressure upon them during periods when a possible conflict of interest could have resulted in frustration and misunderstanding.

Developing literacy programs or scheduling church services, also relates to this economic cycle and should be accounted for if receptors are to benefit. They must be the ones in focus, not the translators. We found it best to segregate men and women in literacy classes, and it was best for the women to meet first, early in the morning. This freed them to go about the rest of their day's activities while the men followed shortly after. We also discovered that it was beneficial to take a break from classes every few weeks allowing a time for group activities farther away from the community. All these considerations arose out of the need to fit ourselves, and the Scriptures, to the Samo economic system. Had we not done so, the translation program would have been less successful because the only people willing to help us would have been individuals marginal to the system: people seeking a way out of economic responsibility, for whatever reason. The need for economic maintenance far outweighs the desire to learn to read, and unless properly scheduled, literacy programs in general may be doomed.

Much of the mythology of a people may relate closely to the environment as well. The creation of land and people will be documented in some way that may tie in well with the translation of the early chapters of Genesis. Many people are fascinated with origin stories and are interested in comparing their stories with others they encounter. This curiosity may prove valuable for introducing Scripture. Many people view themselves as having always lived where they presently reside. Others have elaborate migration tales that trace movement to their present location

(Dundes 1965). Whichever the case, as people point out similarities and differences with their stories and those of Scripture, the translator can assist in the discovery process and translate passages that relate to the particular interests of those being translated.

Economic factors then, are, central to communicating the gospel, whatever form it takes. The ramifications of the economic system ripple throughout the culture and affect all other cultural factors. Communicators should take these factors into consideration and develop programs which will enhance these considerations rather than hinder them. They also need to understand how economic factors affect the source culture and integrate that knowledge with the acquired knowledge of the receptor context. It is this marriage of understanding, bringing two cultures into contact, perhaps for the first time, that is both the thrill and the frustration of every translator.

Suggested Reading

Hiebert, Paul. *Cultural Anthropology*. Baker, 1983. Chapts. 4, 5 & 15.

Leclair, E. and H. Schneider. *Economic Anthropology*. Holt, Rinehart and Winston, 1968.

Sahlins, Marshall. *Tribesmen*. Prentice-Hall, 1968.

Service, Elman. *Peasants*. Prentice-Hall, 1968.

Notes

1. While this is a good idiomatic translation, it may be that future generations of Samo, who know about other building styles, will find this translation less than adequate. A basic translation principle, dealt with later (see chapter 15), is the ongoing need for revisions. Perhaps in a later revision, this focus on the ridge pole, so relevant to the first generation Christians, will need to be changed to bring Scripture in line with an expanding Samo understanding of the world. For the present, however, it is important to encourage new believers with a relevant message that builds upon their knowledge of a world essential to their survival.

CHAPTER FOUR
Ideological Factors

To speak of an ideology normally implies a philosophical or political orientation. The anthropological use, however, focuses on the human universal. All human beings attempt to explain their origins, provide a rationale for present conditions, and make a statement concerning the future. Ideology is "a system of beliefs, explaining the nature of [the human] relation to the cosmos, accompanied by a system of observances based on these beliefs" (Hammond 1964:283).

Ideology often takes the form of religion, but is not a religion in itself. Strictly speaking, the beliefs of the atheist, humanist, and agnostic are not religious, but provide people with a sense of personal well-being and security analogous to those with strong religious convictions; they serve the same function. Every culture has a system of beliefs and observances which provides its members with a reason for being and a rationale for much of their cultural activity. This is the focus of this chapter.

IDEOLOGY VS. RELIGION: THE PEOPLE'S VIEW

Anthropologists have long been interested in religious ideologies. Even before extensive field work began, they eagerly read reports written by missionaries living among peoples in far off places. In analyzing these materials, they developed terms for describing what they read and observed; often reflecting their own dualistic views rather than those of the people studied (Frazer 1933). Therefore, the anthropological literature on religious phonomenology uses many dichotomies to describe what anthropologists have observed: sacred-secular, magic-religion, polytheism-monotheism, etc. Christians have done the same thing when lumping the peoples of the world into Christian—Non-Christian categories. Unfortunately, this tendency draws attention to the extremes of each continuum rather than focusing on the realities of the belief system as followed by the particular people being studied.

Tylor (1891) developed a scale of supernatural beliefs to help anthropologists analyze data (Figure 4:1). These were essentially evolutionary stages in the development of ideological beliefs. *Animism* characterized a belief in a soul or indwelling spirit that affected most animals, plants, and objects in the environment. *Animitism* was the belief in impersonal power, a spiritual force (later popularized as *mana* from the South Pacific concept). These forces could direct a favorite weapon to the mark, or inspire awe for some aspect of the environment (such as a volcano). *Polytheism* described a hierarchy of gods who all have power to affect life within the cultural context of those who worship them. These gods are often ranked and a supreme being rules over those who reign in various localities. *Monotheism* was the religion of the more enlightened cultures: the belief in one God who reigned supreme, often created the world as known to the adherents, and expected their reverence.

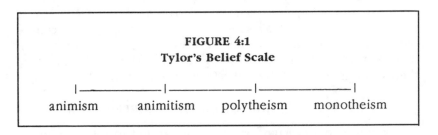

FIGURE 4:1
Tylor's Belief Scale

| ———————— | ———————— | ———————— |
animism   animitism   polytheism   monotheism

If he were writing today Tylor would, no doubt, crown the progression with *agnostic humanism,* the belief that humanity can exist without 'religious' encumbrance and create its own destiny. This obviously evolutionary scheme has been largely rejected by modern anthropologists, but the terminology often forms a framework for the description of a religious system. Tylor's progression is really a dichotomy with specific stages between the extremes defined. As Durkheim studied a wide range of cultures, he noted patterns, some of which reflected mundane or *profane* activities and others more directly related to belief systems which he labeled *sacred* (Durkheim 1965). This descriptive device is still widely used in anthropological literature.

When trying to understand the religion of the Trobriand Islanders, Malinowski saw people worshiping in churches on Sunday, and performing magic in the gardens during the week. One system seemed to have little effect on the other. People blatantly performed 'religious' ceremonies (supplication) or 'magical' rites (control of supernatural power) as situations dictated. His *magic* and *religion* dichotomy was designed to explain what he saw (Malinowski 1948).

Writing in 1960, Titiev noted that many of these descriptive dichotomies did not fit the reality of activities described. Much activity, he noted, could be 'profane' with 'sacred' overtones, e.g. gardening which includes preparation of the ground, planting, weeding, harvesting, etc., but often depends upon some type of spiritual activity (magical spell or prayer) for success. Unfortunately, he proposed another dichotomy to get around the problem, describing *calendrical* or recurrent rites and *critical* or intermittent rites (Titiev 1960).

More recently Hiebert has discussed belief systems with respect to the *empirical* (that which is of this world and can be studied) and the *transempirical* (that which is transcendent and other worldly). In his scheme people bring the extremes of the dichotomy into relationship through ritual and ceremony (Hiebert 1982a).

All of these explanations help a communicator describe the lives of the people studied to others who do not share that ideological experience. But the perspective is external to the system rather than on the needs and concerns of those who hold to it. What is really important here is understanding ideology as part of a people's total way of looking at life. We are really interested in the assumptions upon which they base, not only their ideological practices, but all activities of life.

How do people organize their ideological system and integrate it with their daily lives? This is the real question, for as bearers of the gospel, we are concerned in how that message will be understood and made relevant by those who receive it. Understanding their ideology, their beliefs and values, and what they mean will be of far greater importance to translators than knowing the technical definitions for the extremes of various dichotomies. Our concern when presenting the good news is how people understand the supernatural forces and their responses to them in culturally appropriate behavior patterns. We turn now to discovering these ideological factors.

TOWARD DISCOVERING IDEOLOGICAL FACTORS

Understanding the ideological system of the context into which Scripture was communicated as well as appreciating how the same Scripture will impact the modern receptors is essential if we are to effectively communicate the gospel. Therefore, as with the economic system, we must attempt to understand an ideology from the perspective of those who use it. Our concern is how a people's ideology helps them cope within their world and what that means to them. What are the supernatural forces they must deal with and what are their manifestations? What are the types of ideological practices which help people cope with these supernatural forces? Who are the practitioners who assist mere mortals in this interaction? These questions form the basis of a people's ideology and assist in our inquiry.[1]

Types of Supernatural Forces

What is the range of supernatural forces that a people believe affect their lives and what is the relationship of living human beings to those forces? Do the people have a concept of a High God—one who transcends everything else? Many societies do, some don't, and many of those that do have him or her so transcendent as to be unconcerned with the affairs of real people (Richardson 1981:53-55). Unable to identify with an all-powerful, unconcerned God, many people believe in a wide range of local gods and goddesses who rule over regions, localities, fields, forests, etc. Who are these beings? Do they have names? What is their relationship to the High-God? What do they do? How do they interact with human beings? Are they viewed as good or bad?

What other spiritual forces must people deal with? Are there angels and demons in their world? How are these perceived in relation to the 'higher' supernatural beings and the 'lower' human beings? What powers do they have and how are those manifest? Throughout Melanesia people believe in spirit beings that inhabit the environment and affect nearly everything people do. These beings, however, have numerous manifestations; some groups name the spirits that inhabit certain localities (a deep river pool, a sink hole in the forest, or a cave), while for others the spirits in general live throughout the region and are a pervading force that demand constant vigil. Such is the Samo concept of *hogai* who pervade the forest, wreak havoc in gardens and even creep into houses to bring death. I learned of these beings when I went to meet a plane bringing supplies. I returned to find my wife upset by a Samo man who had spent the entire day wandering around the house. In discussing the matter with him he explained how I had abandoned my family and left them vulnerable to spirit attack. All he had done was fulfill the crucial role of 'spiritual protector' while I was gone. As we discussed this, I learned much about the Samo perception of supernatural forces: of the need to carry weapons at all times, the importance of camouflaging oneself with grasses and leaves in order to be invisible to the *hogai*, the male responsibility to guard a work site while women produce food and the constant vigil necessary when walking the forest trails. Indeed, the *hogai* control nearly every Samo movement.

Using the principles of the observation-questioning technique, watch what people do and listen to what they say about these activities. Use this information to formulate key questions that will help people explain their beliefs to you. Observing practices will trigger questions that lead to discussions of spiritual forces with which people deal. Recall the Apostle Paul's discovery of the unknown god in Athens and his masterful use of that concept to discuss the reality of Christ with those philosophers (Acts 17:16-31).

Another area of ideological concern is the nature of death: what it is, what causes it and the relationship between the living and the dead. At what point do spirits of the living depart this world and enter another, if another exists? When do ordinary spirits of the dead become ancestors? How do they affect the living; do they help, cause trouble, or act as mediators with the supernatural beings? Understanding these concepts about death, human spirits, and ancestors may shed light upon human relationships with the supernatural and a people's concept of life as they know it.

These concepts can be diagrammed (Figure 4:2) to reflect the nature of supernatural forces and their relationship to human beings. Of particular interest to us are the concepts people have of these powers. Reflecting that understanding may require a re-ordering of the chart. What for them is natural, supernatural? How do they perceive that which is absolute? How does this contrast with the non-absolute? What terms do they use to describe all this? These terms may turn out to be crucial to communicating the gospel.

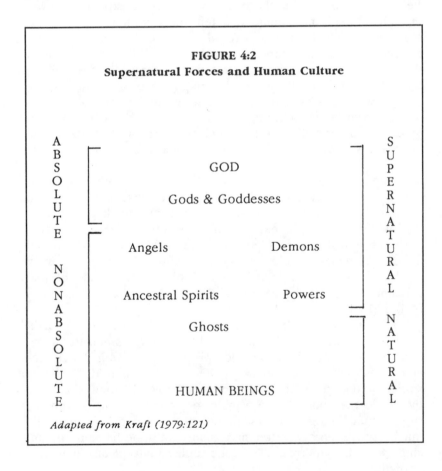

FIGURE 4:2
Supernatural Forces and Human Culture

ABSOLUTE

GOD

Gods & Goddesses

NONABSOLUTE

Angels   Demons

Ancestral Spirits   Powers

Ghosts

HUMAN BEINGS

SUPERNATURAL

NATURAL

Adapted from Kraft (1979:121)

Types of Ideological Practices

What behavior patterns do people associate with these supernatural forces? What are the rituals and ceremonies associated with them, i.e. how do people contact the supernatural and why? What 'magical' formulae help the crops grow better, and to whom or what are they directed? How are music and dance, drugs, incense, prayer, preaching, feasting and/or fasting, taboos of all types, sacrifice, and any type of symbolism used to affect supernatural power? Is this viewed as worship or coercion of some type? As you observe these activities, formulate questions that will encourage people to respond, while at the same time reasoning through their belief system in a way they may never have experienced before.

For example, by watching a mother gently waken her sleeping child so they could go home, I discovered the need to understand the relationship between a human spirit and its disembodied counterpart; two different states for the same entity. When asking questions about my observation I learned of the need to allow time for the spirit, which may be wandering in a dream, to repossess the body. Often an awakening child remains sleepy for a period and the mother explains that the 'spirit' has not yet returned. Gently awakening someone is in no way considered 'sacred', but has far reaching spiritual implications that require an understanding of the Samo concept of a person as a combination of body, spirit, and bones (Shaw 1976). The Samo view of decomposition provides a pragmatic key to this aspect of their belief system. After death, established when the spirit permanently leaves, the body decomposes and only the bones remain. Treatment of the body and the handling of the bones reflect Samo beliefs in keeping with kinship responsibilities and social organization. The departed spirit, however, goes to the top of a special tree from whence it is carried to the 'house of living ancestors' where it lives until, eventually, it will cycle back to indwell another human being giving a new body its substance. It is essential then, to understand the Samo concept of 'soul', either as part of a human being or dwelling in the spirit world. As this illustration indicates, observation and questioning may lead to discussions that appear totally unrelated to the initial observations. Such incidents, however, reinforce the integrated model of culture—pursuit of one aspect forces interaction with all others.

An interest in why a sleeping child (or anyone else) is not hurriedly awakened, leads to an understanding of a broad and complex ideology which permeates many Samo activities.

A people's mythology may also be very helpful in understanding many of their ideological practices. Recognizing that myths are not untrue stories, but rather serve as the corporate repository of truth—a validation of how things got the way they are—we can study them to appreciate a people's understanding of their reality. What cultural themes run through the myths and how do the stories illustrate them? Often mythology is used to validate certain activities, or justify unexplainable occurrences such as natural catastrophe.

Types of Ideological Practitioners

Who are the practitioners who assist their fellow human beings in their interaction with the supernatural powers and principalities? In some societies, religious practitioners assist as part time specialists (shaman) while in others full time priests assist people in their need. Shaman tend to be somewhat more individualistic, assisting in crisis when necessary. Priests, on the other hand, tend to relate to group needs (however culturally defined) supplicating the gods on behalf of the people. This trend led to Titiev's dichotomy in which he saw part time shaman being more active in critical contexts, while full time priests were more in focus during established ceremony. This set of relationships tends to be characteristic of peasant peoples who utilize a *folk religion* in their personal lives while subscribing to a *state religion* that affects their national context. Eliade has written extensively on shamanism, detailing the various manifestations of this phenomena (Eliade 1964). Every cross-cultural communicator would do well to become acquainted with this classic work. These religious specialists can teach us much about the supernatural world.

Life Cycle and the Ideological System

Another helpful area that can assist in understanding ideological issues brings the life cycle into focus. What are the major stages of life assumed by the Biblical authors as well as the people to whom you are ministering? How is life perceived? What periods of life do they celebrate? What are the periods when ritual and ceremony are important? van Gennep's classic work on rites of passage can be helpful here (van Gennep 1960). Figure 4:3 lays out in a very etic manner what are often important life cycle phases. Our interest is in which phases people recognize and how they are structured to give meaning to life. How are these critical stages recognized? What physiological or social manifestations are necessary to trigger an appropriate cultural response? When does a child become a true human being? What signals death and what does death mean? Appropriate questions can only come out of effective observations of people's actual behavior.

FIGURE 4:3
Stages in the Life Cycle

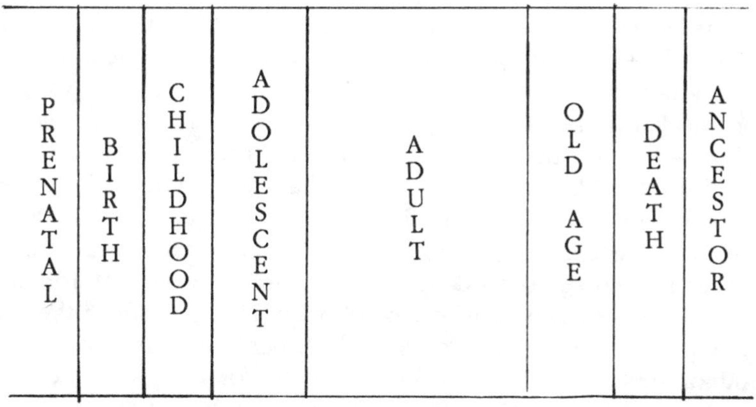

PRENATAL	BIRTH	CHILDHOOD	ADOLESCENT	ADULT	OLD AGE	DEATH	ANCESTOR

I recall my surprise when I discovered that my favorite old man would not have an elaborate funeral. I had seen funerals for younger men that were very involved and mentioned to a brother how I wanted to be there when old Umo died. He did not understand my reasoning and explained that they could hardly wait for Umo to die so he could be of some use to them. As an old man he was useless except for some baby-sitting. But dead (physically) meant that his spirit could go off to the spirit abode and there be an assistance to them in a variety of ways. The elaborate rites for younger men had to do with ascertaining the cause of death through divination and a genuine sense of loss to the work force. Such a pragmatic approach to death heightened my awareness of the dramatic differences in our respective worldviews. More importantly, the cultural distance between the Samo, my own post-industrial culture base, and the Scriptures I wanted to translate, was made plainly evident.

How does the local view of life and death, and the stages in between, relate to Scripture? How are these ideological concerns and practices reflected in lifestyle and what affect will that have upon the way people understand God's Word? What does the Bible have to say about these concerns that are so real to them? It is to these issues that we now turn.

IDEOLOGY IN THE COMMUNICATION PROCESS

As bearers of the good news, we must not degrade Christianity to the status of a religion. Christianity is concerned with worldview, the basic meaning of life. Thus the message we bring and the Scriptures we translate need to permeate all of a cultural system—activate the potential of that culture for Christ. If Christ can fulfill people's lives, it must happen within the cultural context that enables them to live in a manner consistent with their worldview, of which their ideology is an important part. At points where allegiance to God violates culture, people are forced to make a choice. This is where worldview change affects the basic assumptions help by a society. The critical issue is allegiance to God or to their belief system. A choice for God will inevitably result in worldview change. Those changes, however, must relate to the structure of the cultural system in order to bring it in line with God's Word. The Scriptures are full of stories (case studies) that illustrate fundamental changes in ideology while people continued to live as full members of their culture.

Throughout Scripture we note a power struggle between the forces of good and evil. Similarly, when God's Word comes into contact with cultural contexts that are in opposition to it, a power encounter ensues. Much Christian witness has taken place throughout Melanesia at the point of spiritual confrontation

(Tippett 1967). The same could be said for mission enterprise the world over. When Scripture comes in contact with the forces of evil, like Job, people are caught in the struggle. Confrontation is at the heart of the great commission. It comes as a result of the Holy Spirit speaking through the message (including translated Scripture) to affect the hearts of people buried in their ideological base.

In short, people do not need to stop being members of their culture in order to be Christians. That is an extractionist view that must go out with colonialism. Rather they should establish a relationship to God through Christ (Jn. 1:12, Rom. 8:17) and appropriate that relationship to all others within the human realm and the entire supernatural arena that characterizes so many ideological systems.

This matter of allegiance to Christ, who fulfills the culture, greatly assists the cross-cultural communicator who wishes to present the gospel in a relevant way. As people become Christians, they need to be encouraged to integrate their beliefs and practices into a relevant worship of God. If they performed magic for good crops, they need to bring God into the gardening process and pray in a culturally appropriate way for good crops. This introduces the whole idea of functional substitutes that has been widely discussed.

Writing on the "Flaw of the Excluded Middle", Hiebert (1982a) addresses this concern for relevance. While ideology is primarily concerned with "other worldly" issues—the cosmos—it has dramatic implications for "this world". People want answers to life's questions—who they are, why things are as they are, what to do to avoid calamity, and how to appropriate spiritual power. These are issues that much of the ceremony and ritual of ideological systems around the world are designed to answer. Only Scripture provides a better answer. This concept of the "middle zone" is important for Bible translation efforts, for it is here that the reality of Scripture (the ultimate reality with an "R") meets the perceived reality of a people's beliefs and values (a limited reality with a "r"). An adaptation of Hiebert's model contrasting generalizations of Non-western, Western and Christian beliefs and practices is presented in Figure 4:4.

FIGURE 4:4
Ideology and the Christian Message

T R A N S E M P E R I C A L	Non-Western (Animistic)	Western (Humanistic)	Christian (Biblical)	S U P E R N A T U R A L
	gods	Religion (Church)	GOD	
	spirits		Satan	
	powers		Angels	
			Demons	
	rituals	EXCLUDED	prayer	
E M P E R I C A L	ceremony	MIDDLE	use God's power for living	N A T U R A L
	Relation-ships	Science (Work) medicine mechanistic	Daily activities	

Adapted from Hiebert, 1982a

God, as stated in chapter 1, works in and through culture. Relevance is the key for understanding ideological beliefs as they relate to the broader worldview. That must be the arena of interaction—God relates to people in their context—the incarnational principle is still in force. If we can use our understanding of a people's ideology to determine appropriate passages that will demonstrate God's concerns with real life issues, people will see Scripture as having answers for living life to the fullest. What needs are reflected in ideological beliefs and practices and what verses answer those needs? Knowing the deep concern for avoiding the ravages of spirits, translators can choose portions dealing with 'spiritual warfare' and translate them for the people. Knowing their fears of sickness and death, translate passages identifying how Christ dealt with these human problems.

As people relate Scripture to their own beliefs and values (comparing origin stories, noting similar migration patterns, and understanding that other cultures also deal with spiritual issues) they will appropriate Scripture to their own context in a way similar to the original recipients. Through the power of the Holy Spirit, the Word can bring about change in the hearts of those who respond and experience a shift of allegiance. In discussing Genesis chapter 9 with a group of men one day, one suddenly blurted out, "you mean to say that God doesn't want us going on cannibal raids?" Not being a cannibal, I had never considered this passage from that perspective. However, since God told Noah that He had made human beings in His image and was not pleased when they were killed, the application to cannibalism was, indeed, relevant. My brother went on to indicate how they had not understood the government's concern with cannibalism, and why national pastors had told them that raiding was bad. He told me I was the first to make sense on this issue. I quickly responded that it was not my words that made sense, but God's— the power of the Holy Spirit communicating to the Samo that their culture was contrary to God's desire for them. God cares about human life and they can appropriate that concern to their daily living. What a powerful message for them.

As people apply God's truth to their lives, and use forms that are expressive for them, their culture will be fulfilled. People can but live the abundant life within their cultural context. Properly translated Scripture can fulfill their 'search for salvation' both for this life and throughout eternity.[2]

Suggested Reading

Eliade, Mircea. *Shamanism*. Princeton University Press, 1964.

Hiebert, Paul. *Cultural Anthropology*. Baker, 1983. Chapts. 8 & 19.

Taylor, John. *The Primal Vision*. SCM Press, 1963.

van Gennep, Arnold. *The Rites of Passage*. U. of Chicago Press, 1960.

Notes

1. Many peoples of the world have, through their contact with expatriates, developed the awareness that 'outsiders' do not always agree
   with or approve of their ideological beliefs and practices. Thus one
   of the basic concerns of translators is to gradually, over time, break
   through this trust barrier and ensure the people that whatever they
   say is all right. Many a religious system is deeply buried under smiles
   and assenting nods and it takes time to break this down and
   communicate true concern and interest in their system as it functions
   for them. Despite the arduous task, the results are well worth the
   effort. This demands, however, that we communicate an attitude of
   openness to the people at all times on all subjects.

2. It is important to note, here, that while the most natural, idiomatic,
   translation is preferable, and allows the spirit of God to work in
   people's lives, it does not guarantee results. In fact, through history,
   people have responded to the Word despite inadequate translation or
   miscommunication resulting in misunderstanding. Take for example
   the Ethiopian eunuch in Acts 8:26-40. Undoubtedly a changed heart
   led to his attempt to understand Isaiah 53. He did not understand
   and, therefore, needed a translator, someone who could explain in
   terms he understood. God provided that translator in the person of
   Philip and the eunuch acted on his new knowledge to express
   himself in baptism. Many others responding to dreams and cultural
   evidences of God have searched for the truth and responded when
   God's Word arrived. However, in all these cases, complete understanding was only possible after (1) the Scripture was made available
   in some form and (2) the Holy Spirit enlightened them to the realities
   of God's grace.

CHAPTER FIVE
Kinship Factors

Kinship studies are the stuff of anthropology. Ever since L. H. Morgan wrote *Systems of Consanguinity and Affinity of the Human Family* in 1871, anthropologists have been enthralled with kinship. This is largely because kinship offers a quick handle on a culture. Kinship is quite easily codified and can be quantified without an excessive amount of input from the people of the culture. Given our integrated model of culture, the features which dictate the reasoning behind a kinship system will probably affect other cultural aspects as well, thereby giving insight to the total cultural system.

In this chapter the focus is on understanding the kinship systems of both the source and the receptor in the communication process. For example, many receptor languages require that the relative age of siblings be indicated, but Mark 1:16-20 is not clear who was older: Simon or Andrew, James or John. In many societies, effective translation demands an indication of the relative age of these groups of brothers. Something as simple as this can result in people misunderstanding Scripture, not because it is translated wrong, but because the translator's unawareness of such detail may introduce unnecessary focus that results in people missing the intent of a passage. It is to this focus on who the relatives are and how they are classified that we now turn.

THE IMPORTANCE OF INTERPERSONAL RELATIONSHIPS

Anthropologists generally recognize four basic types of kin relationships: (1) *consanguineal* - those who are related by actual genealogical ties of some kind, (2) *affinal* - those related by marriage, (3) *classificatory* - distant relatives classed as close relatives, e.g. FB = F, or MZH = F[1] and (4) *fictive* - those who are not related at all, but are incorporated into the system and have

69

kin terms used for them. In determining the usage of kin terms, anthropologists often use the genealogical method. By studying genealogies for each community member, a researcher can identify the terminology used by people for individuals in all possible relationships.

Inasmuch as anthropologists write to specific audiences in major languages other than the one using the specified terminology, writers are forced to gloss the kin terms (and other linguistic labels) using the terms of the literary language. As a result, readers tend to focus on the meaning of the term in their language rather than the intent in the kinship system being described. Thus, the term *uyo* in Samo can be glossed 'mother' but means far more than genealogical mother to the Samo. For them, the term designates all women who are genealogically in a M, MZ, MBD, and FZD relationship to a given speaker. This classificatory usage, specifying females who are widely scattered both spatially and generationally, indicates the term has significantly broader meaning in Samo than 'mother' does in English. For the Samo, *uyo* indicates women of father's age group from whom one can expect to receive food regardless of where they live. It also designates women of one's own age group who may become wives. Thus a gloss such as 'nurturing woman/potential wife' would be better than the primary usage, 'mother' (see Shaw 1974a, 1974b, and 1976 for details of Samo relationship terms).[2]

The focus for cross-cultural communicators as they become involved in living with people is not on the details of the genealogical system, but rather on the meaning of the relationship terms as they are used in reference to real people. What kind of behavior is triggered by the use of a term and what implications might that have for the communicator? How does terminological usage reflect behavior patterns and how does that relate to the broader culture of which kinship is but a part? For the answer we must be involved with those who use the terms in their daily activity. We need a methodology that relates terminology to behavior which, in turn, gives insight to the meaning of the terms.

As we interacted with the Samo, there came the day when they greeted me using the appropriate 'brother' terms, followed by appropriate terms for Karen and the boys. The occasion was our return after a period of absence. I was delighted, not just because they were accepting us in this way, but because this implied new relationships based on insider roles. Along with this new terminology, however, went new responsibility. Soon we were besieged with requests for various items: canned fish, matches, and soap. I became indignant with these requests, in part because we had not been asked for things before, but also because I suspected we were being used—brought into the system in order to be exploited. Later I was humbled as an older brother explained that travelers always returned with gifts in order to reestablish their kinship ties. Inasmuch as we did not realize this, they were helping us learn by requesting gifts from us. They had to teach us what it meant to be Samo, and this was their way of doing so. They had adopted us into their system in order to incorporate us. Without this incorporation we would remain outsiders, untrusted ones, perhaps even enemies. The only way for them to interact effectively with us was to integrate us into the structure of their kinship system in word and deed.

In short, kinship terms serve as an identification, a label, for people who are variously related to each other. These terms are linguistic designations for how the society expects people in these various relationships to act. Conversely, how people act in specific relationships is a cultural manifestation of the meaning of the terms used for those interaction patterns. We turn now to developing a way to discover these patterns and the terms that signify them.

TOWARD DISCOVERING KINSHIP

As a cross-cultural witness you want to be thoroughly in-volved with the people. Following the observation-questioning technique learn to recognize people and notice who interacts with whom, when and where. Try to learn people's names (if that is culturally appropriate) and the terms they use for each other. As you hear these terms, notice who uses them, in what contexts, and what the circumstances are. Make notes of these observations; describe what you see and how you felt if you were involved. In this way you may begin to recognize family groupings or important relationships, and the essential behavior patterns per-tinent to them.

Your expanding notes on all this interaction will equip you with material from which to ask questions about actual events in the community. You will become aware of certain recurring patterns on a daily basis. Does the time of day dictate a focus on different groupings (men chat around a fire in the evening while women visit as they care for young children, or morning and afternoon rush hour)? How do work patterns, (already discussed with respect to economic activity) affect interpersonal relationships (gardening, marketing, or office parties)?

Jesus understood the Samaritan pattern of women gathering at the well for water in the morning and evening. This knowledge allowed him to point out one woman's lack of conformity to cultural expectations (Jn. 4:5-30). A discussion of the reasons for her behavior followed. A shift from the cultural norm may signal a place for the effective introduction of the gospel.

The family has long been considered a basic social unit, and so it often is. The family results from a marriage which produces children who grow up interacting with parents and siblings as the culture dictates. Therefore, procreation yields children who are related to the parents by consanguineal kin ties, i.e. by descent. Because this is the only biological way to produce children, anthropologists have viewed genealogical relationships as basic to kinship systems anywhere on earth. Hence the anthropological preoccupation with genealogy and classificatory systems based on the cousin terminology used in a prominent society using that system (Eskimo, Iroquois, Omaha, etc.). While cousin terms may be helpful as anthropologists compare notes they may not offer much insight for a communicator concerned about how people organize and label their relationships.

What is a biological fact can be drastically altered by culture. People adopt children and use kin terms for them. Individuals move around associating with different people at different periods in their life cycle. Those in constant close association may find it useful to use kin terms despite the fact that they are not kin at all. Their association is more critical than the genealogical relationship they have with people they seldom see. The rationale behind various types of clubs, religious, social, age, and initiation groups can all have an effect on the terminology used to identify relationships.

In many cultures, the family is, in fact, a close knit unit that brings members into close association with each other. Family members tend to be important to each other, especially in kinship societies. Often in such a context, individuals that are not family, but live in close association are also viewed as being important to the social interaction and family terminology is extended to the wider group. Features such as residence, adoption, initiation, alliance, religious affiliation, education, socio-economic factors, and many more, can all be crucial in determining kinship terminology and may be complementary to, or even supersede, genealogy.

For example, among the Samo, kin terms are used almost exclusively in place of personal names. In order to use a given term, the speaker needs to know where a person lives. If within the same longhouse community the terminology reflects close family ties. Within the community, the use of sibling terms or parent-child terms requires knowledge of the initiation structure, i.e. time of initiation and age with respect to the speaker. For individuals who live outside the immediate community, one needs to know if they are allied in some way; if not, they can only be enemies. Residence or, more broadly, location, initiation, and alliance are central to the Samo kinship system and far surpass a need for genealogical knowledge. An anthropologist using a genealogical model can, in fact, predict correct usage, and categorize the Samo Kinship system as a form of Omaha (Shaw 1976). However, this information tells us nothing about how the Samo use the terminology and what it means to them. A translator, however, needs to know how the worldview is reflected in interpersonal relationships and the terminology used to reflect them, for that will affect how people understand Scripture.

It is here that Goodenough's concept of *identity, status* and *role* is useful (Goodenough 1965). *Identity* establishes a position in the social system. This is the linguistic label or kin term, e.g. *uyo. Status* relates to the rights and duties of the identity. These are the behavioral expectations of the people with respect to the identity; *uyo* are expected to provide food. *Role* is the actual performance of rights and duties: the actual behavior of individuals in a particular relationship. How do *uyo* act out their status in real life situations? What happens if they refuse to give food? Individuals, then, act out the expectations prescribed by the usage of a term.

Another key concept inherent in this discussion of identity, status, and role is *reciprocity*. Role behavior assumes an interactant (another person) with whom the individual, terminologically identified, interacts. Thus kin terms are often stated in dyads, as Hsu calls them (1971), or pairs of terms: husband-wife, father-son, mother-daughter, brother-sister, etc. Each set identifies a pair of culturally defined roles and appropriate behavior for these roles varies greatly from culture to culture.

As you determine these relationships, keep a notebook with a separate page for each identity you discover. This will expand as you note the various behavior patterns inherent in the term and develop questions to help you understand the meaning of the term in relation to all others. All the terms you collect will reflect patterned behavior between two people.

Studying these dyads can produce a wealth of information on behavioral expectations. Questioning individuals in each dyadic relationship can help you anticipate behavioral patterns and what happens when expectations are not met (as with the woman at the well). Gradually you will build an understanding of how kin terms are used and what they mean within the cultural context. Such understanding will serve you well as you begin to translate the meaning of Biblical terms into the receptor language. Remember that language is symbolic of behavior. The terms reflect behavioral expectations of the society. It is important to be aware that Biblical truths may be misunderstood if a Biblical character acts inappropriately from the perspective of the receptor. Use the terminology which will indicate the correct meaning for those who now receive Scripture for the first time.

For example, in some cultures the concept of God as a 'heavenly father' may not be very comforting because of the cultural status of a father in relation to his child. In such cases, the passage using this term must be analyzed to determine if it was intended to be used literally or if the meaning reflects the nature of a warm, loving relationship which might be best translated using a term reflecting a similar meaning in the receptor language, e.g. God, the mother's brother, in some Melanesian societies.

As you learn about these relationships take note of who in the society is qualified to make changes in the customs, distribute new information, present supernatural truth, mediate in arguments, and discipline when necessary. Such information will lead to understanding the authority structure of the society as it relates to kin responsibilities. What roles are outsiders assigned and what are the behavioral expectations associated with being an outsider? How do outsiders become insiders and what behavioral changes are necessary to effect such a change? All these questions develop a deep awareness of the status-roles associated with the various dyads designated by the kinship terms.

Hsu has used the principle of reciprocity to formulate his "hypothesis on kinship and culture" (1971). Though highly controversial and much debated in anthropological circles, the concept can be of great help to a translator seeking to understand the effect of behavior on terminological usage. Hsu maintains that one dyad, with its inherent status-roles, tends to determine the attitudes and actions of people who use that kinship system. These attitudes and actions (for what he calls the "dominant dyad") may affect all other dyadic relationships within that terminological system. Thus, within the industrialized nations the dyad of greatest significance is probably husband-wife. This is the relationship that establishes a family and all family members relate to each other based on the attitudes and actions of these two individuals. They have specific rights and duties with respect to each other and together establish an exclusive unit. Should this relationship be broken, divorce, i.e. a broken home, occurs and all other relationships are adversely affected (Bohannan 1971).

To discover the dominant dyad for the group of people you are working with necessitates returning to your notes. About which relationship have you accumulated the most notes? Who interacts most often? What are the interests of the people so associated? How does behavior with respect to that relationship affect other dyads? Develop questions that will force the respondents to think through their associations and, perhaps, in a new way, express what they do and why it is important to them. Listen to discussions among the people. What interaction patterns captivate their interest and are often the focus of discussion? What relationships give way to others and which one seems to dominate when people are forced to make a choice? Which dyad when disrupted creates the most dissonance with respect to other relationships? This is probably the dominant dyad.

KINSHIP AND THE COMMUNICATION PROCESS

With reference to the communicator's interest in meaning, it is essential that there be an understanding of the emic categorization of kin. Hence I have not attempted to detail the genealogical methods used by anthropologists. Rather the focus here is on discovering what people do and say about their relationships. Such an approach, though perhaps not anthropologically elegant, will develop in the translator an awareness of the meaning attached to the various terms as used by the people for whom the translation will be produced.

The communicator who is totally involved with people and appropriates their lifestyle to the extent possible, will find the use of the proper kin terms a distinct advantage. If this is to become a reality, you will need to be taught what the terms mean so you can enter into dynamic relationships with those around you. Remember that the terms label culturally appropriate behavior, hence you must be ready to use the behavioral patterns correctly, not only in your personal interaction, but in the translation as well.

Why should a cross-cultural witness be interested in an emic understanding of a kinship system? Why is it necessary to know which dyad predominates within a culture? The answers lie in the need to communicate Scriptural meaning within the new context. Utilizing the kinship terminology in the communication of God's Word, can go a long way toward convincing the receptors that God is real. Couched in the context of receptor expectations and concerns, the reality of the message will be convincing. God has a sense of understanding for all patterns of interpersonal relationship. Our responsibility is to discover what those associations mean and communicate the truth of relationship to God in those conceptual patterns: the patterns implied by the use of specific kin terms.

If the dominant dyad for a Biblical culture is not the same as the receptor than adjustments need to be made (either by substituting dominant dyad for dominant dyad or communicating the importance of the Biblical context and what characteristics compare in the receptor). The dominance of the Father-Son dyad in the Old Testament Hebrew culture may be very much misunderstood in a matrilineal culture in Polynesia. Since meaning is in focus, and the receptor attaches different meaning to the father-son relationship, the dyad reflecting the same meaning, intended by the author, should be discovered and used if the receptor is to understand the same message.

Scripture is full of interpersonal behavior (husbands to wives, parents to children, siblings, slaves to masters, rich to poor, and the in-group to the out-group). What do people in Scripture passages call each other, i.e. how do they appropriate kinship terms? Knowing the relationships subsumed by the use of the various terms, the meaning of that behavior must be communicated in the new context. Without this knowledge a communicator is at a distinct disadvantage and runs the risk of miscommunicating important information.

The Apostle Paul's letter to Titus provides an excellent example of the need to understand and appropriate kinship material. Titus is a detailed discussion of interpersonal relationships. Chapter 1 emphasizes the relationship of elders to their families as well as other members in the church. The relationships extent between believers based on sound doctrine is the focus of chapter 2. Finally, chapter 3 relates to the believers' interaction patterns with unbelievers. It is impossible to translate Titus without a thorough knowledge of the kinship system of both the Cretan culture, in which Titus was planting a church, and the social relationships of people in the receptor culture. The book of Titus is about relationships (leaders to the led, old women to young women, old men to younger men, slaves to masters, etc.). Translators must be careful to ensure that correct meaning is communicated by employing the terms appropriate to usage and meaning for those who now receive the message. The effective communication of God's Word may depend upon it.

Suggested Reading

Bohannan, P. and J. Middleton. *Kinship and Social Organization.* Natural History Press, 1968.

Hiebert, Paul. *Cultural Anthropology.* Baker, 1983. Chapts. 7 & 11.

Hsu, F. L. K. *Kinship and Culture.* Aldine, 1971.

Schusky, Earnest. *Manual for Kinship Analysis.* Holt, Rinehart & Winston, 1965.

Notes

1. The symbols used here for kinship terms are widely used in the anthropological literature. They are generally mnemonical, using the first letter of each term in English (or a combination of letters) to represent the term. Thus Father is F, Mother - M, Husband - H, etc. The most notable exception to this is the symbol for sister which is Z in order to distinguish it from an S for Son. Therefore MZH is a reference to Mother's Sister's Husband, MBD = Mother's Brother's Daughter, FZS = Father's Sister's Son, etc. See almost any basic anthropology text, or Schusky's *Manual for Kinship Studies* (1965) for a complete listing.

2. The meanings of these designations will vary with the relationships extant within a society. What people mean by a term we may gloss as 'mother', may be very different relationally for them. We must consider this in our interaction patterns as we associate with them thereby matching our actions to the language we use.

CHAPTER SIX
Social Factors

Whereas kinship is the study of relationships between individuals, social structure deals with groups of people as they interact. Kinship focuses on individuals while social structure has groups of people as its primary concern.

This area of anthropological study tends to be complex, reflecting a long history of development. There are many ways to classify social groupings, and a variety of theories around which the data can be organized. Our focus here will be to define some of the more accepted groupings used by anthropologists and then to note how the Biblical and receptor cultures fit into this classification. The important thing to remember is that no society fits directly into this etic framework. It serves only as an initial model for data collection in a particular society, receptor or source. This terminology establishes definitions that help communicators determine which specific groupings a society recognizes, how they are structured, and what the meaning of each group is. This is a more culture-specific approach to social interaction.

THE MATRIX OF SOCIAL INTERACTION

The primary question in this section is: how do people group themselves? Some of the common etic social groupings that anthropologists use are defined as follows.

Nuclear Family: This group consists of the male and female parents accompanied by their children. This family has only two generations.

Polygenous Family: This two generation family is composed of multiple spouses (male - polyandry, or female - polygamy) and their children.

Extended Family: This three (or more) generation family consists of a male or female head, the married children of the head and their spouses and children.

Lineage: All families belonging to this group trace their descent from a common, known ancestor. The ancestor was a real person, and often there may be attempts within the lineage to demonstrate a *line* of descent that is *pure,* thus establishing a *right* of descent. It is common, though not imperative, that people marry outside this group, i.e. it is usually an exogamous grouping.

Clan: Clans include two or more lineages each of which can trace their descent to a common, mythical (perhaps totemic) ancestor. Often exogamous, the common ancestral tie binds this group for various culturally defined purposes.

Caste: This group pertains more to peasant societies. It reflects occupational and/or socio-economic position. The people within a caste have a social status that is very difficult to change, making mobility from one caste to another rare. Hence, people usually marry within the caste, i.e. it is an endogamous group.

Phratry: This group is composed of two or more clans that recognize a common bond based on kinship or territorial association. These are often a group of allies who interact within a recognized land area. These groups, in turn, are set apart from similar groups who are often considered enemies. Phratries may be endogamous or exogamous, depending on the social context.

Moiety: This grouping is common in Oceania and highly developed among the Australian Aborigines (Radcliffe-Brown 1931). It consists of one half of an equally divided society. A moiety is almost always exogamous. Group identity and interaction patterns are variously defined.

Peasant - Elite: Based both on economic and social status, this division of a society serves to establish group relationships. It does not necessarily imply poor versus rich (respectively). There is a symbiotic relationship in which the peasants utilize materials provided by the elite. The elite also provide religious and political protection in return for goods and services.

Phyle: First used by Hogbin and Wedgwood (1953), this term designates a linguistic boundary, i.e. a language or dialect. It is seldom an organized group that gets together or acts as a social unit, but is useful for understanding linguistic relationships.

Other Groups: Many other factors serve as criteria to establish social groupings: age, education, occupation, politics, prestige, religion, sex and wealth to name a few. In Japan, the company is the focal group and company loyalty is intense. In the U.S. a host of criteria delimit membership in clubs of all types including gangs, churches, and occupations of all sorts. Unlike the more genealogically focused groupings of kinship societies, however, these groups are not mutually exclusive; one can be a member of the local Baptist church, the Kiwanis club and an occupational guild all at the same time.

People group and regroup themselves in various ways. Some societies may have all or nearly all of these groups; others may have very few or use different criteria to establish groupings. It is important to understand why people group themselves. What kinds of interaction patterns are relevant both within each grouping and then between the various groups? A certain size may be necessary for group and/or personal survival. Relatives mean protection and the way people group themselves may provide information about the way a society views itself. Which groups are relevant to the society you seek to reach and why?

TOWARD DISCOVERING SOCIAL STRUCTURE

Though the rationale for much of this etic list comes from the descent principle, people use a variety of ways to expand their relationships. You need to discover these rationale and apply them to interaction with the people of the society you hope to reach.

Anthropologists often begin a study by mapping the groupings they see in a community and/or region. This can be a useful technique for you as well. Within a community, a map may reveal family units and the way they cluster may suggest other types of groupings. In the early part of our field work among the Samo, I drew a map of Kwobi village (see Map 1). On it I indicated the position of each longhouse and its community of origin prior to aggregation, the number of people living in each house, and the heads of households (not included here). This community was something I could observe, map out and interact with. It was a tangible entity composed of nuclear families who interrelated within a household that was controlled by a male head called the *ayo*. A longhouse, then, by the above criteria, appeared to be a type of extended family. These households were, in turn, functioning within a village of which I was now a part.

On a larger scale, you can note the location of communities and how they juxtapose with respect to marriage, peaceful or military interaction, relationship to the land or any other characteristics people use to distinguish groupings. This should reveal valuable information about what the society considers socially important. For the Samo longhouse groups in a village had a rather loose association, residing at a location primarily at the request of administrative officers. These households, however, had previous ties based on the alliance structure established through sister exchange. It was on this criteria that they responded to administrative requests to re-group (see Map 2).

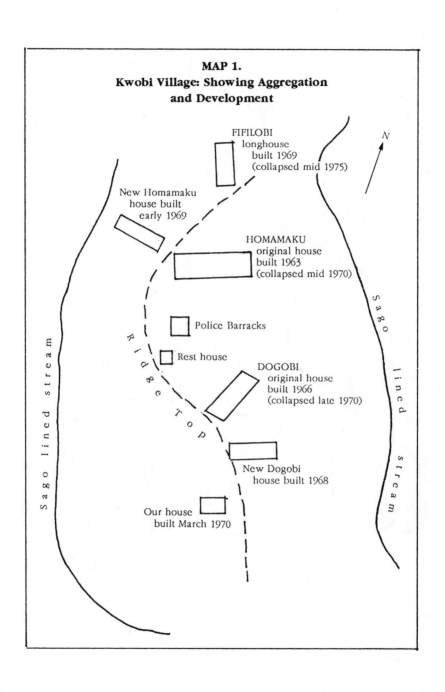

MAP 1.
Kwobi Village: Showing Aggregation
and Development

FIFILOBI
longhouse
built 1969
(collapsed mid 1975)

N

New Homamaku
house built
early 1969

HOMAMAKU
original house
built 1963
(collapsed mid 1970)

Sago lined stream

Police Barracks

Rest house

Ridge Top

DOGOBI
original house
built 1966
(collapsed late 1970)

Sago lined stream

New Dogobi
house built 1968

Our house
built March 1970

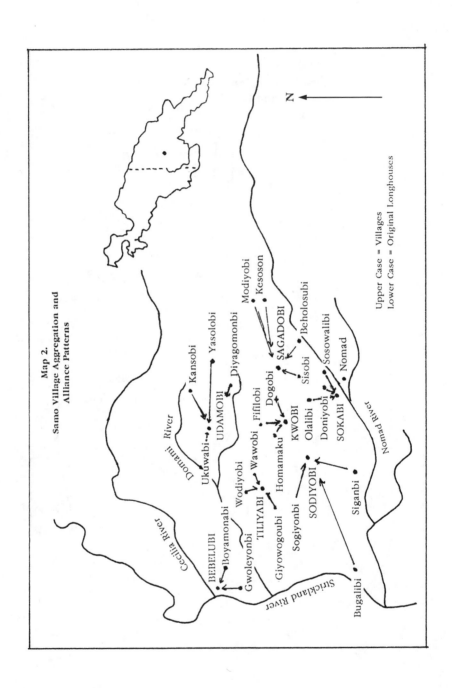

Map 2.
Samo Village Aggregation and
Alliance Patterns

Upper Case = Villages
Lower Case = Original Longhouses

As you work with the maps try to discover the linguistic labels used to identify groupings. There may also be recognized groups that are not named but are considered important. For example, the Samo have no term that designates the nuclear family, yet that unit is very obvious and recognized by the people as the unit for procreation. These family members, however, live within the context of a longhouse where they interact with other families. The household is a named unit that forms the basis of their identity, people who sleep together in the same location.

What does membership in the various groups imply? What types of actions are expected by members and how does that affect their interaction with members of other groups? In short, the identity, status and role distinction established for kinship terms pertains to social structure as well.

Are the various groups hierarchically structured so that each specific group fits into groupings at each successive level, or do people order their groups in another, more cultural, way? Studying the dynamics of group interaction will greatly assist in developing your understanding. The continued use of observation and questions based on that observation will enable a translator to develop an awareness of the social constraints affecting group behavior. Gradually a system will emerge that reflects the values and interaction patterns of the people. This is why collecting good data is so important. The original map, complete with a census, (or listing) of all included individuals is a valuable tool. The labels on this original map, however, are in constant flux as you develop your understanding of the group.

For example, using the etic groupings list, I initially chose to view the village, rather loosely, as a patrilineal phratry. Kwobi, was one phratry/village in a dialect grouping of seven other villages, all very similar in structure. This served as a tentative hypothesis, based on observation, for a description of Samo social structure: nuclear families, extended families, phratry/villages, and a phyle.

As we learned the Samo language, we discovered terms for the various groupings. We could find no term corresponding to nuclear family. The smallest terminologically recognized group was the household, and the term *monsoon*[1] literally meant 'house'. It identified people living together (sleeping together in the Samo terminology) in the same longhouse. Another term, *oosoo buoman,* identified a group of men who exchanged sisters for wives. This term literally translates, 'those who sit together'; exchange groups are the only ones who can be trusted to sit down peaceably. This group, then, was a reflection of the alliance structure between communities. Those who exchanged women formed an alliance structure that eventually served as the basis for deciding who would assemble into villages.

Another important grouping for the Samo is designated by the term *ton,* 'talk'. It focuses on those who speak a common language or dialect. Thus the Samo were distinguished from the Kubo who lived to the north of the Domami River, the Honibo and Gebusi to the south and east of the Nomad River, and the Pare to the west of the Strickland River. Notice the importance of rivers as boundaries between groups. Not only were people differentiated on the basis of linguistic affiliation but they were also referred to as *hatooman,* 'enemy', if there were no alliance ties between them. Thus enemies were those who lived across a river, separated both linguistically and geographically. Within the boundaries one was free to exchange a sister for a wife (endogamous patritocal phratry?), but one raided and ate enemies.

FIGURE 6:1
Etic and Emic Comparative Terminology
for Samo Social Structure

ETIC	EMIC
Nuclear Family	
Extended Family (household)	MONSOON (longhouse)
Phratry/Village	OOSOO BUOMAN (allies)
Dialect/Language	TON (talk)
	HATOOMAN (enemies)

The terminology used by the Samo for their groupings gave a very different perspective of their social structure than what I worked out based primarily on observation (see Figure 6:1). The focus for the Samo is on their interaction patterns based on where they live and with whom they exchange women. Residence and alliance are the keys to unlocking Samo social structure, not the genealogical interaction between primary family members that I first assumed. This difference in basic assumption is crucial, for it is the difference between what I, as an outsider, considered important and how the Samo view their group interaction. Hence the inclusion of enemies as part of the structure was crucial for them, but I missed it. Since it is their system that I needed to understand in order to anticipate their reaction to various terms used in Scripture, it was essential that I use their terms and know what they implied as I translated.

This rather extended example serves to reinforce the importance of determining what is emic for those who receive the gospel, and how to proceed in discovering it. So long as I operated with my view of their social structure, I made mistakes because my assumptions were different than theirs. Once I began using their criteria, though I still made mistakes, they were able to tell me in their terms where I went wrong. I learned their assumptions and could make corrections based on them.

SOCIAL FACTORS IN THE COMMUNICATION PROCESS

It is important to understand the social structure of the source culture. If receptors are to appreciate what is happening socially in the Scriptures, translators must communicate the meanings and intentions of the source.

For example, the tribes of Israel do not conform to the anthropological use of the term 'tribe' which is increasingly avoided in the modern literature. All Israelites in the period of the Kings spoke the same language and interacted in a wide variety of ways. In effect, Israel was one nation, united under a leader and interacting with the rest of the world as an entity of considerable importance (I & II Samuel, I & II Chronicles, I & II Kings, etc.). These tribes were, nevertheless, important social units that probably correspond more or less with phratry (Anderson 1969). The land was divided on the basis of group size and need (Joshua 13-21) and the family heads (clan leaders?) determined their property and were responsible for developing it. These groups continued to grow and some of the sub-tribes became known for their various task-oriented foci: soldiers, artisans of all types, and shepherds. The best known specialized tribe was, of course, the Levites who were not given any land at all, but were divided with respect to their priestly responsibilities as musicians, guards, accountants, and, of course, tabernacle/temple workers (Joshua 21, I Chronicles 24 - 26).

These aspects of the Israelite social structure will need to be communicated with respect to the receptor culture's social system. What did it mean to be a member of a particular Israelite tribe? What rights and responsibilities did people have between themselves and to the group as a whole? Without this focus on meaning, demonstrated by using terms that convey similar meanings to the receptors, misunderstanding of the Scriptural setting and how it worked for the Israelites may result.

On the other hand, many peasant groups, in the world today, have structures which are very comparable and not much adjustment in the translation is necessary. Every receptor situation is different and it is the communicator's responsibility to adequately understand both the source and receptor contexts in order to use appropriate terms that will convey the message intended by the Biblical authors.

Take the concept of levirate remarriage, and harems, for example. The social focus in Old Testament peasant culture was on the maintenance of the family name, on survival of the family as a recognizable unit in the culture. It also affected their right to property, who would receive it, administer its use, etc. Without an heir the rights were nullified and the name lost. Thus to take a brother's wife and raise a family in his name was to maintain one's brother's honor as well as one's own for having acknowledged him in this noble way. On a broader scale, taking wives into a king's harem was a means of maintaining relationships with other nations. This was international politics, and very serious business. The apparent polygamy that resulted from both practices was only a by-product of the survival focus and apparently inconsequential from the people's perspective.

Because of the focus on the husband-wife relationship, communicators from industrial societies tend to lose sight of this larger picture. It becomes an issue of culture clash rather than a means of communicating the gospel. Some translators may even avoid translating these passages for fear that people will use them as an excuse to continue practices which the outsiders view as sinful. We should not make a bigger issue of such concerns than God does. Like Him, we must rely on time, the revelation of the whole of Scripture (through translation) and the power of the Holy Spirit to use the Word to change lives. Our understanding of both the source and receptor social structure can serve as a catalyst for making people aware of what God is saying to them through His Word. Unfortunately, these are matters that have often been misunderstood by outsiders and, therefore, not clear to receptors. Translators who are culturally similar and can identify with both the source context and receptor needs and concerns can make a difference in such cases.

In the early stages of translation, we can assist the process of social understanding by focusing on passages of Scripture which reflect the same broad culture type (Kinship, Peasant, or Industrial). Though in a different time and place, modern receptors appreciate the similarities and the translation process will be less complex. When we began translating for the Samo, we translated the book of Genesis. The kinship focus on origin stories, migration, and the interactions within a growing family were not entirely dissimilar to the Samo setting. When we read the translation of the flood story, they told us their version. When we translated the Abraham story, heads nodded with understanding as Abraham struggled with Lot, worried about his progeny, and migrated to Egypt to find food. As the clan grew and in-house rivalry set in, the Samo understood. If God included such stories in his "Book" then perhaps He could be interested in their similar concerns and struggles. Perhaps He cared when floods or drought devastated their food supply. Perhaps it matters to God that they maintain harmony within a longhouse as their cultural ideals dictate.

The Samo translation of Genesis established, for them, an awareness of a great *Ayo*, who oversaw all that took place within His creation. In ways reminiscent of a household head, God was interested in the welfare of the people, their relationships with each other and could (if provoked) punish those who went astray. God is indeed "our authority person", the one in control of the seen and the unseen, including the bush spirits they fear so much, and "all who sleep in the places throughout the earth." What an impact our understanding of social structure had upon the Samo translation! God is *Oye Ayo*, 'everyone's caretaker or authority person'. Psalm 23 is meaningful indeed.

Choosing social contexts that are compatible with people's expectations will ensure their attention is drawn to the truth of the message rather than to the strangeness of the social setting. Avoiding strange customs at this early stage also provides the communicator time to develop an understanding of the source culture and improve translation skills to present them more effectively. Inasmuch as all Scripture is in some way affected by a social context, and all of life in present day cultures is directly related, in some way, to social structure, this is an important concern in the communication process.

Consider, for example the whole matter of marriage. Marriage rules can tend to be confusing because of the wide variety of ways and reasons for establishing a marriage. Marriage is often a means to define relationships between two social groups and those broad relationships may be more important than the husband-wife relationship that results. As Samuel Johnson noted long ago; to the contract of marriage, besides the man and woman, there is a third party—society. This must be reflected in the translation process as well. Interestingly, these matters are often more confusing to an outside translator who comes from another culture type, especially if that culture has a more individualistic worldview.

These matters of social concern demand analysis, just as do all aspects of the culture. They are important factors in the communication of God's Word. Translators become the bridge for understanding between the source and receptor cultures. Undoubtedly, a wide variety of forms will be quite different and these will vary again if translators come from yet another culture type. Therefore, developing an awareness of the social structure is an important part of the translation task and the effective communication of the gospel.

Suggested Reading

Bohannan, P. and J. Middleton. *Marriage, Family and Residence*. Natural History Press, 1968b.

Hiebert, Paul. *Cultural Anthropology*. Baker, 1983. Chapts. 9, 10, 12-14.

Keesing, Roger. *Kin Groups and Social Structure*. Holt, Rinehart & Winston, 1975.

Notes

1. Samo has six phonemic vowels, including three back vowels: U, O and 'ɔ'. In order to represent these sounds in the orthography, we chose to symbolize the O with a double o: 'oo'. All vowels can also be nasalized, and orthographically nasalization is symbolized with an 'n' following the vowel. Hence *m̨sǫ* is represented by *monsoon*, 'house'. This eliminated the need for diacritical marks and is the reason why Samo orthography, rather than phonetic symbols, is used here.

CHAPTER SEVEN
Political Factors

In face to face societies, political organization is closely associated with kinship and economic aspects of the culture. Among the Samo, the primary means of controlling behavior is through the relationship between older and younger brothers. Initiation and the establishment of the moral order through the mythology provide the framework in which brothers teach their younger siblings what is right and wrong. If not obeyed, some form of punishment results. In more technologically advanced societies political constraints are implemented, not through brotherly love, but by public institutions given the right to make and enforce laws for the good of the citizens.

Radcliffe-Brown characterizes political organization as being concerned with the control and regulation of force: social control (1965). This social control, however, takes place with respect to two spheres of influence: (1) within the group (however defined) and (2) without, as the in-group relates to the rest of its "world". This suggests Nadel's discussion of tribal societies as organizations for "war without and peace within" (Nadel 1942a). Such definitions of political organization establish the duality of territorial and social control (Keesing 1958:289ff). Features that characterize political systems are (1) common membership and loyalty of people who recognize a prescribed territory as theirs, (2) an internal system of group control and welfare, and (3) a system of external relations. Following Hoebel (1954), the internal system of control can be labeled "law" and the activities of interaction with other groups can be called "government". Such labels relate to any level of socio-economic adaptation and provide a model for understanding political structures. This highly simplified model allows communicators to focus on laws pertaining to behavioral control within a group (either in the Biblical source or the receptor culture) and governmental relationships of people across recognized boundaries.

For example, the Law of Moses pertained to relationships within the Israelite nation. It was established to specify relationships between the people and their God (vertical-supernatural focus) as well as among themselves (horizontal-natural focus). As they entered the promised land bitter warfare characterized their relationship with those they sought to displace. Such tribal activity frequently characterizes the people we try to reach, and may provide the basis for identification with Scripture long before the reality of the gospel message, epitomized in Christ's death, burial, and resurrection, makes much sense to them.

THE POLITICAL REALM

Law

The concept of "Law", defined as the use of social control within a defined group, serves as a means to maintain harmony and preserve order. The smaller the group to which the laws apply the greater the necessity to keep order and yet the greater the informality when doing so. Laws establish the culturally accepted behavior beyond which people are not expected to go. As depicted in Figure 7:1, no one can live up to the ideals of a culture all the time. As long as their behavior conforms to the norm, however, the cultural expectations are met. Occasionally a society will permit people to go beyond the norm, they will tolerate behavior for particular reasons (such as behavior at a party or ceremony, that goes beyond the normal bounds of decency but because of the context is permitted). Behavior beyond these bounds is negatively sanctioned, i.e. it is punished in culturally appropriate ways. This whole range of behavior patterns represents the actual or "real" activities of cultural members—what they do as they live out their lives within this particular context. It is important to note that correct behavior for one group of people may not conform to that of any other. Change also affects what is considered correct and results in the norms of a society being in constant flux. What is tolerated behavior today, may become expected behavior tomorrow. Thus we note that cultural norms of behavior are closely tied to a

people's beliefs and values. As values change, so do the norms
and the nature of the negative sanctions that are brought to bear.

FIGURE 7:1
Culturally Appropriate and Inappropriate Behavior

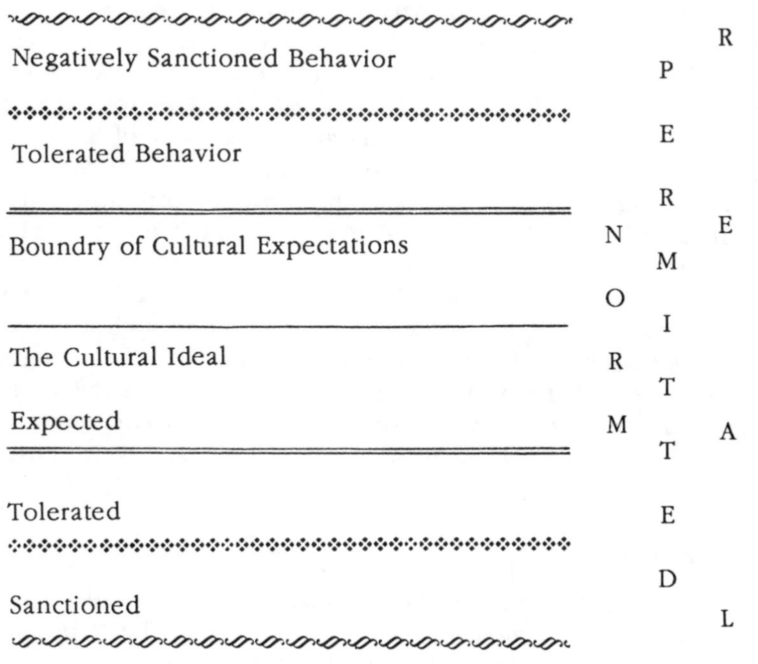

Negatively Sanctioned Behavior   P   R

Tolerated Behavior   E

Boundry of Cultural Expectations   N   R   E
                                                        M

The Cultural Ideal   O   I

Expected   R   T

                                             M   A
                                                        T

Tolerated   E

Sanctioned   D   L

   When the cultural norm is disrupted, society runs the risk of
disintegration. In order to reduce this problem, social control is
essential. Control can range widely from the use of shame to
some form of capital punishment. Ridicule within a society (or so-
called sub-culture of a larger society) causes embarrassment
which encourages the wayward individual back to the behavioral
norm. More severe forms of punishment may be necessary,

depending on the nature of the infraction. Going beyond the culturally expected behavior patterns can be tantamount to a cultural definition of sin. When the values of a group are violated, i.e. when an individual knows what is right but does not conform, then the behavior is culturally defined as sin. It just so happens that Scripture reinforces this cultural view point (Jas. 4:17).

Those who ensure justice are also part of the political question. Who are the cultural defenders? In small scale societies each member is, in some sense, responsible for social control— maintaining harmony and balance within the community and between the community and the broader culture (both physical and spiritual). Large scale societies, on the other hand, depend on institutionalized enforcement with an elaborate police force and court system. Who these mediators are is the study of leadership. There is a wide range of behavioral patterns dependent upon ascribed versus achieved leadership: group consensus at an informal, tribal level, or national elections and formal procedures of law and order.

The changes throughout Biblical times are a fascinating study, tracing the Israelites from a loose tribal structure with a designated leader such as Moses, to the sophisticated ramifications of a justice system that was tied into Roman law during the time of Christ. All this is a necessary part of the study for communicating forms and background that reflect political factors in Biblical times.

Government

While the discussion of law is related to an internal focus on social order, government turns the focus beyond the 'group' and relates people to other similar social groupings. As pointed out in the introduction to this chapter, group definition is often based on territorial factors, land boundaries beyond which people are viewed as 'strangers' or 'enemies'. Thus warfare is often an expression of government infractions against another group (territorial, social, or cosmic). This is true whether discussing an isolated people group or a nation building a nuclear stockpile.

The larger the defined group, the more intricate (and formal) the relations within the society and the broader the relations with other groups. In kinship societies, the focus is primarily upon inter-group activities relating to alliance and defiance. Thus, the

Samo use trading parties as an excuse to spy on an enemy longhouse. In the New Guinea highlands one group expressly states their marriage preference as "we marry our enemies". This relationship obviously has impact far beyond the husband-wife dyad—alliance is the focus.

In peasant societies, the interaction is primarily inter-status, between the peasantry and the elite. Though much of this may in fact be viewed as "law" it has broad ramifications for "government" as well. Much of what has been viewed as peasant uprisings in various parts of the world are, in fact, efforts on the part of peasantry to overcome what they view as oppression by the elite. These "independence movements" are, anthropologically speaking, manifestations of group interaction and, therefore, in this model can be classed as government activity.

Industrial societies, on the other hand, involve themselves in international politics with all the manifestations of the nightly news. The complexities of this political inter-dependence between nations is not in focus here, except to point out that what nations do on an international scale is, politically speaking, very similar to the activities of small scale societies jockeying for power with respect to their land and those who live upon it.

TOWARD DISCOVERING POLITICAL ORGANIZATION

As you develop relationships with people, apply the observation-questioning technique to the political realm as you have for the other sub-systems. Begin to notice what upsets people. How do they handle these frustrations? While interacting with people question them about various types of activities already observed. Which kinds of behavior outside the expected norm are punishable by supernatural forces and which are in the province of human retribution? By keeping a list of these actions you can begin to function within a people's cultural constraints. Such behavior will avoid your being considered culturally inappropriate, or even "sinful" in certain situations. We certainly do not want to condemn the gospel message by violating people's expectations of good or proper behavior—we want to be viewed as Christian.

In order to develop this kind of understanding, it is necessary to build trust through quiet interaction and making observations for a time before asking specific questions. Questions should relate to the circumstances of your observations. The questions may then lead to further observations encouraged by information or volunteered by people who describe violations and punishments which you have not observed. This is extremely helpful data for building an awareness of the system of community justice.

Notice how negative sanctions are handled by members of the society. Who is responsible for maintaining the "laws" of the community. How is violation determined? How is the type of punishment determined? Who are the local leaders and how do they relate to these infractions? Is there a system of village courts? If so, how do these relate to the broader court system of the nation of which the community is a part? Is punishment specific to each case or is there a standard sanction for the particular violation or class of actions? In short, you should be interested in how people view right and wrong and what is done about it. What is their emic perspective of their political system?

Do not just concentrate on negative behavior and appropriate sanctions. Contrast it with positive activities. What are the qualities of good people? What kinds of activities follow on these ideal qualities, i.e. how do people who conform to the rules act? How does the society reward this quality behavior; what are the positive sanctions? Such information will give valuable insight as to how the people expect others to act, even if they don't always measure up to expectations. This may give at least a partial answer to how Christ would have behaved had He come to this group. With such an understanding, not only can you try to act appropriately, but will begin to determine how the Christians of the society will act as Christ fulfills them in their cultural experience. As people become Christians, they will desire to live within the constraints of the political system and thus gain influence and respect from other members of the society. They will begin to receive the positive sanctions reserved for people who live up to local ideals. They may also be questioned as to how or why they are living as the culture dictates they should (when others find it hard to do so). By living this way, they will receive the blessing of God as they live up to His expectations as well.

As you develop this kind of political awareness, activities relative to "government" are also taking place. Various activities bring several groups together. Often inter-group activity involves some form of confrontation. What precipitates such an event and what are its manifestations? What is the means for defusing confrontation? What is the role of leaders on these occasions? Other group activities may be amiable, demonstrating peaceful interaction. What is the basis of peaceful relationships and what can change those relationships to less hospitable coexistence? How are these alliances established? What is the purpose of establishing such relationships? What are the responsibilities of groups so related and how are they affected by the leadership of both sides?

What aspects of leadership encourage others to follow? Such information may be helpful in determining the authority structure within the society and how you may relate to it. Cultural outsiders should not become leaders, but must know the authority system in order to gain access to power. Working through this structure is essential if a missionary program (including translation) is to have validity and be accepted. Obtaining the approval of the leaders and working through them to affect the society with God's Word is the goal. If, on the other hand, you are a member of the receptor context, using leadership roles and working as an advocate for change from within the system can greatly assist in communicating the gospel.

ON THE NATURE OF SHAME, GUILT AND SIN

Learning what the people of a culture define as sin can be important. It is necessary to understand a people's values and note how those relate to Scripture. It is also important to fit in behaviorally wherever possible. Outsiders should avoid going beyond the boundaries of the cultural norms in order not to be a stumbling block to people of that system. Where the reverse is true, and the communicator is called to go beyond the boundaries of conscience (if it truly is that and not cultural difference) there is an ideal opportunity to begin communicating the Biblical message. At the very least a comment such as, "God says something about that in His Book, and I hope to tell you more some day", can help point people in the right direction and establish your role in the community.

In an excellent discussion on the cross-cultural definition of sin, Dye (1976) contrasts shame and guilt. Most face to face societies depend on shame and retribution, through gossip, to keep members within the cultural norm. Accordingly, an activity is bad because the individual is caught, thereby disrupting group harmony. Disharmony can be social (as in the case of disrupted relationships when Samo brothers fight) or it can be cosmic (as when a Papago Indian affects the universal balance by inadvertently killing a desert horned toad). The result, in either case, is disequilibrium until the imbalance is corrected through rehabilitation or ritual of some sort. The individual involved is shamed because of this disharmony (the *result* of the action) not because of the action itself. If no one is the wiser, there is no disruption, no bad consequences, except for the lack of inner peace that may result from fear of the consequences, should the action be discovered. Shame, then, comes as a result of external forces and negative sanctions being brought to bear on the offending party.

Guilt, on the other hand is an attitude in which the offender feels shame and a need for a restoration of balance regardless of being caught: an internalized shame. Conscience is also important, creating each person's point of awareness of what is right and wrong. Therefore, conscience relates directly to cultural values as they are reflected in people's expectations (Rom. 2:15,16). Scripture teaches that every person is aware of what is right, though that awareness is strongly affected by culture. Conscience, then, is the principal channel through which the Holy Spirit convicts and enlightens. What they know to be culturally appropriate behavior but do not do, for them that is sin (Jas. 4:17). It is also likely that the guilty party feels shame when their sin becomes evident. If people are unable to conform to their own cultural standards—their ideals—how much less can they expect to measure up to God's? As people realize their inadequacies, they will begin to rely upon God's strength to live up to cultural standards where appropriate. As they acquire Biblical standards, they will begin to recognize discrepancy between their own cultural norms and God's. This begins the process of bringing cultural behavior into line with God's expectations.

Following this principle, Christ comes to assist all believers in being better culture bearers, those who measure up to the expectations of their culture. Christ in the culture will help believers live up to cultural ideals rather than being caught in the morass of real behavior with its wide fluctuations within what is permitted by the culture (see Figure 7:1). This is not to say that the Scriptures will allow for cultural actions that are contrary to supracultural absolutes laid down by God. Rather, God's Word critiques culture. When activity contrary to God's Word is culturally permitted, people are forced to make a choice: change the culture to conform to God's law, or go their sinful way. Scripture translation can be a tremendous aid at this point.

You need not tell people what is right or wrong. Rather, by establishing the trust necessary to communicate effectively, you can present Scripture which allows the Holy Spirit to work in that context. Such was the case when the Samo heard Genesis chapter 9 for the first time. For them to follow God's injunction and cease raiding and subsequent cannibalism was far more meaningful to them than obeying the authority of the colonial government or missions. On the basis of God's Word they decided to adjust their culture. The fact that this also conformed to the "outside" influences of government and mission was a convenient fringe benefit. The point was that the Samo came to realize the true rationale for the "outsider's" injunction—it emanated from God, not from mere human beings.

It may be appropriate, however, to focus in the early stages of a translation project on those passages which conform to activities assumed to be appropriate. If Scripture can be seen to confirm some of their ideals then God will be seen as one who affirms their culture rather than standing against them. Such was the case with the Samo ideal of "brotherly love". Brothers care for each other, assist in procuring food, acquiring wives, and protecting wives and children. God, as the *ayo,* provided in Christ, an older brother with whom they could establish a warm relationship. They could relate to Christ much as they could a physical older brother who often carried a leadership role. Thus they knew the kinds of cultural activity he would validate and which he would punish. Working from such a familiar relationship, they could add to their knowledge of God and His Son as they received more Scripture. There was much they did not know or understand about God, but this relationship (which they themselves often failed to execute in a culturally appropriate way) provided an excellent avenue to communicate to the Samo who Christ was and what He intended to do: fulfill the Law, maintain relationships (Mt. 5:17-19).

Communicators need a thorough understanding of the cultural norms, sanctions that are brought to bear for infractions, and what the list of critical offenses are. This awareness will assist in predicting, or at least anticipating, the effect translated Scripture will have on the people when they receive it. It is also helpful to know the expectations within the source culture in order to anticipate local reactions to Scripture which presents a list of culturally defined behavior often different from their own.

POLITICAL FACTORS IN THE COMMUNICATION PROCESS

Having developed a good working knowledge of the political organization of the receptor culture, the translator can compare and contrast that with the system found in Scripture. What aspects of the scriptural system are similar to that of the receptor, and which need explanation? For example, among the Higi of Nigeria, a woman, behaving as Naomi instructed Ruth in establishing a relationship with Boaz, would be severely reprimanded. The translator, then, needs to communicate the Hebrew cultural contrast in such a way that young Higi widows do not misunderstand and behave inappropriately in the Christian community. Other aspects of the book of Ruth require little or no cultural adjustment.

Whatever is needed, simple transfer or an explanation of cultural dissimilarity, translators should ensure the original meaning is clear. The historicity of the Biblical context is without question, functional substitutes should not be inappropriately interjected to make it appear that Ruth (for example) handled the situation as the Higi would. Rather this historical incident should be recounted with an appropriate indication that this behavior was within the norm for Jewish culture, though clearly different from that of the receptor culture. People should not assume that this historical context equates with the way God dictated it. God works in and through culture and will meet people whatever their cultural context—even Moabites, enemies of the Jews.

The emphasis here is on appropriating political understanding to the effective communication of God's Word. So much of what takes place in Scripture has political implications: the activities of the Nation of Israel, the politically complex situation at the time of Christ, the very interaction between Christ and his adversaries. Much of this can and must be explained with respect to the local political situation if it is to have any meaning to those who read Scripture for the first time.

There is a sense in which a translation project expands a people's awareness (of themselves and others), bringing them to an understanding of a broader world, both past and present. We have an important role in assisting people in this process. However, we must be more than adept consciousness-raisers. Our involvement, along with the translation, must convey a sense of meaning with respect to relevance for life. We should make the source believable to receptors of very different times and places. Too often books such as *How the Jews Lived* are made available to people with the feeling that we have done our cultural job. Receptors, in my experience, find little relevance. The transfer of information must be done in such a way that the whole of a culture is recognized as having value and customs are related to that context, not the reverse. More importantly, God relates to people in each culture, and the people who live within those various contexts need to see His principles communicated in the Biblical context which can then be applied to their specific situation.

This is the challenge for every communicator. Present Biblical cultures as believable wholes, not just a tangle of various factors with no particular relationship. Cultures (both source and receptor) can only make sense as whole systems. Having analyzed a cultural system into its various parts, we now turn to an integration of these cultural forms and demonstrate how they operate within a specific context to manifest a people's worldview.

Suggested Reading

Cohen, R. and Middleton. *Comparative Political Systems*. Natural History Press, 1967.

Hiebert, Paul. *Cultural Anthropology*. Baker, 1983. Chapts. 16 and 17.

Mair, Lucy. *An Introduction to Social Anthropology*. Oxford University Press, 1965. Chapts. 7-9.

CHAPTER EIGHT
Culture as a System

The focus thus far has been on the various cultural sub-systems and how understanding them assists in the cross-cultural communication process. These cultural factors are manifestations of deeper level concerns that all cultures must handle. What makes this surface level culture work? How can we develop an awareness of the deep level sub-conscious that drives each culture and makes it unique? Space does not allow for a detailed presentation of all the analytical procedures necessary to adequately understand what has come to be called *worldview* (Brown 1983, Hiebert 1986, Kearney 1984, Redfield 1983, etc.). The focus here will be on developing a methodology which takes world-view into account in the cross-cultural communication process.

THE WHOLE IS GREATER THAN THE SUM OF ITS PARTS

The tendency of communicators, especially those who come from an industrial perspective, is to analyze without reassembling that analysis into a unified whole. It is easy to become excited about discovering the various cultural factors and forget to notice how each affects the other. The objective here is to avoid an over emphasis on analysis and attempt to see the system as it works to formulate the lifestyle of those who adhere to it.

A culture must be viewed as a system. People interact within the *rules* to maintain and uphold the basic, often subconscious, and unspoken tenets of the culture. These rules are what make the system work. They make individual actions somewhat predictable, thereby allowing people the freedom to focus on important things rather than being overstimulated by the necessity to process every smile or gesture for its meaning. Culture gives people the freedom to develop themselves within a context; it provides a sense of being at home.

The five sub-systems of culture can be summarized (perhaps at the risk of oversimplification) as a series of interaction patterns: *economic factors* focus on interaction with the environment; *ideology,* interaction with the supernatural; *kinship,* interpersonal relationships; *social structure,* group interaction; and *political organization,* interaction with the rules to maintain law and government. Interaction is the glue that holds all these factors together. Interaction with respect to one factor ensures interaction with all others. Perhaps yet another example from the Samo is in order.

Early in my study, I was struck by what appeared to be a sharp sexual division of labor. Women worked closely together in the home and garden, often to the exclusion of men. Similarly, men spent a lot of time together in activities of their own. I soon discovered that those men who so interacted were, by Samo definition, brothers. Brothers, it turns out, work together as a group and their individual reputations depend upon their group identity. Furthermore, all this interaction goes far beyond the kinship focus on rights and duties between male siblings. Relationships pertain to *economic activity* (hunting, gardening, and even raiding), *ideology* (participating in ritual and ceremony, protecting the community against harmful spirits, and performing the countless rituals which serve to keep an individual alive), *kinship* (interacting with each other and anyone else inhabiting the communal longhouse), *social structure* (arranging the exchange of sisters for wives, and interacting with male exchange partners), and *political organization* (disciplining younger siblings, managing the alliance structure, and arranging for large scale raids against enemies). All this is implied in the relationship between brothers. The Samo know this. For them it is assumed knowledge. I, on the other hand, had to learn all this in order to become a responsible brother.

The relationship is epitomized in the phrase "brothers don't fight". Anything that affects group solidarity has strong negative sanction and fighting would disrupt relationships between the very individuals that serve to maintain the community and the economic, religious, social and political system in which that community exists. Therefore, fighting between brothers is guarded against and becomes the focus of myths, individual behavior patterns, and discussions around late night fires. The relationship between Samo brothers can become a means of describing the entire culture as manifested by the myriad of things people do in their daily activities, including a strict division of labor.

The importance of this relationship and the way it is integrated with the whole of Samo culture alerted me to the fact that this was a core theme. The theme is: "brothers maintain group solidarity", but in Samo is stated negatively in the phrase, "brothers don't fight". The focus is on the male sibling relationship and the worldview perspective is provided by the way the relationship and associating theme flow throughout the activities of people in the society.

The whole, then, is greater than understanding the sum of the various cultural parts. These factors combine and recombine to manifest the underlying meaning of the culture. This introduces a discussion of worldview and how a development of this concept enables communicators to focus on the system of which the cultural factors are but aspects of the whole.

WORLDVIEW

There are various worldview models that are helpful here (Hiebert 1983, Kearney 1984, and Kraft 1979 are perhaps the best known). Without elaborating the models, Figure 8:1 portrays the basic idea.

Worldview provides the basic assumptions upon which the society operates. The culture is set up to maintain and protect these basic values or themes. This cultural core is reflected throughout the universals with which each culture deals. This is part of being human, of being created in the image of God as finite beings. All people must deal with relationships, both within the group and beyond (definitions determined by studying the kinship and social structure). Everyone has a concept of time and space which is dictated by the core assumptions of their worldview. There are many ways to organize time and space and these, in turn, affect behavior in a dramatic way (as I discovered after I lost my wrist watch in the jungle). A concern for cause and effect and the value of ideas, things, concerns, etc. are all part of what every society must handle. Of course, the area of classification is the easiest to analyze because people use their language to classify. As people speak they naturally classify and how they classify provides a wealth of information about their worldview.

Unfortunately, outsiders learning a language often spend more time analyzing the language at a desk than with the people who speak it. Anthropologists have captured this area of classification in the study of ethnosemantics.

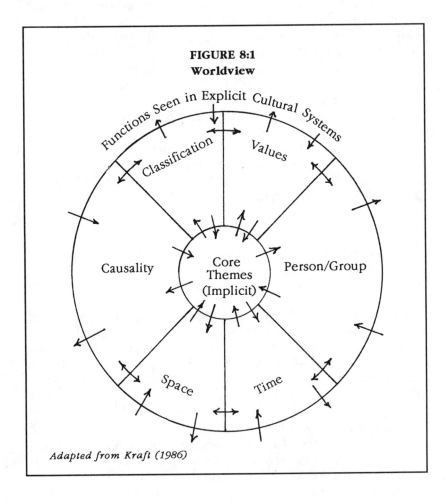

FIGURE 8:1
Worldview

Functions Seen in Explicit Cultural Systems

Classification

Values

Causality

Core Themes (Implicit)

Person/Group

Space

Time

Adapted from Kraft (1986)

Notice that this discussion relates, so far, to the inside of the diagram, the integration between all these worldview considerations and the core themes. All this, in turn, affects people's behavioral patterns as they live out that worldview. It is this observable behavior, the surface structure of the culture, that establishes an outsider's contact with the people. Interaction, bonding, must be with them in their world, where they live, in the way they talk about it. Only as we observe and question the surface activities, can we hope to begin to delve into the deeper layers of the culture and derive the meaning.

TOWARD DISCOVERING WORLDVIEW

Cultural meaning comes out of worldview themes, but these cannot be assumed (an outsider has the wrong set of culturally predetermined assumptions). A methodology that will help ascertain the premises upon which people base their daily decisions is needed. People don't act out worldview themes, rather themes work together to create the rationale for people's actions. Therefore, we must begin by studying surface level behavior and work deeper into the cultural meanings beneath the behavior patterns. Hence the emphasis on the Observation-Questioning Technique.

The best methodology for discovering worldview is explicated by Spradley (1979 and 1980). He combines observations and questions with an analysis of cultural domains, taxonomies, and their components. The combined analytical procedure helps develop an understanding which may expose the core themes—the rationale for behavior (Opler 1945). This discovery procedure is briefly outlined here.

Domain Analysis

Domains are cover terms that act as categories for organizing all the units of a culture. Stated more broadly, they are the discreet units into which people divide their world: colors, kin, disease, things of all types, activities, etc. Every domain contains many smaller units which are included in the domain because they share a specific semantic relationship. All languages appear to have a rather limited set of semantic relationships which they use to organize their world (Casagrande and Hale 1967). According to Werner and Topper, semantic relationships can be reduced to three universal types; (1) inclusion—X is a kind of Y, (2) attribution—X is defined with respect to its attributes, and (3) sequential—X is defined with respect to stages (Werner and Topper 1976).

A domain, then, is characterized by a name or "cover term". Included items are related to the cover term by a semantic relationship and form a set defined by common criteria. For example, kinship forms a domain that includes many terms used to reference individuals in various relationships to each other. All these terms are in an inclusion or attribution relationship to the cover terms, i.e., they are all types of kin terms. A good way to discover recognized domains is to combine a cover term with a question which allows people to list the items included under that term: "what kinds of kin (or anything else) are there?". This may elicit a response such as, "There are people who live in our community and people who live elsewhere". Clearly these are relatively large cover terms into which many included items can be placed, e.g. types of kin in the household, and types of kin outside. This takes us to the next step, building a taxonomy.

Taxonomic Analysis

A taxonomy shows the relationships among all the included terms in a domain. A taxonomy reveals subsets within a domain and shows how they are related to the whole. Thus there are different levels of specificity within a taxonomy and the lower levels are included in the meanings, i.e. semantic relationships, of higher levels.

The taxonomy in Figure 8:2 demonstrates the way levels contrast within a semantic relationship. Each of the included items under the generic domain *man* relate as kinds of human beings in English. But what kind they are is affected by contrast, either the sex of the individual or their age. Sex, however, is a more inclusive contrast than age. A taxonomy, then, divides a domain into subsets based on levels of contrast. This example also demonstrates the linguistic complexity of meaning, since the category *man* appears at each level and means something different (human being, male—opposed to female, adult—opposed to child).

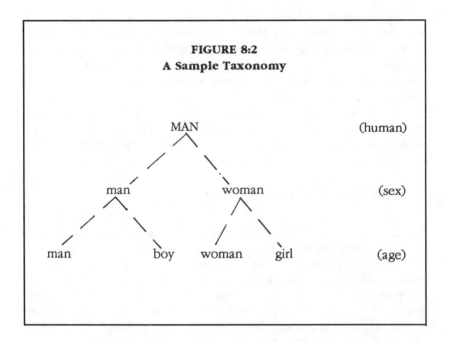

FIGURE 8:2
A Sample Taxonomy

When isolating the taxonomic contrasts of a domain in the receptor culture, look for similarities based on the same semantic relationship. Try to discover additional included terms and obtain definitions (or reasons) for including them under this generic designation for the domain. As you add new terms you may discover various contrasts which result in branches to the taxonomic tree diagram you are building, e.g. all items are types of people (similarity) but some are male and others are female (contrast). Use question frames to check your inclusive levels: "Are men a type of people? Are boys a type of people?"

As you build the taxonomy you may discover larger categories. (Q) "Are people a type of something else?" (A) "Yes, people are part of the animal kingdom". (Q) "What other members of the animal kingdom are there?" The answer may be a long list of types of fauna common to the environment of the people. Your job is to organize these lists into categories and demonstrate the contrasts between the various sub-groupings. Remember, at this stage, these groupings may reflect your etic (or outside) perspective.

As you build a taxonomy you need to test your hypotheses for contrast groups with the people who use them. Elicit their responses by having them actually place the various items into groupings (or write the names of items on slips of paper and have people organize them) and explain their criteria for doing so. Another method is to group items and have people tell you what is right or wrong about your groupings. Attempt, where possible, to obtain their response, or rationale, for assigning members to a particular category. This concern with the reasons for ordering leads us into componential analysis.

Componential Analysis

Despite the apparent mysticism surrounding this subject, it is a useful step in worldview analysis. The process of identifying domains, their included items and the contrastive features which set them apart, provides the methodological framework for determining the components which establish the criteria for inclusion or exclusion in a specific sub-set of a domain. The linguistic process of determining the rationale for the inclusion of sounds within a single phoneme (represented in an alphabet by a single character) provides the theoretical base for this process.

The attributes for each sub-set within the taxonomy combine into a bundle of meaning that contrast it from all others. This can then be displayed as in Figure 8:3.

FIGURE 8:3
Components of Meaning

Domain & Included Items	Dimensions of Contrast	
MAN	Sex	Age
man	male	adult
woman	female	adult
boy	male	non-adult/child
girl	female	non-adult/child

The componential definition for *woman,* in English, is an adult female. This is in contrast to other adults who are male, and other females who are not adults. No components of meaning are shared with *boy,* male children. Once the criteria for contrastive sets have been determined, the results can be displayed in a semantic chart often called a paradigm. The primary distinctions above relate to sex and age which are displayed in Figure 8:4.

FIGURE 8:4
A Semantic Paradigm

	Sex	
	male	female
adult	man	woman
child	boy	girl

Age

Once you have constructed such a display, you can discuss it with people. Suggest criteria for inclusion of new items, or identify new items and notice the response. Throughout this refining process, be especially aware of reactions to your group-ings, criteria, or rationale. Do not force them to agree with you, rather elicit their responses and notice where they agree and disagree. Many of these components, or criteria, will reoccur in many domains. These reoccurrences may suggest points of overlap between domains and give clues of cultural themes within the worldview.

Theme Analysis

Themes relate closely to the worldview definition given in chapter 2. Themes are deep level assumptions that affect behavior and relate to a total cultural setting. Most cultural themes, then, are implicit, taken for granted and demand that the researcher make inferences. Discovering themes requires identifying basic assumptions (criteria, contrasts, etc.) that occur over and over again in many domains.[1]

For example, throughout our analysis of Samo kinship, I noticed that people were identified with respect to their place of residence (where they normally sleep). Terms for people within that context were different from all other individuals (Shaw 1974a). When analyzing plants, the concept of where the plants occurred was critical. If there was any confusion about a plant, they would ask, "Where did you get that?". All plants are classified with respect to their location in the forest, swamps, gardens or open areas. As we learned the Samo language, we discovered that locational words and affixes abounded, indicating where things were in relation to the environment (upstream, downstream or at the top or bottom of a ridge). In fact, 81% of all Samo sentences contain locational information (Shaw & Shaw 1973). Clearly, location, manifested by how things are placed with respect to each other, is a theme for the Samo. Our interest was to understand the ramifications of holding to such a concept behaviorally. It is more than a focus on the worldview universal of space; it affects all other concerns, relationships, classification, causality, etc. What are the manifestations of locational thinking throughout the cultural sub-systems? What effect will that have on their understanding of Scripture and of us who bring it?

Whereas each of the other analytical steps has a particular methodology, theme analysis demands involvement. It is an application of the previous analytical steps to life. Thus one is searching for overarching themes that serve to unite the countless domains within a culture. Discover the cultural criteria for determining people's behavior, the common concerns that appear at all levels of the culture.

It is important, however, not to depart from the previous steps when extracting themes. The whole point of going through this "developmental research sequence", as Spradley calls it, is to assist in arriving at the themes or worldview assumptions that make this particular culture work, i.e. what people must know in order to live and act appropriately within the culture (Goodenough 1956, see chapter 2 for a discussion of this concept as it relates to a definition of culture). To this end we utilize these analytical procedures and apply them to the holy task of effectively communicating the most important message people will ever hear. It could be that the nature of their response will depend on the way it is presented. As communicators we must strive to present God's message in a relevant way—their way. Only then will it have meaning for them, for as we noted in chapter 2, they will derive meaning with respect to their frame of reference: the receptor worldview. Figure 8:5 is an attempt to represent the process of understanding worldview—to represent this research cycle and show how it generates a gradual awareness of worldview themes.

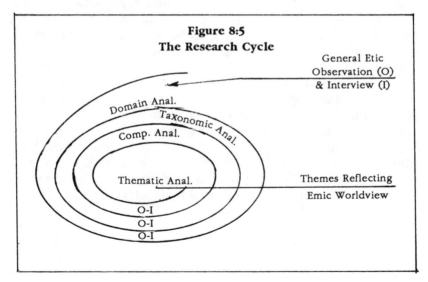

Figure 8:5
The Research Cycle

General Etic
Observation (O)
& Interview (I)

Domain Anal.
Taxonomic Anal.
Comp. Anal.

Thematic Anal.

Themes Reflecting
Emic Worldview

O-I
O-I
O-I

To this end translators study the cultural system: the whole as well as its parts. It is the necessary knowledge without which the translation (no matter how exegetically faithful, or how linguistically accurate) will fail. Translations must act appropriately or they will not be taken seriously; they will not be viewed as relevant. They may even be misunderstood and thereby become bad news, instead of the good news of our Lord and Savior Jesus Christ.[2]

> So Jesus said to those who believed in him, "if you obey my teaching, you are really my disciples; you will know the truth, and the truth will set you free" (Jn. 8:31,32).

The more cultures are transformed by His Word, the freer people will become. Human culture at its integrative best still falls far short in its ability to perform this liberating function. Therefore, the first step in the communication of the gospel is to identify with and understand the cultural context. Then, out of empathy and understanding of the people's needs (the areas in which the culture fails to liberate), we can provide the truth that will set them free. What are these unliberated areas that all cultures struggle with? Fear, a sense of shame, guilt, suffering—all are culturally defined and ought to be understood in order to effect a meaningful communication in the context where these inadequacies prevail. As the Word is brought into these contexts, people become aware of a higher source, a source that can free them to be the people they were created to be. Culture gives people the freedom to develop themselves within a bounded context. God fulfills them within that context, enabling them to live an abundant life, however that may be defined. An exegetically and linguistically accurate translation of God's Word is only half the equation. The other half takes the receptors into account and seeks to meet their needs and fill them with joy (Ps. 16:11).

Suggested Reading

Foster, George. *Traditional Societies and Technological Change*. Harper & Row, 1973.

Hiebert, Paul. *Cultural Anthropology*. Baker, 1983. Chapter 18.

Spradley, James. *Participant Observation*. Holt, Rinehart, & Winston, 1980.

Notes

1. The interesting thing is that when an outsider states a worldview theme people often respond with a gesture or a look that says, "Well, of course; that's obvious!" Such a reaction can be very frustrating when, after long months of investigation, you finally see a theme emerge from the analysis. These "obvious" themes, however, are seldom explicated by the people who live them out. That is why worldview themes are difficult to ascertain—they demand analysis. Yet, once discovered, they seem mundane and obvious to those who use them (Hiebert 1985:111).

2. This does not imply that the translator must know everything about the receptor worldview before starting to translate. Rather, having developed trust and working from an attitude of constant learning and reevaluation (the process), translators do the best they can. There is much yet to learn about the Samo worldview. What is important is that I continue to revise and make adjustments to keep the translation in line with my knowledge. Of course, culture is in a constant state of change, necessitating constant changes in the translation, i.e. revision is an important part of a translation program: it is never really complete. Translation is a long process indeed. As the process relates to a need to identify and understand the worldview to the extent possible, so does the product. People need to identify with it and/or interact with it—make it theirs. From such an understanding they can then make valid decisions that affect their worldview, i.e. worldview change will take place.

PART II

TOWARD APPRECIATING CULTURE

The discovery of the cultural sub-systems and their integration to form surface level cultural manifestations that reflect a deep level worldview provides the foundation for the rest of the book. Thus far, the focus has been on ways to discover cultural context. Anthropology assists in this process—understanding the culture in which the message is and will be structured. Now we strive to understand the impact of the context on the text itself. What kind of cultures did the Biblical writers communicate to? How do these compare with cultures we see around the world today? What affect does the communicator's culture have on the transfer process from source to receptor? Now we turn attention to appreciating the transcultural process that affects any communication experience.

CHAPTER NINE
Cultures of the Old Testament

As we look at the cultures of the Old Testament we see an application of the three cultures model introduced in chapter 2. Socio-political changes are a dynamic part of the unfolding Old Testament story. In Genesis we see people with a kinship approach to life. Abraham may have raised up a nation, but in the early days he, his family and servants had a kinship system. Abraham approached the people around him in a very tentative but relational manner. Confrontation and warfare were never far away. The social structure of the day was based on personal relationships and group interaction, e.g. the twelve sons of Jacob fathering the tribes of Israel. This remained the case until well after Israel possessed the land under Joshua's leadership.

During the period of the judges, a subtle change began to take place. The Israelites were settled on the land, established in one place, and able to develop what God gave them. They began to view themselves as a people, a nation, rather than a collection of tribes. Their allegiance to God gave them a commonality, a bond of fellowship, and their relationship to other nations was on the basis of their peoplehood. Thus by the time of the kings, Israel had become a peasant type culture. There was increased emphasis on agriculture, the priests were in control of the religious system, and an elite had developed around the royal court.

This shift from kinship to peasant culture makes the Old Testament a culturally complex collection of writings. There is not one cultural type represented in the Old Testament Scriptures, but many. The Old Testament basically traces the development of a nation and God's providence over His people. However, as a people, they progressed through these two cultural types and by the time of Christ we see another shift to the beginnings of an industrial culture type, characterized by urbanization along with internationalism and colonialism in the dominance of the Romans and the impact of the Greeks. We will deal with this complexity when considering the New Testament period (chapter 10).

It is essential, then, that we appreciate the three cultures model and apply it to the cultural complexities of the Old Testament period. Without this understanding we cannot hope to communicate the meaning of that period to modern receptors. Inasmuch as God is receptor-oriented, it is within these contexts that we must understand the message people received. Recent studies relating to the anthropology of the Old Testament are helpful in deciphering the Old Testament contexts and their cultural implications (Johnson 1964, Gottwald 1979, Rogerson 1979, and La Sor, Hubbard & Bush 1983). This is particularly exciting as anthropological insight from cultures around the world are used to develop a deeper appreciation of the Hebrew worldview (Wilson 1977, Wolff 1981).

THE IMPORTANCE OF UNDERSTANDING THE SOURCE

The variety of cultural types in the Old Testament may be a distinct advantage to the Bible translator. Except for the increasingly post-industrial nations, much of the world today is familiar with the social and economic circumstances explicated in the Old Testament. One of my Nigerian students exegeting the book of Ruth, commented frequently on the parallels between the way people did things in the times of the Judges and his own Nigerian culture: the importance of the levirate, kinsman redeemer, and the function of inheritance were very similar (Guli 1984).

It is this receptor familiarity with kinship and peasant contexts that necessitates a need to understand these cultural factors. In many ways the non-industrial people of today's world are much more familiar with the realities of relationships, spiritual understanding, and political structures to which God spoke than most translators who come from an industrialized context. For this reason they may also be much closer to understanding God's message throughout the Old Testament. Thus it may be reasonable to assume that translation projects for these people should begin with portions of the Old Testament which they may perceive as being more relevant than the New Testament.[1]

This is not to say that the New Testament is unimportant to people in kinship or peasant type cultures. The whole of

Scripture is God's Word and it is "useful for teaching the truth, rebuking error, correcting faults, and giving instruction for right living" (II Tim. 3:16). However, beginning with a Greek philosophical argument may not be the best starting point in communicating God's message to people who live in kinship or peasant societies. We need to begin by presenting a message that people can apply to their own situation—make relevant to daily life.

A BRIEF LOOK AT OLD TESTAMENT CULTURES

To implement this study, I will use the five cultural subsystems of the previous section as an outline.

Economics

A good Bible Atlas with lots of pictures can be very useful. Many parts of the world today closely resemble the environment described or implied in much of the Old Testament. In these areas, the description of the flora, fauna, climate and geographical features will be unnecessary. In other parts of the world, despite an understanding of the basic kinship or peasant cultural patterns, the setting will need to be elaborately explained (such was the case with the Samo living deep in a swampy rain forest).

Material culture (the things people had, and how they used them) is important. Many forms familiar to receptor cultures today are similar to those used in Biblical times: tools, clothes, eating utensils, houses, etc. The meanings attached to those forms, however, may be quite different, e.g. Elimelech's relative removed his sandal and gave it to Boas thereby relinquishing his right (and responsibility) as the next of kin (Ruth 4:7,8). Among the Higi of Nigeria, the same meaning is conveyed when the deceased's bow and arrows are handed to the one who will marry the widow.

Economic process (the ways people utilize their material culture and social processes to derive a living) is also important to effective communication of Old Testament meaning. It is necessary to understand the meanings of various divisions of labor, forms of exchange, distribution of goods, concepts of time and space, etc. For example, the story of Jacob rushing in with food to receive the blessing before Esau (Gen. 27) may be severely misunderstood by industrial peoples unfamiliar with the importance of the birthright and methods of hunting and shep-

herding, etc.[2] The study of modern peoples living in an environment and circumstances similar to Old Testament times, added to
a growing body of archaeological research, provide helpful
sources of information regarding Biblical economic patterns.

Ideology

God's interaction with people is the primary topic of the
Bible. How people develop this relationship in light of their own
ideological beliefs depends, in large measure, upon how it is
presented to them. His message to Israel throughout the Old
Testament was to put Him first, acknowledge Him and He would
direct their every activity. This ideological perspective did not
begin as a fully developed concept. It was a gradual learning
process that took thousands of years.

As God called Abram, He identified Himself with the creation. Abram knew little or nothing about God but he listened and
obeyed in faith. No wonder so much of Scripture is devoted to
remembering this individual through whom "all nations will be
blessed" (Gen. 12:3). Gradually people came to know God and
related to Him in a variety of ways. Translating these portrayals of
God and His relationship to people will be of great assistance to
those who do not know Him. How can they believe in One they
do not know and how can they know unless they receive the
word in an understandable form (Rom. 10:15)?

It is also an immense assistance to local understanding to use
a term for God that people understand, a term they already know
and use to represent supreme, supernatural power (Richardson
1982). God revealed himself to Israel as the *I am* (Ex. 3:14), the
one present in their daily activities. He was not known as God
(an abstract noun), but as Yahweh (a personal name), implying
relationship and personality (Loewen 1985, 1986). Nor did the oral
speech forms distinguish between small and capital letters at the
beginning of a word. He was known by what He did: create,
provide, protect, comfort. He was contextualized by His presence
in word and deed. What better way to discover God than the way
Israel did (or should have): recounting His acts hearing the stories
of His acts among the Old Testament peoples. This so-called
"story theology" (Macky 1981) helps modern recipients identify
with what has gone before and brings them to a fuller understanding of the "God Who is".

The constant contrast throughout the Old Testament between the true God and the gods of all other peoples needs to be adequately understood. The Old Testament is full of what Tippett calls power encounters (Tippett 1967). God was constantly demonstrating that His power was superior to all other gods. He did not claim the non-existence of other gods; he said, "Worship no god but me" (Ex. 20:3). He did not depreciate the power of other gods, but He often demonstrated that He was more powerful. As we learn about the receptors and provide materials to develop their understanding about God and who He is, we should allow the Holy Spirit to perform a change of heart attitude, or worldview in them. We must also be careful not to stage a power encounter. It must come naturally so people can learn how God relates to their situation. It needs to be their discovery! Remember how long it took Abram to understand what God was trying to do? And the revelation of God changed over a period of several thousand years. How dare we rush those who know so much about the supernatural powers into committing themselves to a new and powerful God they know nothing about!

Not only must we understand God and His relationship to people throughout history, we must also discover the nature of religious practitioners. Who were the religious leaders in the Old Testament? What was the contrast between priests and prophets? What were their roles in relation to the people and the nation of Israel? How did the priesthood degenerate to the condition Jesus so vehemently chastened? How can this understanding, communicated through the translation, assist people as they utilize their cultural patterns of religious practice to establish a new church? Answering this question assumes a knowledge both of religious practice and leadership in the receptor culture.

Another ideological interest is the relationship of myth (not to be confused with untruth) to the Old Testament Scriptures. Most of Scripture, and especially the Old Testament, was passed from generation to generation as part of an oral tradition. It was not written down until much later. This in no way depreciates its value. In fact, from the perspective of many peoples in the world who understand and appreciate oral history, it validates and heightens the Bible's effect. It places Scripture into a tradition that ties it to a more definite reality. As translators, we need to learn how to utilize the oral styles of both the source and receptor, instead of capturing God's truth in only a written style that forces literacy. Using oral styles encourages people to identify with the patriarchs, the conditions under which they lived, and the meanings God intended to communicate to humanity (Klem 1982).

Following the ideological changes through the Old Testament can be very helpful for people today. The worship patterns, with an emphasis on various communication styles (dance, music, poetry, narrative, etc.) all relate closely to what people already know. They can be encouraged to follow these meaningful forms rather than introduced patterns that may not be so meaningful. Giving people the freedom to employ worship styles that come out of their culture and an understanding of Old Testament forms provides them an opportunity to relate to God meaningfully through worship.

Kinship

The Scriptures are filled with relational information and genealogies. Obviously great importance was placed on knowing who one's ancestors were and how one was related to them. Throughout both Old and New Testaments reference is made to Abraham, Isaac and Jacob. What are the implications of these reminders? The focus of a genealogy can be determined by the individuals on the list. This does not mean one genealogy is correct while another wrong; rather it indicates a variation in the authors' purpose and this must be considered along with the message that was intended for those who originally received it.

Among the Nakanai, on the north coast of the Island of New Britain, genealogies are often recited orally for the purpose of validating ownership or lending credibility by establishing rights (as for example in having the right to perform a certain ritual). When they encounter a genealogy in Scripture, the Nakanai take careful note of the meaning intended in the listing of ancestors. The genealogy in Matthew chapter 1 is of extreme consequence to them. It establishes the validity not only of Jesus, but of the whole New Testament upon the truth of the Old Testament patriarchs (Gela 1985). The Old Testament paves the way for the New!

Understanding the kinship terminology and the relationship patterns implied by such use can shed great light on our understanding of the importance and use of names, the first born, male siblings, and the birth right. Translators should focus on the meaning of these culture traits rather than on the degree of divergence from their own cultural practices. What did the father-son relationship mean to the Israelites and how did God use it to communicate to them? What was implied in the husband-wife dyad and how does that relate to so many references to prostitution? Unless we understand kinship patterns in Scripture, we cannot understand the meaning of specific passages based on the recipient sharing those relational presuppositions. Without this background we complicate the transfer of information through the translation process.

Expatriate translators require caution here. Coming from a primarily non-kin perspective where the focus is on individual decision and identity, relational patterns within a kin based society may not be considered important. The tendency to ignore kinship affects the translation of passages, such as genealogies, that others consider crucial. Most cultures, even in today's world, identify closely with the Biblical focus on group activity and relational behavior that benefits all in the group, however that is culturally defined. Perhaps this is part of the reason for the rapid growth of house churches in China and why they did not develop until after the missionaries left.

Social Structure

How did the Israelites group themselves and what did that imply about their cultural system as well as how God spoke to them? The organization into twelve tribes establishes each as a large clan. The themes that permeate the whole of Scripture regarding this type of division and family relationships are extremely significant, but often lost on readers from industrial societies. Peoples of a kinship culture, on the other hand, are quick to pick up on these interactive patterns between groups and how they apply to an understanding of God (the ultimate Patriarch). His relationship to people as well as creation, and the meaning of that interaction through time provides the story line of Scripture.

How were alliances set up and maintained among the Biblical societies? What was the role of women in establishing and maintaining a marriage? These questions pertain to who could marry whom and the many strict injunctions against marrying foreign women. What was the role of betrothal, cross-cousin preferential marriage, the levirate, inheritance, and concubines? How did the harem act as a political buffer against the hostility of neighboring nations? God knew all this and perhaps it provided the reason He did not want Israel to have a King (I Sam. 8). But now we are talking politics and we note the integration of political and social structures. This was certainly as true for Old Testament times as it is among kinship and peasant peoples today. Much research is needed in order to develop an understanding of this crucial and far-reaching aspect of Biblical cultures.

Political Organization

Central to understanding political organization in the Old Testament is an understanding of law. Beginning with the Mosaic Law God clearly explicated a means of internal behavior control. What happened to this simple law is a fascinating study of the cultural development of jurisprudence. The elaboration of the Levitical law—the Talmud, and its effect upon development of a religious elite—is all part of this story. It was a gradual process that the prophets and Jesus himself understood and spent much time speaking against. The function of the law had been developed far beyond its cultural necessity to maintain order within the nation. It had become a tool for religious manipulation by the religious and social elite.

Turning outward, warfare and intrigue marked the political relationships of Israel with surrounding neighbors and beyond. God's power was often evident, especially in the early stages of nation building. What were the influences of government on the nation and what effect did that have on their later history? The Hebrews were very much influenced by the surrounding nations, lending credence to the importance of studies on these cultures as well. Solomon's temple was built by Hiram, a Phoenician, who implemented a plan similar to that of temples in other key cities. There was also a healthy trade between the nations, and warfare played a significant role in Israel's beginning as well as its fall and exile. The interplay between Israel and the nations around her provide the context for much of Scripture, both Old and New Testaments.

The underlying political themes that flow through Scripture (human greed, desire for power and control, and the sovereignty of God who is truly in control) permeate international politics today. The principles are much the same; the scale is simply global rather than regional (although in Old Testament times they thought the political implications to be global as well). Knowledge has expanded our understanding, so will the translation we produce.

DISCOVERING OLD TESTAMENT WORLDVIEW

Worldview analysis takes time, especially when the subject comes from ancient cultures and the primary data are texts in dead languages, and archaeological investigation. Yet, as communicators, it is necessary to take the time to acquaint ourselves with this background material. Without a basic awareness of the Biblical context and the assumptions of the people who lived in it, we will be handicapped in communicating the meaning of Scripture to people in the modern world.[3]

To begin, we must reaffirm that there are many cultures and more than one cultural type represented throughout the Old Testament. With this in mind, attempt to focus on kinship or peasant passages and note the interaction patterns of people in those contexts. Read through a passage and note the concerns that are repeated. Throughout the desert wanderings of the Israelites the focus is on food, water, discontent and warfare. During the period of possessing the Land, the emphasis is on warfare, power, righteousness, and obedience. How are these various emphases communicated in the actual incidents of Scripture? A good question to ask is why the author (and the Holy Spirit) chose this particular incident over some other? What does this story portray about the culture, about God's purpose with respect to the people involved? How does such information affect future generations that will hear what has been preserved?

A helpful tool for worldview study comes out of myth analysis. A myth often acts as a means of unifying thought patterns and portraying ideal behavior for those who hold to it. A myth can be analyzed by recognizing three parts: the *moral* (the overriding message of a story), the *themes* (cultural foci within a story) and *motifs* (the cultural manifestations used to demonstrate the themes (Shaw 1972).

This model provides a means of analyzing Biblical materials to derive cultural meaning. What motifs are used to demonstrate the themes and how are they arranged to develop the moral? When a passage is chosen, a more in-depth analysis following Spradley's developmental sequence (chapter 8) may be in order. Such analysis fits into the exegetical steps necessary to understand the semantic structure of a passage, (chapter 14). In effect, worldview analysis is cultural exegesis just as semantic structural analysis is linguistic exegesis. Both are essential for an adequate job of translation as well as preaching, discipling, and teaching.

"God cares about people". This can be considered a worldview theme that encompasses the whole of Scripture. From the creation and the special position given Adam, to the focus of the epistle writers of the New Testament on the relationship between a loving, caring God who reconciles human beings unto Himself, this theme comes through. Many of the Old Testament case studies seem to specifically focus on this theme and are told and retold to reinforce to both the Israelites and all the peoples around them, that God cares. Discovering that they are part of the creation and, therefore, recipients of God's care can be *revelation* for a people group receiving God's Word for the first time.

The discovery of these worldview themes and morals will give communicators a deeper appreciation of both the cultural situation and the meaning of the message communicated to the original receptors. This, then, provides the area of needed transfer to the receptor culture. When translators note that certain passages or topics overlap with concerns or worldview themes of the receptor, they should mark them for translation early in the program. As people relate the Biblical passages to their own context they will apply God's truth to themselves. Such was the case when old Hogwanobiayo drew the application of God's injunctions to Noah and applied them to his own cannibalistic practices. God cared so much about the people whom He created that He did not want any other created being, human or animal, interfering.

Keep in mind that worldview is integrated. It links all the various cultural assumptions. Therefore, insights gained through linguistic analysis may also shed light on cultural concerns. When reading Scripture, note the discourse style and structure of the communication, how a subject is introduced, developed and concluded, and the various devices used for emphasis, argument, transition and communication flow.

For example, when reading the Old Testament note how often something is repeated. In the first few chapters of I Kings (and many other passages as well) Western readers tend to become bored because the same thing is repeated in several ways: the incident, a repetition of the incident (often through a quote), and finally a summation or later reference which reiterates the event once again. This linguistic structure is reflective of the Hebrew language which, in turn, focuses on scenes that bring out the intended meaning. Repetition is a linguistic device for emphasis in many languages (English is far more cryptic and parsimonious than most). These repetitions, then, may contain themes which are important in communicating the message. They may contain the moral which encapsulates the meaning of the passage. Therefore, noting linguistic style (how the language develops focus, draws attention to what is important, develops an argument, or connects the parts of a story) can relate closely to the culture of those who speak the language, revealing important truths.

Despite the variety of worldviews portrayed throughout the Old Testament, the basic means of discovering them is the same. We can also apply the methodology to the message itself. What, in effect, is God's worldview as portrayed through what has been included in Scripture? Is there a supra-cultural worldview? What is the message God is trying to communicate through each of the themes and motifs we analyzed throughout Scripture? Once we understand what God intends to communicate and how the language and culture transfers that meaning into reality, we can see how the people of Scripture responded. This understanding will assist in communicating the same message into the context of modern receptors. It will also affect their response to the message.

Understanding God and His interaction with people through language and culture is what theology is all about. Some theologians are beginning to realize the importance of cultural studies (Bush and Butler 1985). This trend toward giving the study of Scriptural cultures some priority is long overdue and I applaud it. Hallmarks of theological study such as systematics, may be little more than viewing God through Western cultural glasses—glasses assembled by the industrial complex. As finite human beings, we cannot hope to fully understand God. This perspective from which God is viewed is cultural by its very definition. The communicator's cultural viewpoint needs to be expanded and critiqued by those of the source and receptor. In fact, translators might learn something important about God and themselves if they would rediscover and apply this process to their own understanding. Much of what we call Christianity in the world today is a reflection of reformation liturgy, music and theology not Biblical forms as such. Glimpses of God through other cultural experience may help defuse the tendencies to communicate God's message and intent from one's own perspective. Such a broadening of self-awareness will serve to develop a greater freedom to break out of the cultural shells that encase every society and to recognize the responsibility to communicate God's Word in as culture-free a manner as possible (Donovan 1979).

Developing an awareness of Old Testament worldview is an essential part of the translation/communication task. This can be done by studying cultural manifestations with respect to each of the cultural sub-types and how they together form an integrated cultural system. The concerns that serve to integrate the system provide us with cultural themes that reflect a worldview.

Suggested Reading

Robinson, Wheeler. *Corporate Personality in Ancient Israel.* Fortress Press, 1980.

Wilson, Robert. *Sociological Approaches to the O.T.*

Wolff, Hans. *Anthropology of the O.T.* Fortress Press, 1981.

Notes

1. When translators from an Industrial type culture are working with peoples of kinship or peasant cultures and focusing on the Old Testament, there is the potential for the greatest cultural misunderstanding. Receptors often share much more in common with Old Testament cultures and values than those who translate for them. In many cases translators have identified more with the cultural situation of the New Testament. They get excited about the incarnation as God's fulfillment of prophecy, and Paul's philosophical arguments. From this keen cultural interest they assume that everyone else shares these concerns and relates to them. Translation projects have

been known to bog down because co-translators, unable to see relevance in Paul's complicated thought patterns and argumentation, lost interest in the project. The culture type of the translator, without question, has a dominant effect on the entire translation project and expatriates should be aware of it and avoid the cultural tendencies that could get in the way of receptors understanding God because they misunderstand the context in which God spoke.

2. We often assume an understanding because of our Biblical background gleaned from sermons based on these passages. But preachers primarily attempt to contextualize for their audience and apply the concepts to modern technological society. While this is as it should be, it makes sermons poor sources for cultural information other than material pertaining to the particular audience.

3. Perhaps it is best to remember that Western culture is a very recent development. People have lived with values and beliefs common to those found in Scriptures for a lot longer than industrial systems have been around. Their perspective, then, may offer us opportunity to learn what God was communicating in a context that was more like the one with which they are familiar.

CHAPTER TEN
Cultures of the New Testament

The inter-testamental period was stormy. Much was happening in the world: the rise of socio-political interdependence epitomized by the Roman empire, increasing urbanization, a developing class structure, a consolidation of business ventures. All this brought tremendous pressure on the peasant cultures that had developed in the Bible lands. Interaction patterns throughout the region were changing from relationships based on kinship or social status to interaction based more on individual initiative, and commercial enterprise. Though not specifically industrial in type, the shift in focus resulted in a socio-political complex that included colonialism, slavery, business cooperation, and internationalism that suggests a cultural complex not at all unfamiliar to the world today.

Many of the philosophical issues present today were in place by New Testament times. The Gospels tend to reflect a more rural, agrarian lifestyle epitomized in many of the parables Jesus told. The Apostle Paul, on the other hand, deals with themes that reflect urbanization and commercial concerns. He understood loneliness and individuality from which he drew many of his examples. He understood the Greek worldview and appropriated it for effective communication. Thus, translators from the West feel more comfortable reading the New Testament. However, they should not allow this feeling of familiarity to lull them into complacently reading or translating without adequate cultural analysis. Much of the New Testament is still far more similar culturally to most receptor cultures today than to post-industrial society.

New Testament times were distinct from the Old Testament period, yet were heavily influenced by them, as well as the interval between the Testaments. A sense of history gives us an appreciation of a rich cultural backdrop characterized by cultural

135

diversity, but moving towards greater cultural integration. Change is central to understanding the context in which the incarnation occurred and the new covenant was communicated. We now turn our attention to it.

THE CHANGE OF CULTURE TYPE

The increased interdependence of political entities in New Testament times is probably the most obvious indication of a gradual shift from tribal and peasant culture types to what could be called a pre-industrial or *commercial* culture type. During the inter-testamental period there had been a sharp rise in urban drift, and large numbers of people were living in cities: Athens, Corinth, Ephesus, Rome, and Jerusalem. Alexandria boasted one and a half million people and had production lines for the making of many standard items. The New Testament world was also characterized by frequent travel and the cultural intermixing that resulted. The road system developed by the Greeks and expanded by the Romans provided easy access to cross-cultural fertilization. People of the time appear to have taken this for granted as evidenced by the listing of nations in Acts 2. This freedom of movement contributed to the wide spread of the gospel "in Jerusalem, in all Judaea and Samaria, and to the ends of the earth" (Acts 1:8). Those who were more provincial still had to deal with cross-cultural issues (recall the discussion between Paul and Peter in Gal. 2:11-14).

Within Palestine, there had been a cultural shift following the exile. As people returned from the dispersion they brought a wide variety of experiences, cultural complexes and religious beliefs. Thus, Jerusalem at the time of Christ was a cosmopolitan city with a far more eclectic nature than during the time of the kings. It was also heavily influenced by the nature of the political present: the Greco-Roman influences, especially the colonial presence and lack of self-rule. Perhaps this is why religious independence was so important to the Jewish leaders—they had no other way to express their authority.

Going beyond the life of Christ and the Palestinian context, we see a world in which Christianity took root, a world outside of Judaism—the Gentile world. It was the Greco-Roman world of Athens with its philosophers, Ephesus with its religious eclecticism, and Rome with all its sophistication. It was a complex world teaming with cultural diversity. As in the Old Testament period, we find the gospel message interacting in a variety of cultures, but the focus is much sharper, the time period much more compressed, the integration more specific. We turn now to a discussion of these cultural factors and look specifically at the times and conditions of the New Testament world and the influence that had upon the continuation of God's communication with humanity through the writers of Scripture.

A BRIEF LOOK AT NEW TESTAMENT CULTURES

As with our discussion of Old Testament cultures, it is helpful to apply the cultural sub-systems model to the New Testament. What were the environmental, ideological, social and political forces moving through the world to make the cultures of New Testament times what they were? How is the New Testament different from the Old? How do we communicate these differences to present day receptors?

Economic

There was a radical change in the economic structure of the world by the New Testament era. The environmental conditions of Palestine in New Testament times were probably not much different from those of the Old Testament period. What was different was the human response to it. Through a change in material culture, and a shift in economic technique, people had altered their environment. The economy was different (though still primarily peasant, especially in the rural areas) and reflected cultural shifts.

For example, during the Old Testament period the labor force had been family oriented, people working together in kinship groups to accomplish necessary tasks (the sons of Jacob working together, the Israelites occupying the land and possessing it by family groupings, etc.). By the time of Christ a less personal form had been adopted and hired help was frequent. The parable of the hired hands is a case in point (Mt. 20:1-16). The fishing industry on the Sea of Galilee, though often a family business (Zebedee with his sons James and John, Mk. 1:15-20) included common laborers. Food was, to some extent, mass produced as evidenced by the parable of the rich man who tore down his barns and built new ones (Lk. 12:16-19). His business was producing food for those in the urban centers who could not produce their own. Then as now, economic specialization was the order of the day. Artisans and laborers performed their respective jobs and used the earned pay to purchase necessities: Jesus was a carpenter, Paul a tentmaker. The system depended upon commerce and the exchange of money; the dominant economic relationships were commercial. An awareness of the inter-testamental period with its apocryphal writings, as well as historians such as Josephus can be helpful in understanding these economic shifts.

While it can be argued that the economy depended on human and animal power (there were no fuel powered machines), the interaction patterns of the day were distinctly different from Old Testament times. The kinship and peasant emphases had undergone a shift to individualistic tendencies in a commercial environment that resembled modern cultures. This was particularly true in the urban complexes, though Palestine was by no means exempt. Economically, rapid change was part of the cultural expectation. The economic forms and meanings were in a stage of transition similar to that experienced by modern receptors. Understanding these cultural shifts between the Old and New Testaments can serve to assist people as they adjust to changes in their own socio-economic context.

Ideology

The ideological struggle between Christ and the dominant Jewish religious system permeates the Gospels. The Book of Mark is primarily devoted to documenting these ideological differences (Kingston 1975). This interaction centered around the way God's laws had become the Jewish Religion. Christ was arguing for the spirit of the law, while the Jewish leaders were interested in perpetuating the letter of the law which benefited them rather than the people they served.

This ideological climate was further complicated by the Greek and Roman philosophies which placed great emphasis on humanism and class society. Though not a focus in the Gospels, the latter comes to the fore in the epistles. We can note this difference throughout the book of Acts as Paul and others interact in Jewish synagogues or with other ideologies. Paul's sermons in the book of Acts are a fascinating study of ideological and cultural adaptation with receptor-oriented communication as the focus. Paul knew and understood the complex ideological and cultural world of his day and he used it to his advantage. There is much we can learn from his methodology which applies to today's world (Allen 1913, Gilliland 1984).

As we study the New Testament in preparation for translation, it is essential to note the extent that ideological considerations permeated people's lives: a shift from organic to mechanistic, from an awareness of a supreme, transempirical God to many lower, local gods. What were the particular ideological concerns and how did they affect lifestyle? What was the perception of those who originally received the Word with respect to the spiritual realm? How did these beliefs affect the way they understood God's truth? Put another way, how did Christ understand the belief system of his day and how did he speak to it? This, of course affected the authors of the New Testament, especially when the audience was different than the one Christ addressed.

Throughout the New Testament we see a pervasion of spirit beings and their impact on humans; Christ seemed to constantly relate to demons and the people who were possessed by them. Spiritual forces often dominate Paul's writing, reflecting both the beliefs of his receptors and the reality of the spirit world that Westerners have largely rationalized away. The importance of religious structures, full time religious specialists and mythology (both Jewish and Gentile) demonstrates the highly developed ideological context of New Testament times and writings. The many references to the Old Testament are a conscious attempt to validate circumstances and arguments and reveal a heritage which had on-going effects upon the receptors. This heritage is, in large measure, a product of cultural development and it is this development that we must understand in order to effectively communicate the message of the New Testament. A friend of mine recently commented on what he feels is a travesty of translating the New Testament and publishing it without the Old: the latter contributes to and sets the stage for the former; both are God's communication to human beings.

The ideological climate of New Testament times, with influence from religions throughout the world, was a complexity similar to that found today. In many cases recipients have similar beliefs and values. By focusing on these and the Biblical answers to them we can build credibility and develop an awareness of the New Testament context.

Kinship

By New Testament times the focus on relationships had broadened somewhat from the family to relationships outside the kin or work group. Greater urbanization brought people into contact, not so much with respect to their family ties, but more in relation to their roles. The developing complexity of roles thus demands some analysis on the part of the translator.

Christ had much to say about the family, comparing the human relationships within a family to the relationship between God and those who, by faith, put their trust in Him (Jn. 1:12ff). The dominant dyad for the New Testament was probably brother-brother, evidenced by the brother sets among the disciples and Jesus' references to relationships to God through Him. The Apostle Paul extended the brother relationship from the family to the broader interaction with all Christians as family members. Yet, there are equally as many references to neighbors and to interaction with people in a wide variety of roles, both Christians and non-Christians.

The New Testament demonstrates a gradual shift to relationships beyond the family, though by no means disregarding the importance of family. This emphasis shows a gradual shift to a greater degree of individualism, a factor that was affecting relationships during New Testament times even as it does today. In receptor contexts that focus on kinship and peasant styles of human interaction this greater sense of individualism may need to be explicated, implied information made clear as necessary. We must, however, avoid cluttering the translation with supplementary material that is not part of the original communication. Clearly, relationships are central to Christian interaction, and many of those associations are detailed in the New Testament writings.

Social Structure

Much as the family structure was changing, so was the interaction between groups. The social units of the culture, namely the tribes of Israel and their respective interaction, had largely broken down as a result of the exile. Though clan lines were known, they had lost some of their emphasis except, perhaps, for the Levites who maintained the religious structure and acted as a religious elite.

The relationships between peasant and elite, part of the pre-exilic cultural complex, were shifting to relationships between social groups within a nation and beyond to those in other nations. While in exile the Jews had been oppressed; they were, for the most part, the slaves, the social outcasts (exceptions were Esther, and Daniel who spoke on behalf of their people). Once back in the land their social ordering turned more to artisan groups and class structure. Governmentally they were ruled by a foreign elite and their ideological system was controlled by their own religious elite.

Marriage patterns were also in a state of flux, raising other issues of relationship and social order including the status and roles of women and the changing nature of the husband-wife relationship. Christ's many references to marriage, John's comparison of the marriage supper of the Lamb to a wedding feast, and Paul's many illustrations using marriage, all point to an increasing importance of the husband-wife dyad within New Testament cultures. This relationship again demonstrates the cultural shift between the Old and New Testaments.

Understanding the cultural dynamics behind these changes can be a great help to translators trying to communicate these differences to members of a receptor language and culture. It is also important for Western translators to recognize their own cultural bias at this point, particularly with respect to the dominance of the husband-wife relationship and its social consequences. It must not be assumed that this same perspective is shared with the New Testament writers or by present day receptors. These matters demand study and cultural awareness as the translator communicates the New Testament message to others. That message represents a gradual social shift which affected many relationships, both individual and group, including the dominant dyad. Understanding that shift and the message implied in it is useful for effective translation, especially if the receptors do not share that social perspective.

Political Organization

The political complexity of the New Testament era is one of its most prominent characteristics. The Roman empire dominated politically, but there were innumerable local political concerns that affected the message being communicated by the Scripture writers.

The disciples were clearly confused about Christ's real motives. Theirs were largely political; they expected to usher in a temporal kingdom. The circumstances of Christ's trial provide a study of the religious-political interplay between the Jews and their colonial rulers: the church and the state, law and government. The Roman influence was primarily political, dealing with civil law, keeping the peace, maintaining the road system and a far-flung colonial empire. Military overtones were never far below the surface (Daniel-Rops 1962, Edersheim 1976).

The circumstances surrounding the Apostle Paul's trial in Jerusalem and Caesarea were directly affected by the relationship between the Roman government and provincial administration. Paul's dual citizenship led to confusion and injustice as well as many good illustrations of the political climate of the day. It was a complex time politically that worked for and against the communication of the gospel.

Internal politics, or law (in anthropological terms), was also in a state of confusion. Many of the patterns relating to the Law of Moses had long since been institutionalized. Christ specifically said He came to fulfill the Law, to renew the spirit of the Law and reduce the heavy yoke of obeying minutiae as represented in the religious system (Mt. 5:17ff, Mt. 11:28-30). Religious law was the primary means of social control in Jesus' day: condemning adultery (Jn. 8:3-11) and work on the sabbath (Lk. 6:1-11), controlling tithes (Mk. 12:41-44), and encouraging prayers (Lk. 18:9-13). These religious or internal laws, however, were often in conflict with Roman laws. This was the heart of the controversy surrounding the crucifixion. Jewish religious law affected their internal affairs, giving them the right to punish Jesus (but not to inflict the death penalty, Jn. 18:31,32). The external Roman system, in contrast, gave Jesus the right to a fair trial (Jn. 18:38). Such conflict characterizes much of New Testament writing; the Apostle Paul often discusses the interaction of believers with the governmental system and their relationships among themselves based on

God's law (Rom. 4-8, and many of the practical portions of other epistles).

Such political complexity may be quite foreign to receptors today and will need some explanation. Interestingly enough, many receptors find themselves in similar circumstances as they deal with colonialism, regional factionalism and secession movements. Internal tribal laws (codes of behavior) often conflict with the law of the land. Much of the New Testament is good news to such people as they apply Biblical principles to present day contexts.

DISCOVERING NEW TESTAMENT WORLDVIEW

Unlike the Old Testament that is a record spanning several thousand years, the New Testament is much more compressed. It deals specifically with the life of Christ and the period of time immediately surrounding that life span. Thus the cultural context is much more focused. Doubtless there was change during the 70 years of New Testament writing, but they are not of the magnitude discussed for the Old Testament.

Of primary concern as we look at New Testament worldview is the difference of focus between New Testament and Old Testament themes. What cultural themes recur frequently throughout the New Testament writings that are different from the foci of the Old Testament? The answer largely reflects the change in culture type: greater individualism, political concerns, and ideological issues that reflect an attempt to break away from institutionalized forms of religion (a product of the inter-testamental period) and return to the meaning of heart concerns as expressed by David and the prophets. Such a focus is important today where change is taking place at an increasingly rapid pace in every society. No people are immune to encroaching change brought about by interaction with a wide variety of people, including cross-cultural communicators.

In documenting this focus on change, we must consider the New Testament view of the Old Testament. What effect did the Greek worldview have on the translation of the Old Testament? How did worldview affect the way New Testament people understood the message of the Old Testament? As the various writers quote the Old Testament in order to validate a particular point, what effect did Greek worldview have on their interpretation and how they used the quote? Since so much of the New Testament is based on Old Testament prior reference, we must fully understand the contrasts between Hebrew and Greek world-view and the impact of both the Targums and the Septuagint on that understanding.

There is a considerable literature over the nature of Hellenistic influence at the time of Christ (Goodenough 1953, Hadas 1959, Hagner 1973, Tarn 1952). Were the New Testament writers primarily influenced by Greek philosophy and, therefore, culturally disembodied from their Hebrew roots, or did those roots play the central role? It is not my intent to resolve this debate. It does, however, appear that perhaps both sides have validity. Greek was the trade language of the day, allowing wide geographical interaction while speaking a single language, though some question the extent of use beyond the market place (Sevenster 1968). The Septuagint was available and widely used by Jews in the diaspora. Much of the New Testament was originally written in Greek, not Aramaic, the language of the Palistinian countryside. This was a reflection of the importance of Greek culture and philosophy on the world of that time.

On the other hand, the writers of the New Testament were profoundly affected by Judaism, their heritage shows in the constant references to the Scriptures. Many of the themes of the Old Testament (care, judgment, peace, etc.) are reflected in the New. In fact, to appreciate the New Testament, a thorough background of the Old is essential. Though writing in Greek from a primarily Greek perspective, the Apostle Paul was profoundly affected by his religious training at the feet of Gamaliel (Acts 22:3). John's writings, as well as those of the book of Hebrews, appear to be a synthesis of Jewish and Hellenistic thought, the religious tradition and conceptual background of the former plus the language and philosophy of the latter. This richness of both traditions blends in a series of writings that totally mix the two, linguistically Greek, but conceptually Jewish (Hengle 1974, Sevenster 1968). Judaism and Hellenism should not be viewed as two discrete cultural complexes; they interact to give the world of that period a distinct cultural integration. This complexity provides the atmosphere in which the incarnation took place. This was the world that spawned Christianity, a rapidly growing church, the spread of gnosticism, and the rise and fall of Christian persecution

(Foxe 1926). The diaspora enabled the Jews (wherever they were) to bring a broader perspective to the ideas of Scripture. These became highlighted in the New Testament: dualism, an emphasis on the spirit world and the impact of divine sovereignty in human affairs.

Clearly then, regardless of the Judaism-Hellenism debate, a thorough understanding of the Greco-Roman cultural overlay is necessary for an appreciation of the New Testament context. That understanding must be brought to bear on a sense of history during the period. Understanding the dynamics between the three culture types assists in respecting cultural differences between the Old and New Testaments as well as between cultures within the world at the time of Christ. How the commercial culture of the New Testament era was affected by and interpreted what went before is critical for an appreciation of that period and its writings, including Scripture (Meyers and Strange 1981).

Relating these cultural and linguistic issues to the exegesis of the New Testament may help develop a better understanding of New Testament theology. What effect did urbanization, individualism, social and political diversity and ideological institutionalization have upon the peoples whom Jesus addressed, as well as on what he said? How did these issues affect the travels and presentations of the Apostle Paul? How did they affect the development of the church, its dispersion, growth and persecution? How did they affect the theology of the day?[1]

These questions are not only relevant as we analyze the New Testament culturally, but pertain directly to how we theologize today. Theology is simply organizing thoughts about God. All people theologize in one way or another. It is a product of our worldview, the human response to the transempirical dimension of culture. To what extent does our worldview affect the way we understand the New Testament writings and the theology we derive from them? If we have this freedom to theologize how do we pass that freedom on to others? As the people of the world receive Scripture they need to organize their own thoughts about the true God. It is the responsibility of the Bible translator to so communicate the truth of Scripture—its meaning—that the receptors can develop their own theology and have it ring true to Biblical themes.

THE COMMUNICATOR'S RESPONSIBILITY

Culture, then, is reflected through all of Scripture. How we and our receptors understand much of God's Word relates directly to the way we perceive and interpret the Biblical context: culturally, linguistically and theologically. In the past considerable emphasis has been placed on linguistic understanding through the study of Biblical languages and this remains an important aspect of translation. From a linguistic appreciation of Scripture we have developed an awareness of the spiritual conditions into which the Scriptures were initially communicated. From this we have written our theology based on what we understood God to be saying.

It seems apparent that culture has not been given its proper place in Biblical exegesis. Cultural study provides us with a greater awareness of the context: the cultural factors, conditions and meanings affecting God's communication with human beings. Perhaps the concerns raised in these two chapters will alert communicators to the need to determine the source culture type and relate that context successfully to the receptor.

What Biblical concerns or themes are reflected in the receptor context and how can that meaning assist people as they live in modern cultures? As we translated for the Samo we asked the question, "If Christ had come to the Samo what would He have said and done?" To answer that question we needed information regarding (1) the Samo cultural concerns to which Christ would have spoken, and (2) an understanding of Jewish concerns with which Christ actually interacted. With regards to the former, we learned of the incredible fear the Samo have of the supernatural forces that surround them: cosmic forces, bush spirits, sorcerers, etc. These concerns are directly related to the high incidence of sickness and death (which is always caused—nothing just happens). They also spend a great deal of time procuring food. As we looked at the life of Christ, we saw him interacting with spirits of all kinds, healing the sick and raising the dead. He also spoke often of daily needs for food, shelter, and clothing.

By beginning our New Testament translation with passages that demonstrated Christ's interest in Samo concerns, they identified with Him. These concerns were of far greater importance to them than His miraculous birth, or even His death and resurrection. These issues, as important as they are, came later (as they do for most believers, including those in the West). People need to view Christ as one who is concerned about their worries, one who can relate to their felt needs (IPet. 5:7). Though speaking to another time and place, much of what Christ said and did has dynamic relevance to the Samo and all other people groups around the world. His relationships are timeless. He cares. This early message allows a translator to eventually put the rest of Scripture into a context the recipients understand.

Bible translators, like other missionaries, can become overwhelmed by the enormity of the task. An adequate analysis of the type suggested here could add considerably to the length of time it takes to do a translation. There is, so far, very little research of this nature available. Such scholarly studies could make a great contribution. The problem of raising issues in a book such as this is that we become aware of how little we really know and how much we need good scholarship. Despite all this, however, it is worth the effort to understand the meaning intended by God in communicating these case studies. It is worth the time spent to understand the worldview parallels between Scripture and receptors. Meaning-based translation communicates that understanding in relevant ways. Receptor-oriented communication and resultant understanding is the goal.

Translation serves as a bridge between the source and receptor. It communicates the meaning intended for the source to the receptor in such a way that the receptor is able to act on the message and understand God. The goal is lives being conformed to the image of God. Cultural studies within an integrated cultural system, such as that represented by Palestine at the time of Christ, should assist cross-cultural communicators in reaching that goal.

Suggested Reading

Malherbe, Abraham. *Social Aspects of Early Christianity*. Fortress Press, 1983.

Meeks, Wayne. *The First Urban Christians*. Yale U. Press, 1983.

Tidball, Derek. *The Social Context of the N.T.* Zondervan, 1984.

Note

1. See Meeks 1983 for a vivid discussion of these topics—they are crucial to understanding the New Testament.

CHAPTER ELEVEN
Receptor Cultures in Today's World

Understanding the cultural conditions which affected the original Scripture writings is vital for effective translation. So too is a thorough understanding of the receptor culture into which the gospel message will be introduced. Much of the focus in Part I of this book dealt with ways to obtain material of use to communicators. Once that information regarding the receptor culture is available, what does a communicator do with it? How does that material affect the translation process? These are the questions to which we now turn.

THREE CULTURES MODEL APPLIED

A quick look at today's world reveals societies of each of the three main culture types. Many of these people groups are experiencing rapid culture change, particularly kinship societies in developing nations. Due to external pressures people are rapidly changing their cultural complexes (material culture, political relationships and even social interaction patterns), but the ideological base of these cultural systems remain, in large measure, the driving force behind the more sophisticated surface structures. Studies have shown that ideological factors in a culture tend to change more slowly than the economic and social aspects (Foster 1973). Thus the same beliefs and values that affected behavior in a culture with a subsistence-based economy now precipitate behavior in a culture with a rapidly growing (and changing) material culture dominated by an outside political force that may have largely obliterated the old political system.

For example, among the Maxikali of East Central Brazil, elders and family heads are strong opinion leaders. Despite government records of "chiefs" described as men of status and influence, specialists in religion and ceremonies, Harold and Fran Popovich were unable to discover a term in the language for this office. After twenty years of interacting with these people, the very concept of such a leader seemed foreign. Interestingly, the dominant society apparently imposed their ideas of leadership on the Maxikali in order to facilitate administration as well as to supply what they considered a cultural deficiency. Traditional leadership was the province of the old men, the wise and experienced family heads who lead as one among equals. They are still expected to provide the necessary leadership to the domestic group and its descendants. The government, however, looks for a degree of bilingualism and an ability to pass along orders. As a result young men, with little or no prestige, are often called *capitao,* 'chief' (Popovich 1980:32-35).

Kinship societies exist primarily on the Island of New Guinea and some parts of the Amazon basin. Small pockets remain in Africa and Asia as well. These are the societies to whom Bible translators have gone in the tradition made popular by William Cameron Townsend (Cowan 1979). Pioneering translators have gone to these often numerically small, unreached peoples and translated God's Word for them.

Peasant societies cover much of the rest of the so-called Third World. These societies, too, are experiencing rapid change as social and political concerns, often a product of the socio-economic system, produce unrest and attempts to instigate change. Many of the large languages of the world represent these peoples and have translations of Scripture available. Many others do not. It is for these groups that national translation projects are most obviously possible and many are now being done under the auspices of the United Bible Societies, Living Bibles International, and newly formed National Bible Translation Organizations.

Most of the industrial nations have Scriptures available to them, often in many forms (Kubo & Spect 1982). Despite this availability, many people in these societies do not know or understand the Biblical message. Could it be that this relates, in part, to the individualistic emphasis? Does the humanistic, cultural impact affect their worldview to the extent they feel no need for God? The exact reasons for these patterns are not the subject of this book, but are a fascinating study of the impact of culture on the development and message of the Christian Church in a cultural context. Morton Kelsey alludes to this in several of his works and draws the conclusion that those "in the Western world live in an age as ignorant of spiritual things as medieval cities were of sanitation and hygiene, not only ignorant, but often contemptuous" (Kelsey 1984:5).

The intermix of these cultural types within the nations of the world, presents communicators with a considerable amount of complexity. Translators increasingly find themselves working on a translation for one cultural group, but that group, in turn, is very much affected by the impact of another. In the Samo case, though very much a kinship culture, they are increasingly affected by the industrial presuppositions of government officers, magistrates, teachers, and pastors. As airstrips have been built and access into the region has increased, the Samo find themselves being introduced to an ever larger world: that of both Papua New Guinea and the West which is dramatically influencing it (Shaw 1981b). The rapidly expanding roads, schools, trade stores, and churches (not to mention the recent discovery of large oil deposits) all affect their rapidly changing interests and concerns.

The world is full of such examples. Affected by change, these culturally complex situations will increasingly characterize the translation context. Most translation programs today include an overlay of all three major culture types.[1] Understanding the dynamics of such cultural interaction is essential for successful translation.

THE IMPACT OF CHANGE

Change is the topic of numerous books and understanding current trends is crucial to survival (Toffler 1980, Naisbitt 1982, etc.). Rapid change in third world countries has resulted in concern among anthropologists for the welfare and survival of the hidden peoples (*Cultural Survival* is a journal devoted to these concerns). Anyone engaged in communicating the gospel should also be vitally concerned about these trends and how they affect the people (Richardson 1977). We must understand ourselves as agents of change and be prepared to assist in the change process as well as helping people step from "darkness" into "light". Historical forces constantly act upon a society to effect worldview change that, in turn, affects their behavior (Kearney 1984:120).

How, then, should we tell people they need to change? How do we tell them many of their cultural practices are Biblically wrong? How do we communicate that they are sinful and need to establish a right relationship with God? How do we change their worldview? We don't. As Christians our desire is a positive response to what God has communicated to all people. We must, then, communicate the message in such a way that people themselves are given the dignity to make a decision based on their worldview, not ours. Their decisions should be a product of their culture, not some outsider's. Changes they make should be based on what God's communication means to them individually and as a group, not on what others tell them.

So often missionaries, in their enthusiasm to reach people for God, give them a list of what God wants. These conditions, however defined, are usually a product of the outsider's culture and, therefore, appear irrelevant to those who receive them. In trying to point the way to God, they create misunderstanding. Rather, the communicator's responsibility is to present truth upon which people can make wise choices and grow in grace and knowledge. Such is the focus of Bible translation as an approach to Christian mission. Translated Scripture gives people a choice based upon their understanding of God's communication, not on what someone tells them about what God has said. As people have more of God's Word, they will appropriate it to change their worldview and resulting behavior. Such change then, is a product of their own understanding and has meaning within their system as a whole. Scripture communicates meaning (truth) and meaning manifests itself in behavioral changes (Shaw 1981b).

No matter how well versed outsiders may be, they can only predict response. Insiders alone can act as innovators who instigate change and act appropriately within the bounds of their culture (Barnett 1953:291ff, see Figure 11:1). If an insider goes beyond those bounds, the political system may bring negative sanctions to bear and both the innovator and the ideas may be rejected (Wallace 1956). Too often this has been the response to the gospel; it has not been seen as relevant. The adherents were somehow peripheral to reality as perceived by those in the mainstream and they, as well as their message, were rejected.

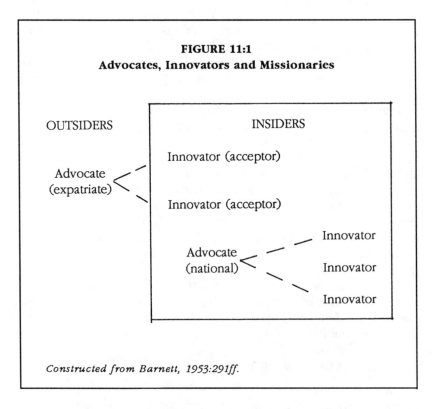

FIGURE 11:1
Advocates, Innovators and Missionaries

Constructed from Barnett, 1953:291ff.

To avoid this, it is essential that we understand the culture to the greatest extent possible: its features, concerns, needs, interests fears, i.e. its system. Those who are leaders within the cultural system, the advocates, the ones who are viewed as the hope of the society, they are the ones who must understand the message and communicate it within their context. They are the ones who can appropriate Scripture so that it makes sense to all members of the society. As they understand, changes will take place because this is God's Word and the Holy Spirit will make it powerful and sharper than a two-edged sword (Heb. 4:12).

As people determine the cultural changes necessary for a response to Scripture, they will know the cultural rationale for change and act accordingly. Knowing the system, they understand how change in one area will affect all others and can make

necessary adjustments. Thus they have an answer for the hope
that is within them (I Pet. 3:15). This is the only way the gospel
can fulfill the culture. Communicators have the responsibility to
make that Word available so people can act upon it.

As gospel communicators, who are outsiders, enter a cultural
situation, a keen awareness of cultural difference is prominent.
Behavioral norms which are expected by their own culture are
constantly being broken or similar behavior has very different
meaning. Overcoming this cultural disorientation is the process of
language and culture learning. Adopting the role of learners or
babies in the culture, they gradually "bond" to the new context
and begin to function within it (Brewster and Brewster 1976,
1982). This will often be difficult, demanding that they set aside
their own cultural rules and roles in order to act appropriately in
the new context. Though the process is disorienting, the cultural
pay-off as outsiders become more like insiders is well worth the
effort. People appreciate attempts to understand, they appreciate
the learning that takes place, and outsiders discover that different
cultural forms are not wrong, just different. This variety of forms
and their wealth of deeper meaning may be a way to appreciate
the broader human condition as well as deepen human respect
for the incarnation.

RECEPTOR-ORIENTED COMMUNICATION

A combination of the worldview discovery model developed
in chapter 8 and the communication model of chapter 2, can
assist those involved in communicating meaning from one context
into another. Part of the communicator's job is to avoid worldview
clash which is precipitated by different cultural contexts. Much of
the translator's time is spent resolving these potential conflicts so
that receptors clearly understand the message intended by the
original author. Worldview studies that focus on the receptor
context, are the basis upon which receptor-oriented translations
are accomplished. Without this understanding, the translator is
only guessing, educated guesses, perhaps, but guesses nevertheless. Of course, no acquired tongue cross-cultural communicator can hope to internalize the whole of another worldview. The
Samo still surprise me. The translator's own worldview will
constantly affect translation decisions. However, with worldview
studies as an adjunct to our task, we will gradually become alert

to the kinds of adjustments necessary and the areas that may prove most problematic. It is at these points that focused study can help avoid miscommunication.

When we were translating for the Samo, we came to the passage in John chapter 6 dealing with the feeding of the 5000. In verse ten it talks about the grass in the area and I immediately sensed a translation problem: which of the many types of grass the Samo know should be used in this context? First we needed to know what type of grass it was that grew in Palestine and might have been on that hillside overlooking the Sea of Galilee. No Bible dictionaries could help us, but clearly it was a type of grass on which people could sit and be comfortable.

Having made a decision regarding the source, we turned to the Samo understanding of grass. Following the process outlined in chapter 8, we discovered two major types: grasses that occur in open places like old gardens and airstrips, and grasses that occur in the forest environment. But grasses are further classified with respect to their growing patterns, amount of seeds, and what they are used for. We could not use the generic term for grass, because it is also used at a lower taxonomic level to specify jungle grasses and is also the name of a specific type of grass (the same problem with the English word *man*). To use the wrong grass name would give the Samo the wrong idea when hearing or reading this story of how Christ fed hungry people. We did not want the focus to be on the wrong thing, the grass. It was far more important for them to understand God's power and His interest in people, people with whom the Samo could identify.

It is the misunderstandings precipitated by people sitting on the wrong kind of grass that detract from the message of Scripture and skew people's perception of God and His communication with the people He created.[2] These cultural clashes can be compared to linguistic collocational clashes which translators work hard to avoid (Beekman and Callow 1974:160-174). What is not well understood is that many so-called collocational clashes are based on cultural factors that dictate the types of things that can come together linguistically. To be aware of linguistic clashes, then, necessitates a cultural sensitivity.

This type of sensitivity can come only through long term experience in a culture, and thorough familiarity with the materials to be translated. As a Melanesian student once told me:

"Cultures are made up of living human beings. There is a constant need for us to interact with the people we are working with, people who have real needs. There must be an element of exchange, of understanding, of appreciation." In short, cultural studies that lead to understanding worldview must be at the heart of every translation project. Only then will the translation relate to receptor needs, interests and perspectives. Only then will the translation have meaning within the community at which it is aimed. The specific messages intended for the original receptors will, then, to the greatest extent possible, be transferred to the hearts and minds of the modern receptors who receive God's Word for the first time. Often the ultimate message of the gospel is not accepted because the vital aspect of communication on the personal level has not been clearly established.

Studying the receptor context is exciting and often productive in broadening an understanding of one's own cultural background. It is much harder, however, to study one's own worldview, because the assumptions are implied in so much of what is lived out. Making these implicit assumptions explicit is very difficult, especially in a mono-cultural context where everyone makes the same basic assumptions. It is a violation or disruption of these assumptions that often produces frustration and stress in a cross-cultural situation. All cross-cultural interaction produces some form of culture clash: a lack of understanding the assumptions upon which meaningful behavior is based. It is to this understanding of the translator's own cultural perspective and its implications to the communication process that we now turn.

Suggested Reading

Spindler, George & Louise, General Editors. *Case Studies In Cultural Anthropology.* Holt, Rinehart & Winston. (A series of ethnographic studies from all over the world.)

Notes

1. There is at least the Scriptural source, the modern receptor and the translator (if from another culture), interacting in the translation process. Add to this the complex overlay within the immediate setting, and the cultural, linguistic, and communicational complexities multiply rapidly.

2. In fact, this example does not pose a particularly serious problem. However, if the translation is full of such culturally incongruous information, the overall impact will be affected. People will not consider the message relevant because it is clouded by so much extraneous material, material that does not fit with their perception of reality.

CHAPTER TWELVE
The Communicator's Culture

The focus now shifts to an area that communicators know best, their own culture. However, so much of what they know is intuitive and buried deep in the sub-conscious. It is not part of their thinking process. As with the source and receptor cultures, the communicator's worldview also structures the behavioral level through the cultural sub-systems. Hence, worldview conditions cultural expectations and when those expectations are not met cross-cultural communicators may assume others to be acting wrong. As outsiders, however, they must realize that it is their assumptions that may be incorrect by local standards—they are the ones behaving incorrectly. In the case of national translators working in their own or related socio-linguistic contexts, it goes without saying that their worldview will more-or-less match the receptors. However, understanding what those basic assumptions are can greatly assist in recognizing cultural blind spots and adjusting for them when relating to the source or interacting with expatriates.

It is the intent of this chapter to help communicators raise their worldview assumptions to a conscious level. Once these values and cultural themes are understood, they can then be compared with others in the communication context.[1] This is perhaps the most difficult part of the cultural discovery process because one's own worldview is assumed and, therefore, seldom, if ever, questioned. At the same time, it is the aspect which most frustrates the communication process. The translator often represents a third cultural perspective and must be fully aware of this and its impact on translating the intended message into a new context.

DISCOVERING YOUR OWN WORLDVIEW

Because of the deep level assumptions made by people of each and every culture, communicators need a definite process for determining their own worldview. This is not only true of the overarching cultural perspective or what Benedict calls the "modal personality" of a culture (Benedict 1934), but also pertains to the specific background and what is popularly known as "subculture". In large, diversified or stratified cultures (such as many of the industrial nations) it is necessary to be more specific, focusing on the homes, schools, and organizations which form a sub-culture (for a good discussion of this concept, see Foster 1973:178-180). Understanding these variations with respect to cultural context could help translators cognitively understand their own values and project those into various contexts in which they find themselves working. The more communicators are able to be rational with respect to their own or other's behavior, the less reactive they will be when confronted with worldview assumptions they do not share, whether those differences be reflected in Scripture or a modern culture.

For example, in the story of the prodigal son (Lk. 15:11-32), Westerners assume that the father rushed out to greet his son, glad for his return and ready to take him back. Writing from a peasant perspective, Bailey maintains that the critical factor here was protection. A father would never run in a peasant society that respects and honors age. But this father knew that if he did not protect his ragged son, the village urchins, dogs, and others who saw him would harass the returnee to the point where he may lose his resolve. In order to protect against that, the father broke tradition and ran to meet his son (Bailey 1980:181-182). This is a dramatic shift in focus based on very different assumptions. It also projects a very different view of God. Such cultural difference will be more easily discerned when communicators are aware of their own assumptions. People are to a considerable extent products of their context out of which come values, interests and concerns.

Not many cultures have had worldview tests developed to help communicators understand their unconscious roots. In some industrial cultures psychological inventories have been developed and may prove helpful, but these do not point directly to cultural factors. Being part of a test-oriented society, undoubtedly affects the outcome of testing. Members of non-testing societies may respond very differently. Each culture, however, needs a means of determining its own worldview. I am aware of only one test specifically designed to encourage self-awareness of values and themes in the American culture: the Basic Values Test (BVT) developed by Mayers (Mayers 1982, and modified in Lingenfelter and Mayers 1986). This concept, however, has application on a much broader basis as demonstrated by Mayers' generation of a values profile for several key Biblical characters: Abraham, Moses, Peter and Paul (Mayers 1982:111-116). This can, perhaps, be used as a model to help communicators arrive at a profile with respect to these values for other cultures. The fact that Mayers labels these "basic values" implies their universality, allowing for cross-cultural comparison. This model is based "on the premises that once these values and their order of importance have been established for an individual, one can also predict his/her probable behavior in a given situation" (Mayers 1982:3). What is needed, of course, is an appropriate instrument to derive the data necessary to arrive at such a determination.[2]

The Basic Values

The basic values are considered to underlie many other values that, in turn, generate various types of behavior that are further affected by the surrounding cultural context. The values are made up of twelve categories that form opposite ends of a continuum. These six continua (with samples of how the values they represent may be expressed) are detailed here in the hope that they can be used to develop materials that will help communicators more readily understand their own cultural values. This knowledge can then be used to temper reactions to behavior generated by contrasting values. This material has been slightly edited and is used with Mayers' permission (Mayers 1982:22-27).

Read through these descriptions and attempt to tentatively place yourself at a point on each continua. On a seven point scale, do you strongly agree or disagree with each statement (represented by the extremes) or do you consider yourself more moderate (moving toward the center which indicates uncommitted)? If you ask yourself how each statement applies to you personally, and place a dot on the continuum for that particular statement, you will probably discover that the dots tend to cluster together for each of the twelve categories. This clustering will give you a feel for your own values with respect to these categories. The difference between the two categories that define each continua represent the tension you feel as these basic issues contrast within your own experience and shape your values.

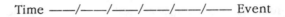

Time ——/——/——/——/——/—— Event

Time-oriented

  a. Time-oriented people will be concerned with the time period.

  b. The time period will be a certain length depending on the intent or purpose of the time spent.

  c. Concern will be given to the "range of punctuality" at the beginning and end of the time session.

  d. The time period will be carefully planned to accomplish as much as possible.

  e. Such people set goals—long, middle, and short range—which are related to some type of time period.

  f. They attempt to condense into a given time period as much as they can of that which is considered worthwhile.

  g. There will likely be a time/money equivalence, or a time-spent/production equivalence.

  h. They will not be overly fearful of the unknown.

  i. They will remember and try to reinforce certain times and dates.

Event-oriented

  a. Event-oriented people are not too concerned with the time period.

  b. They will bring people together without planning a detailed schedule and see what develops.

c. They will work over a problem or idea until it is resolved or exhausted, regardless of time.

d. They live in the here-and-now and do not plan a detailed schedule for the future.

e. They are not much interested in, or concerned with, history.

f. They do not rely on the experience of others, but rather trust their own experience implicitly.

Dichotomy ——/——/——/——/——/—— Wholism

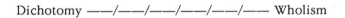

Dichotomizing

a. Dichotomizing people tend to polarize life in terms of black and white, here and there, right and wrong.

b. It is relatively easy for such people to evaluate others (persons, programs, or ideas) on the basis of such dichotomies.

c. They must feel they are right—that they are doing the right thing and thinking the right thoughts—to be satisfied with themselves.

d. They adapt well to the computer.

e. They are highly systematized in terms of classifying and organizing experiences and ideas.

f. The ability of such people to organize and to understand where they "fit" and where others "fit" gives them a sense of security.

Wholistic

a. The parts will have a vital function within the whole.

b. No consideration can be given any part unless it is also considered within the whole. Situations where they must consider one part without respect to the whole produce frustration for wholistic people.

c. Such frustration will likely result in some defensive measure.

d. Wholistic people derive satisfaction through integration of thought and life, whether planned or natural.

e. They feel very insecure whenever they are placed in a category.

Crisis ——/——/——/——/——/—— Non-crisis

Crisis or Declarative

a. Crisis oriented people seek an expert to advise them in a crisis.

b. They try to find the very best authority to use as their most important guide.

c. They like an authority which is easily accessible, to which they can return, and to which they can direct others seeking knowledge. Consequently they read a great deal and use the best written authorities as the basis for decisions.

d. They have a keen interest in . . . history, since they believe that crises similar to this have been faced before.

e. No crisis is entirely new, since there are bound to be similar crises and answers conveyed through information given by an expert.

f. In a learning experience, much emphasis is placed on comprehending the instructor and being able to re-verbalize what has been taught.

g. The responsibility for the learning experience primarily belongs to the instructor.

h. Crisis oriented people trust the knowledge and advice of an expert. Following such advice gives confidence in making decisions.

Noncrisis or Interrogative

a. Noncrisis people expect to select an answer to the question from various alternatives.

b. Security and satisfaction will result from selecting among alternatives. Frustration will come if no alternatives are available.

c. Bitterness may develop later if people find they have not been given opportunity to select from alternatives.

d. For these people, therefore, a new problem arises out of the alternatives selected.

e. Personal satisfaction comes with the alternatives and the ones selected, as well as from the vitality of questions or problems arising from the selected ones.

f. Noncrisis people can, through the events of life, be brought back to the same situation faced earlier and then choose a different answer—another alternative.

g. They will be frustrated with a lecture situation in which an expert speaks.

Object   Person
as Goal ——/——/——/——/——/—— as Goal

Goal-conscious (task oriented)

a. Goal-conscious people are concerned with a definite goal and with reaching that goal.

b. Achieving the goal becomes a priority.

c. They find their deepest friendships with those who have similar goals.

d. When necessary, they will go it alone.

e. Depending upon motivation in attaining goals, they will even be willing to see their own bodies destroyed for the sake of the goal.

Interaction-conscious (person oriented)

a. Interaction-conscious people are more interested in talking with others than in achieving their goal.

b. They derive greatest satisfaction from talking with people.

c. They will sacrifice a goal for the sake of conversation.

d. They will break rules or appointments if they interfere with involvement with another person.

e. Security for them will come in the group—getting to know people and being involved with them.

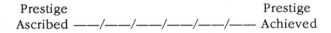

Prestige   Prestige
Ascribed ——/——/——/——/——/—— Achieved

Prestige ascribed (status focus)

a. People who feel that prestige is ascribed and then confirmed by the social group will show respect in keeping with the ascription of prestige determined by society.

b. They expect others to respect their rank.

c. They see a person's formal credentials as important.

d. They will sacrifice to achieve the desired rank and prestige in the society.

e. They play the role status demands.

f. They tend to associate most with those of their own prestige or rank.

Prestige achieved (achievement focus)

a. People who feel prestige is achieved and must be achieved repeatedly will ignore formal credentials.

b. They will consider rather what the person means to them.

c. They will struggle constantly to achieve in their own eyes and not seek to attain a particular status in society.

d. They will work to prove themselves.

e. They will give as much consideration to statements made by those without credentials as to those with them.

Vulnerability   Vulnerability
as weakness ——/——/——/——/——/—— as strength

Vulnerability as weakness (conceal weakness)

a. People who feel that vulnerability is a weakness will take every step possible to keep from error,
    1) double-checking everything they do, and
    2) being methodical and organized.

b. They enjoy arguing a point to the end.

c. They hate admitting mistakes and organize life to avoid making them.

d. They try to "cover up" errors by withdrawal, denial, projection, etc.

e. They will not expose weaknesses or tell stories about their own mistakes.

f. They have a tendency to speak vaguely about areas of their lives that are personal or use euphemism to avoid this.

g. They are rather unwilling to become involved in a new experiment.

Vulnerability as strength (willing to expose weakness)

a. People who feel that vulnerability is a strength do not have difficulty admitting mistakes.

b. They are not too concerned about making errors.

c. They tell stories that expose their own weaknesses.

d. They are willing to talk freely about very personal areas of their lives.

e. They are willing to be involved in new experiments.

You can now compare your profile with others. Within a cultural context, members tend to share positions on the profile allowing Mayers to suggest an average profile for a population. This helps us understand something about that group's basic values.

Generating Values for Other Cultural Groups

Once communicators have developed an awareness of their own cultural values, this information can be applied to the source and receptor worldviews. Taking what was learned from the research suggested in chapters 3 - 10, how might Biblical cultures be characterized with respect to these six continuua? This is complicated by the variety of cultures portrayed throughout the whole of Scripture. Perhaps a generalized profile needs to be developed for the three major culture types found in Scripture. For example, with respect to the Time-Event continuum, Figure 12:1 may be a start.

FIGURE 12:1
Time and Culture Types in Scripture

O.T. Kinship Culture
Time——/——/——/——/——/-●—Event

O.T. Peasant Culture
Time——/——/——/——/-●—/——Event

N.T. Commercial Culture
Time——/——/——/-●—/——/——Event

Developing such an understanding helps communicators compare their own profile with the Biblical perspective which will draw graphic attention to areas of difference and similarity. Differences should signal the need for caution when analyzing text where these differences are implied.

For example, the modern industrial view of time is very much to the far left, focusing on schedules, punctuality and treating time as a commodity. This is reflected in English by such expressions as: "spend time", "save time", and "time is money".

American Post-Industrial Culture
Time— ●-/——/——/——/——/——Event

Such awareness may help develop a greater appreciation for the original context God spoke to and how industrial culture is diverging from it. In light of these differences, what does God say to us?

Once the differences between the Biblical worldview and that of the communicator have been somewhat cognitivized, attention can turn to the receptor—approaching people from the perspective developed in chapters 3 - 8 and 11. If a basic test could be developed to show where receptors stand with respect to these basic values, communicators would have a guide by which to adjust their own behavior as well as to reduce cultural clash between source and receptor. Where the lines of the profile are close, values are somewhat similar, but where they are far apart we can expect varying degrees of cultural clash. Just because the values appear to be similar, however, does not mean one can forget about those areas. The reasons for being at that point on the continuum may be quite different, and may themselves generate cultural clash.[3] Mayers' generation of data provides a starting point for determining the basic values and a profile for a society (Mayers 1982:92ff and 73ff). At the point that the profiles compare, a minimum amount of stress can be expected in the relationship. Where the profiles are more divergent, however, one can expect higher degrees of stress or discomfort (Mayers 1982:96-101).

Since the means of determining values is highly subjective, a degree of consistency in testing is impossible. However, it can give a first approximation of sensitive areas in the communication context. It cannot be over-stressed that this is only an initial measure of value differences. This can, however, assist anyone engaged in cross-cultural ministry by helping to determine necessary adjustments both in personal behavior and in the communication process. Areas that are most divergent may also be areas of greatest sensitivity in relation to culture contact and thus point out areas needing a greater understanding before attempting to translate Scripture passages that relate to those differences.

THE COMPLICATING FACTOR IN THE COMMUNICATION PROCESS

Translators may be the complicating factor in the communication process. As mediators between Biblical and modern cultures, the further removed the translator's cultural premises the more crucial understanding those cultural contexts becomes. This is more than a discussion of meaning. It relates to communication styles, whole cultural complexes (areas of a culture that, because culture is integrated, affect each other to form a set of expectations), and values that underlie behavior.

Missiologists Winter (1975) and Wagner (1983) have used the idea of cultural distance to register the need to distinguish differences between communicator and receptors. Thus, communicators can be described as presenting the gospel mono-culturally E_1 (evangelism within the society of the communicator), or cross-culturally either in a "somewhat similar" culture, E_2, or "a culture which is a great deal different from the missionary's own culture", E_3 (Wagner 1983:170). Inasmuch as "somewhat similar" and "great deal different" are imprecise terms, I attempt here an application of the three cultures model to this evangelistic distance model in the hope that it may become a more effective tool for understanding cultural-evangelistic distance and determining communication and translation efficiency.

Applying the three cultures model to this material results in the following definitions:

E_1 - Mono-cultural evangelism, i.e. within one's own society.

E_2 - Cross-cultural evangelism to societies of the same culture type, i.e. industrial to industrial, peasant to peasant, kinship to kinship.

E_3 - Cross-cultural evangelism to cultural types different from one's own, i.e. industrial to peasant or kinship, peasant to kinship or industrial, etc.

What is important in making these distinctions is the impact of crossing into contexts where different cultural orientations pervade. Each culture type operates on different presuppositions and concerns itself with very different kinds of questions about life and what is considered important. We have called this *worldview* and it strongly affects all that goes on in a context where cultural contact and interaction takes place. Rather than a linear progression of evangelization out from the communicator, we must understand the interactive nature of evangelism. This book has stressed the need for dynamic interaction which results in a learning process in order to identify needs and understand lifestyle so an effective witness may be presented. It is recognizing these type differences and their impact on the relevance of the gospel that is in focus here. Communicators must relate to the local context, cross the boundary between their evangelism models and relate to those in another culture type. The use of the three cultures model, redefines the evangelism distance model, giving the criteria that establish the distinction between E_2 and E_3 —the crossing of culture types.

Clearly those communicating within their own culture will do so on the assumption that individuals receiving the message will share a worldview with the communicator. Thus, jokes, illustrations from the culture, and applications of the gospel will generally be understood. One communicates out of a shared commonality; the message is intuitively contextualized.

Those communicating cross-culturally (whether in an E_2 or E_3 context) do so at greater cultural distance. It stands to reason that the more distinct the culture from that of the communicator's, the more difficult communication becomes. Thus communicators from an industrial background will be most conceptually similar with individuals of other industrial societies[4] and most dissimilar with individuals in societies of a kinship or peasant type culture. The cultural gap to cross (the presuppositions that contribute to worldview) is greatest when individuals operate beyond the boundaries that are created by a culture, beyond the basic assumptions and expectations that are so much a part of one's own worldview.

Taking the Biblical, receptor, and translator's cultures into account, we can anticipate a progressively complex cultural mix, especially when all three culture types are represented in the translation context.

Greater similarity within a culture type leads to a greater ease of communication based on understanding common interests and concerns.[5] It can also affect identification with Biblical ideas. Thus industrial peoples tend to focus on New Testament passages that follow a logic and argumentation that appeals to individualism and personal success. Perhaps this explains, at least in part, the reason for a far greater amount of New Testament translation. Translators from industrial nations tend to identify with the language usage and context in the more urban and commercial setting of the Greco-Roman world.

However, Westerners should not delude themselves into thinking that the New Testament writers shared their presuppositions. For example, in Galatians 3:26-29 the Apostle Paul says that all are "one in union with Christ Jesus" (v.28) and this is possible because of faith (v.26). He then ties faith into a social structure where "there is no difference between Jews and Gentiles, between slave and free, between men and women." Faith, in Paul's concept, introduces people into a new type of community. In industrial societies where the individual reigns supreme, this interpretation is probably not the first inclination of the average Christian. The societal structures force people into an individualistic mold where the focus is on the first person: "I think, therefore I am". For Paul, however, all are "one with Christ". What does that really mean and how does taking it seriously affect the notion of individuality? Paul's "perspective is so radically different that we need to be continuously on our guard against transposing his thought into categories acceptable to our individualistic preconditioning" (Murphy-O'Conner 1982:176).

Communicators operating from the preconditioning of kinship and peasant societies with their emphasis on interpersonal relationships, social control and multitiered status structures will understand such a passage more like the author intended. However, they can expect to have different misunderstandings, i.e. the elite will find it difficult to see themselves as "one" with the peasantry and vice versa. What Paul is saying is, we have a heritage—we are descendants of Abraham—and look forward to an inheritance (v.29), therefore, we interact within a community in order to be of service to one another: "I exist to serve you". This results in an individuality that is "submerged in the unity of creative love" (Murphy-O'Conner 1982:182).

Given an awareness of cultural distance, it seems fairly obvious that the most effective translation should be done by those who have the least distance from the Biblical and receptor cultures, Put another way, the best communication should take place when there is the least cultural distance between source and receptor. This places translators from industrial societies working far from home in a complex translation environment (where both the Biblical and receptor cultures are very different from their own) at a considerable disadvantage communicationally. This, in turn, provides the basis for a strong argument for national translators who can work in their own or closely related languages. We will return to this topic in chapter 17.

As communicators, we should make every effort to know and understand the total context in which we find ourselves. We must, to the extent possible, identify with the situation and translate Scripture within that context to mean the same as it did to the original recipients. This is no small task. We begin with what we know and use that knowledge to avoid the pitfalls of misunderstanding others, either from Biblical contexts or among the peoples of the world who need God's Word. What is our own cultural base, its values, presuppositions, and assumed structure? Recognizing one's worldview as the starting point for effective communication is essential for building understanding from which relationships can develop. Recognizing the cultural distance between ourselves and the peoples represented in the Scriptures we seek to translate, as well as the distinctions between those materials and the people who will receive their message is strategic to effective communication.

The evangelism typing has been included here in order to clarify a missiological concept by applying the three cultures model. Cultural difference can strongly affect evangelism as missionaries have long been aware. Using this model to establish criteria for determining distance on the one hand and the type of evangelistic styles and foci necessary for effective communication on the other is the emphasis here. As communicators of God's Word, we must understand how our own worldview relates to the entire communication context. This, in turn, provides an avenue for more effectively bridging the cultural gap. This section concludes with a discussion of this bridging process.

Suggested Reading

Lingenfelter, S. and M. Mayers. *Ministering Cross-Culturally*. Baker, 1986.

Mayers, Marvin. *The Basic Values*. Biola University, 1982.

Keirsey, D. and M. Bates. *Please Understand Me*. Prometheus Nemesis, 1978.

Notes

1. It should not be ignored that translators and the cultural contexts from which they come are themselves receptor cultures. While this has not been the focus in this book, the relevance of the message and its communication within the translator's culture is also essential. This subject of cultural relevance within a mono-cultural context has been addressed recently by books on "lifestyle evangelism" (Aldrich 1981, Pippert 1979). The gospel must communicate meaningfully whatever the context.

2. If Lingenfelter and Mayers' book, *Ministering Cross Culturally*, is available, or you have purchased the questionnaire booklet with this book, take the 48 item questionnaire and derive your personal profile. Use this to establish a better understanding of your own culturally conditioned values as described by the categories that follow.

3. The Basic Values Test does not focus on rationale for position on the continuum, but only on what that point is and what it means for American culture (and, perhaps to some extent, other industrial societies). Beyond that, considerable research is necessary.

4. Even within an apparent culture type, vast differences exist. Americans with their emphasis on rugged, pioneering individualism have moved a long way from their Western European roots (see Bellah et.

al. 1986). The increasing influence of Asian immigrants is also changing values in American life even as the new environment is changing their Asian perspectives.

5. The success of Campus Crusade's *Four Spiritual Laws* is a good example of a contextualized gospel presentation. Designed to reach people in the American society where the "Laws" were developed, the concern is for the individual who is not feeling fulfilled. Therefore, to learn that "God loves *me* and has a wonderful plan for *my* life" is a significant attention grabber. That, however, is not too exciting to a Papua New Guinea villager who focuses on close interpersonal relationships. If this affirmation is taken to its logical conclusion, it may remove the individual from group to personal identity which could result in isolation and loneliness. This is precisely what the first law is attempting to avoid. Thus, in Papua New Guinea, at least, the four spiritual laws have not been too successful.

CHAPTER THIRTEEN
Bridging the Cultural Gap

The importance of communication in the translation task cannot be minimized. The translator stands as the mediator between the culture of the source text and that of the receptor. Translators are, in effect, bridges between these two entities. Translators are usually bearers of yet another culture, thereby complicating the translation context. They view the original text through their own cultural glasses and relate to the receptor by means of cross-cultural interaction. Despite this cultural complexity, receptors, who are essentially mono-cultural, interact with translators in relation to their own worldview. The more translators relate to them on the basis of that worldview, the more effectively the translation will communicate (Dye 1980:235-237).

CROSS-CULTURAL ROLES

The roles that communicators assume within a cultural context are varied and many. Accepting the validity of the incarnational model discussed in chapter 1, the challenge is to discover roles which assure receptors that we are genuinely interested in their best welfare and want to interact effectively with them. In the initial stages of interaction, so called identification is impossible because the outsider does not know insider expectations of the various roles.[1] This is another reason to encourage those who are able to provide Scripture for their own people.

Cross-cultural communicators do not have the benefit of true incarnation (a birth analogy). They can, however, develop an awareness of culture as presented in this book, and use that knowledge to develop meaningful relationships. There is no substitute for the right attitude combined with years of intimate time spent in observation and communication with people. This is

more than surface level identification, it demands an understanding of and appreciation for a people's deep level concerns
(Hiebert 1982:4).

Perhaps the Brewsters' bonding model can be taken too far.
We do not enter a cross-cultural situation as babies; it would not
be cross-cultural if we did. Rather we come into the new context
with a host of preconceived notions about reality that are
different from that of the group we enter. The Brewsters suggest
another analogy based on adult relationships, that between
married partners. As members of both cultures learn to give and
take, strive to understand what is meaningful and why, and
through it all love each other, bonding will occur and the new
relationship will thrive. The point the Brewsters stress is the need
for a learner's attitude when entering the new context—approach
the situation with a desire to learn and not judge; accept their
view of reality and discover what it means to live by those
standards (Brewster and Brewster 1980).

Our second son, Rob, spent 20 of the first 24 months of his
life among the Samo. Samo was his first language; he was a Samo
kid. He had distinct advantages over us as he began life in that
context. When the Samo women saw Karen nursing him (and his
older brother before him), they realized we were no different, we
shared the human condition. Watching the boys' cultural acquisition and our own adaptation was a good lesson in culture
learning from two very different perspectives. Rob and Rick were
accepted into village life just like other Samo kids and, accordingly, received a lot of attention. If found crying in the village the
women nursed them as they would any other child. This was a
natural process of being part of the community. Our reaction to
these events was crucial to our acceptance and believability.
When the boys had needs, the Samo took care of them as they
would their own, for, in fact, they were. We made that decision as
we entered their community—wherever possible we would do
things their way. The acquisition of Samo culture later affected
our boys' acquisition of American culture. They are richer for it!
The point here is that learning as a baby and as an adult are very
different. Attitude in that learning process is critical. So are the
roles we assume in the cross-cultural context.

It is not my intention to suggest which roles are most
effective—these will vary with the situation as well as the

expectations of the receptor culture. Their interaction with outsiders in the past will have a significant impact on relationships they develop with you. It becomes your responsibility to discover what roles are being assigned and strive to overcome any negative side effects as early as possible. The best way to do this is to interact on a friendly basis from within the context and surprise the people by not living up to their "outsider" stereotypes.

When we first arrived among the Samo, they had two roles for outsiders, neither (from their perspective) particularly complimentary: government officer, and missionary. Both were transient, staying in one place only long enough to deliver a message, then moving on to the next stop. We destroyed that image when we remained in one place for a lengthy period. This stereotype was made clear when, after eight years, our house began to totter on termite-infested posts. My brothers responded with wonder that the house had stood so long—twice as long as they normally expect a house to last. As we discussed my predicament, they said they had not used the best wood because they had no idea how long we would stay. Now that they knew our intent they would construct a house that would not succumb to local infestations: they were true to their word.

Cross-cultural roles are also affected by the expectations communicators have as they move into new situations: how they see themselves, their stereotypes of what cross-cultural workers do and the expectations they perceive the folks back home have of them. All of this may mitigate against accepting insider roles or even investigating them. This is one reason for encouraging prospective missionaries to take anthropology and mission orientation courses as well as to thoroughly familiarize themselves with the context they hope to enter *before* going into it.

Whatever roles missionaries adapt, they need to be roles that relate to people and their needs. Generally these are "insider" roles, roles known to the people and accepted as valid within the cultural context. Often they will be roles which are terminologically identified and have prescribed rights and duties as discussed in chapter 5. While this implies that kinship roles may be best, they are not the only effective roles. Of importance here is the need to be involved with people and know the expectations of the various role possibilities. Interacting in this way develops trust.

There is the potential that cultural expectations will force an expatriate to adopt "outsider" roles, at least initially. Bringing an outsider into the family and developing relationships to other family members is an awesome demonstration of trust we cannot necessarily expect or assume from the outset. The key to developing trust is cultural sensitivity and linguistic awareness. Use the language and act within the cultural rules to be appropriate whenever possible! Such identification and love (so long as it is genuine) cannot go unnoticed, and will bear fruit. Right attitudes will lead to right actions, because the witness, like Christ, wants to communicate the right message in such a way that it will bring the right results—understanding and acceptance!

This raises the whole issue of identification. How closely does an outsider need to identify (much less bond) with the receptor culture, and how much does it really affect the end product? How does identification relate to the things we take with us, the style of housing and the clothes we wear? I remember trudging the muddy trail to Kwobi the first time with fifteen carriers lugging our "essentials": baby crib, tape recorder, two-way radio, clothes, a chair or two . . . I wanted to identify, but what did that mean to the Samo? How would they respond to all this stuff? I eventually learned that my attitude was much more critical than what I was wearing. We built a Samo longhouse, but were the only family living in it. We identified physically, but broke the social rules by not sharing it with others. In fact, regardless of how close we may think we identify, there exists a considerable amount of cultural distancing. No matter what kinship terms are used for us or what insider roles we assume (or may be assigned) we remain outsiders (Reyburn 1960).

It is easy to assume we have identified (bonded) and yet through the eyes of others we may be far from it. We must not delude ourselves! Interact to the extent possible, maintain an attitude of love and concern, and allow the Holy Spirit to speak through our message. As already stressed, the messenger is the message (McLuhan 1967); the people's perception of us will strongly affect what they hear and how they respond. Each context is different, and the blend of communicator, home culture, personality, and all that we do, affects "identification in the missionary task" (Reyburn 1960). As the Loewens (1967) indicate, we are outsiders, and the benefit we bring to the community as a whole will, in the long run, aid the community far more than if we had not gone. Understanding our personal and cultural roots and making a strong attempt to interact (without deluding ourselves) is a good beginning (see chapter 12).

The situation, particularly in the more complex cultural contexts of the urban setting in which many missionaries find themselves today, will to a large extent determine the nature of identification necessary to communicate the gospel. We want to imitate the incarnation, but that is very difficult for culture-bound human beings. This is an area of growing research (Bakke and Vinay 1985, Conn 1987).

For most missionaries it is virtually impossible to make a "for the rest of my life" commitment to relationships within another culture. Our children and our home constituency deserve awareness of both the home culture and the receptor culture. We must avoid "going native" on the one hand and cultural schizophrenia on the other. Realizing that a lasting and complete commitment is impossible, we must not deceive ourselves, or those we serve, with false pretenses. We should recognize that we will not be there forever and prepare all involved to assume from the very beginning that the gospel, the translation and the church that builds on it is theirs. While we assist in its birth and early development it must assume its own identity and become a unique manifestation of God's will among human cultures (Donovan 1978:37-40). While accepting and acting out insider roles, the emphasis must be on the attitude conveyed within the relationships: communication rather than total identification. The members of most cultures will realize (perhaps better than we) that outsiders cannot identify completely. The willingness to relate to them and be part of their context while involved, however, communicates a powerful message which builds trust. Within that bond we can also acquaint them with our cultural background and expand their perspective. This is part of the education process that takes place as culture bearers meet cross-culturally.

A portion of one wall in our Samo house was devoted to pictures of family and friends. When we received pictures from home, or other missionary friends, we put them up. When visitors to the village were brought into our house, it was the first order of business (after introductions) to go through our "family tree". "This is Dan's mother and father, and his little sister. These are Karen's parents, her big brother, little brother, etc. These are Dan and Karen's friends who are doing translation in the Philippines." And on it went, integrating us into the kinship system through the appropriate use of terms for our relatives, and relating themselves and us to the world beyond (not to mention Bible translation for other groups). The Samo discovered they had a bigger "household" than they realized. In other parts of the world, such as Latin America, a similar display of pictures may be viewed as the family's "saints" and thus be totally inappropriate; an incompatible mix of cultural forms and their respective meanings. Sensitivity is essential; what works in one situation may produce culture clash in another. Each context should be analyzed using cultural discovery principles and applying the acquired understanding to the context.

Through culture contact, in effect, a new culture is created. It builds on both the expatriates' cultures and the cultures which they serve. This "biculture" becomes the context for the effective communication of the gospel. Both cultures recognize the reality of the other and work within the interactive context to perform a mission. Incarnation is the Biblical model, "but it does not deny who we originally are . . . Just as God became one with us in order to save us, we must become one with the people to whom we go in order to bring them that salvation" (Hiebert 1982:6). The quality of relationships on the "bicultural bridge" is the major determinant of how well the gospel is received. Relationships are more convincing than facts in most non-industrial cultures. Perhaps the best way to achieve this is through Loewen's "insider-outsider role" (Loewen 1967).

The fact that the Samo co-translators were my brothers made a big difference in the Samo understanding of Scripture. Because of our brother relationship, they had the responsibility to correct me when I was wrong—part of the interaction between brothers is ensuring correct behavior. When I made cultural mistakes (either personally or with respect to the translation) they dutifully pointed out the error (the correctability of the translator is crucial to an adequate translation which may also need correction). When the culture of the source did not match that of the Samo, I had to explain it thoroughly and my brother co-translators had to work out how it fit their worldview. In cases where a worldview clash arose because of differences between God's intended message and the Samo perspective, deep thinking resulted. This kind of searching at the translation desk encouraged the Samo to make cultural adjustments in some cases while reinforcing their behavior in others. As the spokesperson for the source message, I had the responsibility of making sure the information upon which they based those decisions was accurate. Hence I acted as a bridge between the Biblical cultures and the Samo, between God's message and those who received it.

This kind of interaction is not necessary for cultural bearers working within their own culture. For them, the challenge is not how to live appropriately in the cultural context they know best, but how to bridge the gap from Biblical cultures, on the one hand, and encroaching outside influences on the other. They must still act as resource people in helping others bridge the cultural gaps we have already discussed. National translators cannot avoid these kinds of problems, they simply come at them from a different perspective, that of an insider to the particular context—one who explains the outside context in culturally relevant forms.

This type of approach is not easy for well-trained nationals who must fit back into the local context in order to be effective. Mother Tongue Translators (MTT) who are willing to do so have difficulties maintaining local obligations while performing their translation responsibilities. Working in teams helps, but the advantages of bonding already discussed are the very factors that mitigate against a member of the community doing effective translation—there are too many obligations and "distractions". What does incarnation mean for these MTT? How do they maintain the close interaction demanded by the culture and still accomplish the incredible job of translating the Bible? Such concerns demand research and prayer and we must look to the Holy Spirit for guidance. This is God's work not ours, but like the Apostle Paul, we "share in the blessing" (I Cor. 9:23).

UNDERSTANDING THE MESSAGE FROM
A CULTURAL PERSPECTIVE

It should now be obvious but cannot be over-stressed: without an adequate understanding of the source culture translators cannot hope to communicate an author's message effectively across the temporal and cultural chasm separating it from the receptor. The objective here is to understand the source meaning to the extent that it can be adequately communicated in the receptor context, whoever the communicator is. This demands exegesis that takes into account the deep structure of the text so it can be communicated into the new context. That communication however, needs to be in terms of the meaning, the deep structure, of the receptor as well. The surface forms may vary considerably, but the meaning of both the source and receptor texts will—indeed must—be the same.

In the process of translating Scripture, we came across the passage in I Thes. 5:8 that talks about the breastplate of faith and love, and the helmet of a hope of salvation. Faith, hope and love are all very abstract and the Apostle, recognizing this, tries to make it understandable by comparing these Christian qualities with cultural items known to the people of Thessalonica: armor. From the context, it is clear that Paul is trying to encourage them both with respect to their persecutions (I Thes. 2:14, II Thes. 1:4-10), and their future when the "Lord will come as a thief comes at night" (I Thes. 5:2). Protection against surprise, from their enemies and by the Lord, is the focus.

For the Samo, protection is not achieved by wearing armor, rather it comes by utilizing the longhouse as a fortress. Each night logs are stacked to seal off the main entrance and a watch is set. Secure inside, the *ayo*, the one in control, encourages community members. Their faith and trust in the security of the house is a product of their knowing the strength of the logs and the ability of the guardsmen. Hope and love are communicated as the *ayo*, expresses his concern for each one and encourages them. The stacked logs, guardsmen, and personal encouragement provide, for the Samo, the meaning for which Paul used "breastplate" and "helmet" in his communication to the Thessalonians. The forms are very different but communicate the same meanings. For the Samo to understand that meaning it should be couched in understandable forms (Nida and Reyburn 1981, and Kraft 1979, c.f. pp.261-312). For further discussion of meaning transfer, see chapter 14.

In the translation, however, we had to be careful to communicate meaning without jeopardizing exegetical and historical fidelity. Hence a translation that communicated the essence of the metaphor was imperative—as God protected the Thessalonians who trusted Him and encouraged them in their salvation, so He will protect and encourage you. Paul was writing to the Thessalonians in their culture. But if he had done it in Samo what forms would he have used? Without some identification they will see little or no relevance (see chapters 14 and 15 for further discussion of cultural substitutes).[2]

RELATING THE MESSAGE TO
THE RECEPTOR CULTURE

This too, may now seem obvious, but the fact is, the translator is the translation. Dye's research clearly demonstrates that without trust in the translator, the Biblical message will be seriously affected and may have little impact on the receptor. Thus, the translator's lifestyle, the interaction with the receptors, all that we have stated about relationships throughout this book, are critical to the success of a translation (Dye 1980:39-61, 235-260; Gould 1986). This is not only true cross-culturally, but within the communicator's home culture as well. People around us are reading our lives; we are the gospel for them. May we live in such a way that they will be attracted to our Lord through our lifestyle (Aldrich 1981:72-76)!

Good News Encounters

Demonstrations of relevance through life experience are part of the communication process. Dye has combined the ideas of lifestyle evangelism and effective witness in his concept of "good news encounters". To be effective, these depend on a "no interruptions" or "come anytime" attitude. While in the receptor context, one must always be available, regardless of what is happening. Remember that few non-industrial cultures dichotomize or structure a schedule; people will "interrupt" without realizing it. This may be a problem for people who spend a lot of time studying at a desk.

While living among the Samo, we had a routine: work with assistants or teach literacy classes in the morning (when it is cool) and study, translate, and prepare for the next day's sessions on our own in the afternoon. It was always a temptation to turn people aside when they just showed up. On the other hand, much of our learning took place during these casual, unplanned encounters. When people feel comfortable dropping by, you know you have developed friendship and trust. People want to be around. Often it does not demand your full attention, they just want to know what you are doing. Other times, it may take much more than full participation. The feeling of being constantly interrupted communicates to others, and soon the interruptions cease. The problem is that when the interruptions cease so does the ministry—communication is no longer sought or, worse, no longer valued.

Good news encounters have four basic characteristics. (1) They convey love and demonstrate an attitude of concern for those with whom we interact. (2) They take place on the spot— they are part of life. We don't seek them out, but as life is lived, our contacts bring us into situations where we can demonstrate love and be of help to people. (3) They relate to people's needs. Without perceived need, there may be little relevance. (4) They point to God and His Word. We must recognize God as the One in ultimate control. He wants to relate to people—restore the relationship lost through sin. As people recognize God as One who cares about their needs, they may begin to respond to Him. It is up to us to point people His way, to encourage a relationship with Him.

Though expatriates may not be able to preach a sermon or present a translated book in the early stages of their ministry, they can do life-style evangelism. What an incentive for language and culture learning! Obviously the more of the culture you know and the better you can communicate with the culture bearers, the more effective you will be. But the communication of love through right attitude is the all important starting point. Establish good rapport and gain trust as quickly as possible. This is the life approach to evangelism; it is following the incarnational model. Of course, nationals who are already insiders can apply these same principles for more effective ministry within their own cultural context.

As people see this kind of personal involvement, they will become very interested and want to know more. This could provide the motivation for conversion and the development of a local church. Throughout the translation project, we are a living demonstration of gospel relevance. If we are perceived as relevant, then the Scriptures we produce may also be viewed that way. The knowledge that we have a message designated by God to meet human needs serves as an encouragement to codify it into a culturally relevant form. This form, be it a culturally sensitive devotion to ministry, or God's Word itself, can be used by the Holy Spirit to meet human needs (Gould 1986).

One afternoon I was preparing a portion of Titus for translation when my main co-translator walked in visibly upset. Our brother-in-law had come demanding that we return his sister since our sister had run away again. Milo then informed me that as his older brother I had to tell our sister to return to her husband in order for him to maintain his happy marriage. I shot up a quick prayer as the unhappy couple (my sister and brother-in-law) were escorted in. After some casual conversation, I told them I was working on Titus. Building on my understanding of Samo relationships I explained Titus 2:5 where wives are instructed to "be good housewives [and] submit to their husbands, so that no one will speak evil of the message that comes from God". I asked my sister if she lived this way; her response was a mumbled negative. I turned to my brother-in-law and communicated the idea of verse 6, "urge the young men to be self-controlled". This young man had a violent temper and the verse grabbed his attention. I then encouraged both of them to act in a manner that would not allow others to criticize their behavior, prayed with them and extracted a promise to return to their village and work on their relationship.

My little brother was delighted and thanked me often after that. He was later able to work on the passage with a new appreciation for God's concern about proper relationships. The gospel had been acted out in love, on the spot with respect to a particular need that God cared about. It was a good news encounter—a matter of great importance for all of us. It also reflected on the Scripture, the source of the solution to the problem. I had done the Samo thing, enforced right action by appealing to a higher source. Previously the Samo would have turned to their mythology, now they had a demonstration of turning to Scripture for the answer to life's problems. This was a cultural approach to Scripture that they later became adept at using. God, through Christ and the Scriptures, could make a difference in the way they lived.

Use of Communication Styles

In order to respond to the gospel message, people must perceive it as an answer to their needs; there should be an appropriate and respected messenger and an appropriate use of media. This is an area where missionaries often have a problem. Industrial use of media are often forms that are very different from those considered meaningful by the target population. For example, part of nearly every Bible translation project includes a concerted effort to teach people to read and write their own language. The motivation is to have readers for the translated Scripture. From a peoples' perspective, however, there is far less motivation, as most societies can manage quite happily with less than 15% of the population literate (Klem 1982:15ff). More important is the paramessage: in order to understand Scripture people should be able to read it. They feel forced into a foreign model of communication, which by inference places the Scriptures into an "outside" category. Since outsiders and what they bring are often viewed with suspicion, the fact that Scripture is introduced via this outside style may adversely affect receptivity. Where possible, we need to explore relevant communication styles and note how the gospel can be presented so that it appears appropriate. Most of the cultures of the world remain largely oral in nature. Oral communication involves numerous forms that, though different from literary styles, are no less effective as a means to present the gospel. In fact, the Scriptures themselves were, for much of their history, communicated orally using poetry, song and dance to involve the people who received the message.

Discovering and using local forms of communication can be very important to the spread of the gospel message (Klem 1982:159ff). How do people use music, dance and drama? What are their oral styles of communication—poetry, epic tale, proverb, chant, exhortation or animated discussion? How can the gospel be presented in these forms? Bruce Olson gives an account of a presentation of the gospel through a song duel among the Motilone of Colombia. Bruce did not like the chanted form, sung by men swinging in hammocks tied to the rafters. But hours later the old chief climbed down and commented, "God has spoken to us in the song". The whole house turned to Christ, not on the strength of the presentation alone, but because of the relevant form used to present it (Olson 1978:152-153).

Appropriating God's Word

People do not want to put their culture aside in order to accept the gospel. A conversion response comes as people recognize that the proposed lifestyle is manageable. While the gospel will at points challenge their assumptions, on the whole, God intends to fulfill people in their cultural context—make them better members of their society. As people respond to this cultural desire to live closer to the ideal, they will be more likely to appropriate the gospel to their lives. They will be more willing to change their allegiance to God, and begin to be conformed to His image. Out of this atmosphere comes church growth and an application of the message to the local context. As this happens, there develops a growing need for vernacular Scripture—Bible translation becomes crucial to the life of the Christian community. Now the people need the "whole counsel of God" and all a translator's preparation and understanding is brought to bear upon making God's Word a reality to them.

It is at this stage that literacy should be introduced. There will be a created need that the ability to read can fill. Now, however, the focus is on learning more of what God has said and determining what it means for them as a productive society. Not everyone will need to read, but having some who can will be beneficial. Literacy, as other aspects of your interaction, should relate to people in such a way that they can use and adapt it as their own. In this way it enhances truth and understanding—people want to learn.

It is to this end that the long process of language and culture acquisition becomes worth the effort. All the pieces come together. The message has been presented and people respond. The communicator has served as a cultural bridge, a messenger, one who understands the complexities and implications of the local context and uses them effectively. This does not imply that where there is no response we have failed. It does mean that every communicator should have the training and patience to learn the needs of people and apply the gospel to those needs. Missiological research indicates that assessing needs and demonstrating, in culturally appropriate ways, how God can relate to those needs is an effective methodology. Recent breakthroughs in the Muslim world attest to success of such an approach (Parshall 1980).

Bible translation serves this methodology admirably. God has used His Word in countless contexts to bring people to Himself. Having discussed the strategy for understanding culture in the various contexts relevant to translation, we turn now to apply cultural studies to the actual process of Bible translation and the presentation of the good news.

Suggested Reading

Donovan, Vincent. *Christianity Rediscovered*. Orbis, 1978.

Olson, Bruce. *Bruchko*. Creation House, 1978.

Taylor, John. *The Primal Vision*. SGM Press, 1963.

Notes

1. Perhaps this is why God chose the incarnation to begin as a baby born into the cultural situation rather than using the "intrusion" approach. Perhaps this is why Christ waited 30 years to begin His ministry—He did not want to make cultural mistakes that would alienate the people He most desired to reach. Working from the inside of the culture, He knew what was wrong with it and could act as innovator and an advocate simultaneously (Barnett 1953). He could strive toward change by criticizing those cultural aspects which truly went against the intent God had for His creation—hence the confrontations with the religious leaders who sought to institutionalize interaction with God. Christ told them to communicate with God like a "daddy", not a harsh father (Mt. 7:9-11, Mk. 14:35).

2. Translation is on-going. There is no such thing as a completed translation. If a translator uses cultural substitutes to communicate the meaning for an audience that has no understanding of "breastplates" and "helmets" then a future revision may need to adjust for these culturalisms as people's knowledge expands. See the last section in chapter 16 for more on the on-going nature of translation in the life of the church.

PART III
TOWARD TRANSCULTURATION

The goal of a translation is that it is to be "so smooth in vocabulary, so idiomatic in phrase, so correct in construction, so smooth in flow of thought, so clear in meaning, and so elegant in style, that it does not appear to be a translation at all, and yet, at the same time, faithfully transmits the message of the original" (Beekman and Callow 1974:32). The same authors define a "faithful translation" as one which "transfers the meaning and the dynamics of the original text" (p. 33). They then define their use of "dynamics": " The translation makes a natural use of the linguistic structures of the receptor language and . . . the recipients of the translation understand the meaning with ease" (p. 34).

With these definitions in mind, we note a now familiar progression which suggests a basic two-step process in translation: (1) determining the meaning through discovery and understanding of the context into which the message originally came and (2) applying translation principles to all that one knows in order to transfer the text meaning to the receptor culture. Here we combine anthropology and translation principles to produce texts that communicate, i.e. dynamic translations that faithfully transmit the message of the original in forms the recipients understand. Thus we seek to communicate in linguistic and cultural forms that present the source text within the receptor context in such a way that the transfer is perceived as natural and relevant: we strive toward transculturation.

CHAPTER FOURTEEN
Exegesis: Meaning and Culture

The word *exegesis* evokes an image of a saintly pastor poring over well-worn tomes preparing a stately sermon. A glance through any seminary catalog will reveal the importance of exegesis in theological study, first at the how-to level and then, as students become adept in original languages and exegetical skills, at the applied level. They are encouraged to utilize these principles in their homiletics classes and are graded accordingly.

If exegesis is important for pastors who seek to communicate the source message to modern day receptors each Sunday morning, it must be equally as critical for translators. Unfortunately the exegetical tools available are written primarily to help pastors preach, rather than develop a translator's understanding of the source context, lexical problems, and meanings. In short, most commentaries are designed to help pastors interpret source meaning theologically within their culture (hermeneutics is a much more accurate word than exegesis), rather than communicate uninterpreted meaning into other cultural contexts. By its very definition, translation must do the latter. Hence a methodology for determining source meaning is essential for Bible translation.

LINGUISTIC STRUCTURE

To understand the meaning of a text, we must understand the linguistic concept of deep versus surface structure (see chapter 2). The surface structure is the forms: words, sentence, paragraph, and discourse types, i.e. formal features of a language. It also includes the cultural manifestations already discussed in previous chapters. The deep structure is the meaning that is communicated by these forms, including the worldview of a people. A basic linguistic assumption is that meaning has structure (Larson

1984:6). Just as surface forms can be analyzed in terms of their components, e.g. the grammatical, lexical, and phonological units, so deep structure can be analyzed according to "meaning components"—things, events, attributes, and relationals. Deep structure is far more universal than is surface structure, as discussed in chapters 2 and 8. Therefore, if we can apply methodologies for ascertaining the deep structure of the source text, we can transfer that meaning to the surface structure of the receptor language as indicated in Figure 14:1.

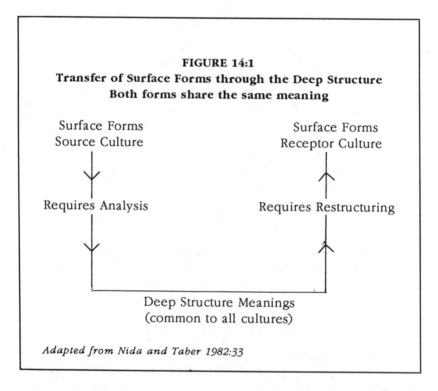

FIGURE 14:1
Transfer of Surface Forms through the Deep Structure
Both forms share the same meaning

Surface Forms   Surface Forms
Source Culture   Receptor Culture

Requires Analysis   Requires Restructuring

Deep Structure Meanings
(common to all cultures)

Adapted from Nida and Taber 1982:33

What impact does culture have on the deep structure? Are there cultural universals of deep structure that can help translators communicate across cultural boundaries? Undoubtedly the three cultures model and the associated features for each culture type offer a beginning point. The communication distance model is also helpful here, giving insight to conceptual differences. These conceptual differences reflect worldview contrasts which, as part of the deep structure, should be more basic than the cultural manifestations of those worldview features/themes. Kearney (1984), Hiebert (1985) and Kraft (1986) all make significant contributions here. This is, however, an area that needs much research. In essence, an understanding of the source deep structure can help translators match these basic concepts with those of the receptor. The theme analysis discussed in chapter 8 relates to these worldview assumptions. This is much more than matching surface structure components, a process that often results in considerable skewing or mismatch.

For example, 'love', *agape,* in the Greek usage is very different from the English usage which is vastly different from the Samo concept. For Greek and English, however, the verbal form can be easily skewed conceptually by nominalizing it. In Samo, a very concrete relational language, not only must the concept be communicated as an action, but the actions of the persons who are 'loving' must be culturally appropriate. In fact, there is no word for 'love' in Samo. Rather, individuals demonstrate their love through caring, encouraging, sharing, and disciplining as necessary. Therefore, translators need to determine what in the surface structure may cause any skewing, exegete the nature of the deep structure event, and restructure to communicate the idea in the new context. Such analysis forces one to think through the meaning of 'love' lexically, semantically, and culturally, a process I call *cultural hermeneutic.*

SEMANTIC STRUCTURAL ANALYSIS

A methodology for analyzing the deep structure of original language materials has been developed by and for translators. Known as Semantic Structural Analysis (SSA), the method seeks to determine the underlying meaning of the communication units within a text. The use of the term *semantic* draws attention to the focus of this approach on meaning. The most significant difference between an SSA and other commentaries is that meaning is more systematically analyzed. A consistent and comprehensive approach is applied whether the meaning is being conveyed by the smallest communication units (propositions or kernel sentences) or by the largest unit (the discourse). The term *structural* indicates there is a structure to semantic content even as there is a grammatical structure. This semantic structure focuses on the meaningful elements of the text and their relationships to each other as they unite to develop the intent and themes the author expected the audience to understand. *Analysis* refers to the methodological approach required to determine the meaning intended by the author within the source context. This focus on the structure of the text within a context makes SSA unique (Beekman et al. 1981:1).

The basic semantic units of communication are called propositions and serve as the semantic units (deep structure) that enable individuals to organize speech using grammatical units (surface structure). These semantic units are linked in meaningful combinations to develop a discourse. Thus a series of related propositions combine to form clusters which interrelate to develop sentences and paragraphs. Continuing the process, paragraphs combine into sections which form the entire discourse. Meaning is conveyed through this overall structure as much as by the individual words. Propositional analysis, as it is often called, is discussed at length in several recent works following Beekman and Callow's lead (1974, Barnwell 1981, Beekman et. al. 1981, Larson 1984, and Nida et.al. 1984). While not specifically labeled 'exegesis', certainly this technique is designed to understand source meaning and apply it directly to the translation process.

The concepts of SSA are summarized in the Appendix. The intent is to encourage translators to use the methodology and tie it into the cultural concerns discovered as a result of applying the principles discussed in this book. Scripture was produced by someone in a particular time, place, and set of circumstances, and it was directed toward real people in a particular context. There is usually a specific aspect of this situational context that motivated the writer to address the receptor. The nature of this cultural, physical, and psychological setting, establishes the relationship between these individuals. The particular details of these motivating factors will obviously have a dominant influence on the shape of the communication. Those factors in the communication situation which are regarded as particularly significant for an adequate understanding of the text are, in large measure, the subject of this book—the cultural factors which affect communicative meaning.

Discourse Structure

The discourse structure and style used in a particular communication is important to the meaning intended by the author. There are four primary discourse types (narrative, procedural, hortatory and expository) each with sub-types and a different focus. Thus a narrative discourse tells a story while an expository text argues for a point. Each discourse type conveys certain kinds of information that was undoubtedly shared by the original author and audience. The criteria for the use of poetic style over straight prose are important to the Bible translator who must present the poetry in such a way that the receptors understand what the author meant. Meaning is conveyed by more than the denotations of the words, the connotative meaning is also very important. What style in the receptor language conveys the mood of David as he sings the Psalms? It may be that utilizing a particular form expressed in songs, garden chants, or poetic style will be far more meaningful than writing down the words and encouraging people to learn to read them.

The variance between connotative and denotative meaning is buried in the deep structure of a text. We cannot reconstruct why a particular author used a specific form, but knowing the meanings of those forms and how they are structured to convey a message, we can utilize the modern forms that communicate similar meanings and thereby translate at a level which communicates as effectively as possible. Use of SSA is a direct attempt to eliminate translators' cultural bias. In this way the source culture can show through to the extent necessary to communicate original meaning, and the receptor culture can predominate as necessary for people to understand.

The discourse structure may also convey meaning far beyond the mere combination of words that are used (Kraft 1979:269ff). A narrative style that adheres to a time line communicates differently than one with a considerable amount of flashback. What linguistic features are used to keep the discourse going, to give it cohesion? How does the author show what is prominent as opposed to background information? What are the cultural fillers necessary for an interesting communication worth paying attention to? These are all part of discovering what the text means.

The Overview

A discourse is arranged in a hierarchical structure which gives a broad overview. This overview shows each unit and its constituent parts. Each unit has a theme (reason for inclusion in the text) and each unit at a particular level combines with other units to form the theme for the unit into which they all fit. This structure allows a translator to keep track of the portion in focus as it relates to all other units in the entire discourse. This semantic outline complete with the themes for each major section provides a summary of the prominent information in the discourse. These are summarized in Figure 14:2 for the book of Titus. The communication units should be described in the order that Figure 14:3 indicates.

Such an order allows each unit to be discussed in terms of the higher level framework into which it fits; and allows the units to be discussed in the order in which they occur. "In other words, the order for the discussion is sensitive both to the hierarchical as well as the linear aspects of the contents" (Kopesec 1980:4). The thematic structure of the book can then be displayed as in Figure 14:4.

What do these ways of developing a discourse convey about the meaning of the text? Furthermore, how do we communicate them when translating into a language which does not use a specific feature such as flashback, for example? How much of the meaning is actually communicated outside of the actual words? Hall (1959, 1976) has demonstrated that verbal communication itself is a relatively small part of the communication process. Perhaps this explains the excitement over some of the newer English translations. Receptors are able to understand the source better because translators have attempted to utilize English styles that convey these thoughts and ideas. Hall maintains that culture is communication, thereby drawing attention to the necessity of taking culture into account in the most significant communication that has ever taken place. God did, so must we.

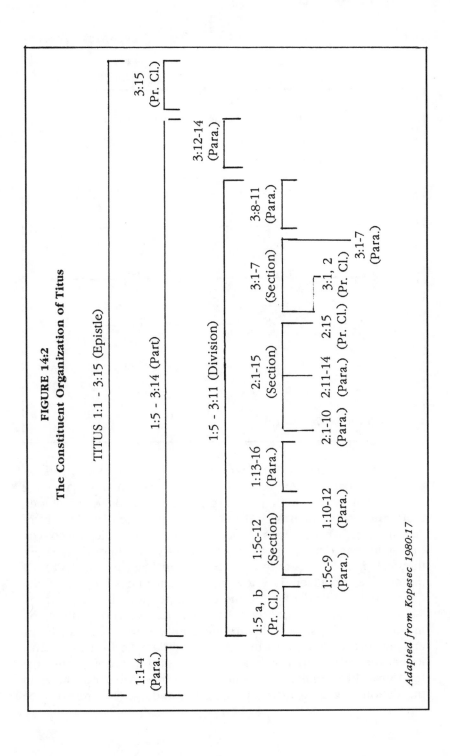

FIGURE 14:2

The Constituent Organization of Titus

TITUS 1:1 - 3:15 (Epistle)

1:5 - 3:14 (Part)

1:5 - 3:11 (Division)

3:15 (Pr. Cl.)

3:12-14 (Para.)

1:1-4 (Para.)

1:5c-12 (Section)

1:13-16 (Para.)

2:1-15 (Section)

3:1-7 (Section)

3:8-11 (Para.)

1:5 a, b (Pr. Cl.)

1:5c-9 (Para.)

1:10-12 (Para.)

2:1-10 (Para.)

2:11-14 (Para.)

2:15 (Pr. Cl.)

3:1, 2 (Pr. Cl.)

3:1-7 (Para.)

Adapted from Kopesec 1980:17

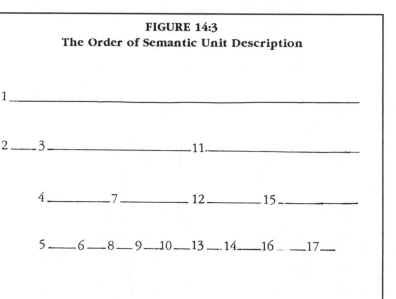

FIGURE 14:3
The Order of Semantic Unit Description

Adapted from Kopesec 1980:4

Nida and Taber (1982) clearly state in their well-known list of translation axioms: "Anything that can be said in one language can be said in another" (p. 4). Yet, as they go on to point out, there are forms (such as poetry) that are "an essential element of the message" (p.4-5). It is difficult, if not impossible, to convey the style and features of Hebrew poetry in other languages, though it is much easier in Chinese than in English (Lim 1986). Of importance, however, is knowing the semantic structure of the poetry and conveying that, to the degree possible, in the receptor. Without an SSA, the translator is much less certain of both the meaning and the style. Utilizing these enhanced tools, translators are not forced to give up in despair and "do the best they can". Rather they can search within the genius of the receptor language for forms that communicate similar meanings. What one loses in translation is gained in receptor understanding: "to preserve the

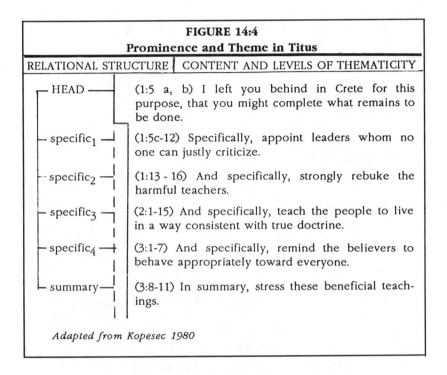

FIGURE 14:4
Prominence and Theme in Titus

RELATIONAL STRUCTURE	CONTENT AND LEVELS OF THEMATICITY
HEAD	(1:5 a, b) I left you behind in Crete for this purpose, that you might complete what remains to be done.
specific$_1$	(1:5c-12) Specifically, appoint leaders whom no one can justly criticize.
specific$_2$	(1:13 - 16) And specifically, strongly rebuke the harmful teachers.
specific$_3$	(2:1-15) And specifically, teach the people to live in a way consistent with true doctrine.
specific$_4$	(3:1-7) And specifically, remind the believers to behave appropriately toward everyone.
summary	(3:8-11) In summary, stress these beneficial teachings.

Adapted from Kopesec 1980

content of the message the form must be changed" (Nida and Taber 1982:5). This is true of style, format, and structure—the surface level forms which communicate the underlying meaning which must not change !

Semantic Structure

At a more specific level, semantic studies of the source text can be a great help in communicating an author's concepts. What do specific words mean in their original context? What other words share semantic components with the word used, i.e. what other words could the author have used? With what concepts does this particular word (or idea) combine? This introduces the importance of multiple meaning. Words, grammatical constructions, even an entire discourse, can have primary and secondary meanings. The secondary meanings give rise to extended usage, the figurative forms to be discussed in chapter 15.

Extended usage provides many alternative ways to express meaning. For example, the forms used in English to express emotions often refer to the heart: 'heartache', 'broken heart', 'warm and cold hearts', and even 'bleeding hearts'. In other languages, the seat of emotions may be communicated by reference to other body parts: liver (among the Binumarian of PNG and the Cheyenne), stomach (on the Huon Peninsula of PNG), and insides in general (among the Samo). None of these body parts are considered the literal seat of emotion. The heart has no more relation to our emotions than any of the other organs. In English the meaning of 'heart' is extended to refer to emotional states. When used in translation, the English reader knows the intended meaning and thinks nothing about it; it is natural. This is what makes translation so complicated, but interesting—ensuring that the flow of communication as well as thought form is natural.

These lexical concerns can be applied to contextual factors from the cultural setting. Appropriate ways of greeting, showing hospitality, expressing opinions, and communicating displeasure or grief are but a few examples. When Jesus admonished his disciples to "shake the dust" off their feet when rejected, He meant: "have nothing to do with them; don't stick around" (Mt. 10:14, Mk. 6:11, Lk. 9:5). What forms in the receptor context convey this meaning? In the rain-soaked jungle, there is no dust, but the Samo have a way of communicating displeasure, a variety of ways, in fact. It is thus important to use the form that most closely convey's Christ's intended meaning: turning one's back, in this case. Similarly the "sackcloth and ashes" of Biblical times needs to be expressed in appropriate forms that communicate remorse in the receptor culture. A literal translation can result in radical misunderstanding, particularly if that form has a different meaning to the modern receptors. J.B. Phillips' rendering of "holy kiss" as "hearty handshake all around" (Rom. 16:16) provides an excellent example in English—it fits the culture.[1]

The Broader Perspective

Bible translators are likely to ask how a technical commentary of this nature should be used, and how it relates to other available aids.

An SSA represents a step beyond the standard exegetical or critical commentary. A cursory comparison of commentaries will reveal a wide variety of alternative interpretations at numerous points in the text. A serious attempt is made in the SSA to arrive at a specific interpretation, taking into account all the factors which are considered to be relevant—the words used, the grammatical constructions involved, the relational structure, the theme of the units, the overall purpose of the document, etc. (Kopesec 1980:13,14).

An SSA incorporates careful reasoning by a number of scholars. Translators can use the displays of the SSA as a special type of commentary, in which their needs have been the primary consideration. An SSA should, however, be used along with other versions and materials. Where there is agreement, translators can move ahead with confidence knowing they have a factually-based method on which to base their interpretative process.

Although the needs of translators are the primary motivation for an SSA, it is hoped that anyone interested in communicating Scriptural truth can benefit. Pastors, who desire to faithfully expound Biblical meaning should find the SSA a real help. Arguments for and against differing interpretations are given and provide a basis for clear communication based on the deep semantic structure of the text along with the attendant situational context.

Auxiliary Translation

On completing the exegesis, translators can make an auxiliary translation which restructures the meanings determined for the source through the particular surface forms (lexical, grammatical and cultural) of the receptor. How does the receptor language communicate the particular meanings, moods and features the author used? With these questions answered, and the help of translation principles, the translator has only to utilize the surface structure of the receptor to communicate the same meanings. Much of this is cultural in nature, e.g. forms of planting seed, arranging labor for specific jobs, types of clothes worn (or not worn), and manifestations of the time concept are only a few.

Such linguistic and cultural studies allow a degree of precision that earlier translators found difficult or impossible. As studies of the Biblical languages and cultures continue, and our ability to understand and apply these studies to modern receptors expands, translation becomes an increasingly exciting job. We should remember, however, that the Biblical languages were human forms of communication, and as such were limited in concept and construction (Nida and Taber 1982:7). Yet, God chose to use them to communicate His truth. Understanding that truth is the responsibility of every translator. As God found a way to communicate within the constraints of the Biblical context, so modern communicators of the gospel must discover ways to present the same concepts to modern people. That is the challenge of translation. Having established the communicational focus, its context, purpose, style, mood and meaning, i.e. having exegeted the passage, we can turn to the translation principles designed to assist in a faithful, idiomatic communication that God can use to present His truth once again.

Suggested Reading

Beekman, Callow & Kopesec. *The Semantic Structure of Written Communication.* Summer Institute of Linguistics, 1981.

Barnwell, Katherine. *Introduction of Semantics and Translation.* SIL, 1980.

Gill, Jerry. *On Knowing God.* Westminster, 1981.

Larson, Mildred. *Meaning-Based Translation.* University Press of America, 1984.

Note

1. This is a somewhat controversial point in translation theory. Basically there are three options. (1) Keep the Biblical form and have a footnote as to its meaning, (2) qualify the Biblical form, e.g. Jesus admonished them to shake the dust off in displeasure, (3) use the substitute and give a note for the original form. In determining what course to take a translator should consider many things including, knowledge of cultural forms beyond those of the receptor culture, the Biblical context and whether a form is used literally or figuratively, and how the material relates to the whole of a passage. While it is true that Jesus and His disciples lived in dusty Palestine, it is also true that the Samo know nothing of dust. How do we remain faithful to the historicity of a text and still communicate the meaning to those who know nothing of that history or its context? Communicating meaning, from the deep semantic structure, provides at least part of the answer. Better to err and communicate what Jesus intended than to confuse and have people not understand and, therefore, perhaps reject the message altogether.

CHAPTER FIFTEEN
Principles: The Translator's Tool Box

Inasmuch as most translation principles contain a variety of cultural material, it is difficult to organize this chapter around the now familiar cultural factors model of this book. To do so would demand handling each translation principle with respect to each cultural factor. Therefore, I depart from this format, appeal to the integrated nature of culture, and note its impact on each translation principle. As Nida has long pointed out, culture enters directly into the sacred halls of translation theory and affects the final product (Nida 1947). Now, with the conclusion clearly in mind, we take up the challenge of relating it to the data.

Translation principles are the centerpiece of any work on translation theory. These principles apply the understanding of structural aspects of the original text to their restructuring in order to communicate in the receptor language. Several excellent texts have been written explicating these principles and how they relate to actual translation problems (Nida and Taber 1982, Beekman and Callow 1974, Larson 1975 and 1984). What has not been well understood is the relationship of culture to these principles. It is to this we now turn.

TRANSLATION TYPES: LITERAL VS. IDIOMATIC

As indicated in Figure 15:1, translations occur on a continuum ranging from very literal to unduly free (Beekman and Callow 1974:21ff, Larson 1984:15ff). This range of types basically divides into two kinds of translation, literal and idiomatic. Literal translation is an equivalence based on surface forms. A completely literal translation is only intelligible when the two languages share many structural features. An interlinear translation is a good example of a very literal translation; it helps the reader follow the original structure. There may still be considerable misunderstanding, however, because of the tendency to use equivalent words rather than equivalent ideas. An idiomatic translation, on the other hand, is based on meanings: the deep structure. Forms with equivalent meanings are substituted whenever they interfere with the transfer of meaning from the source to the receptor.

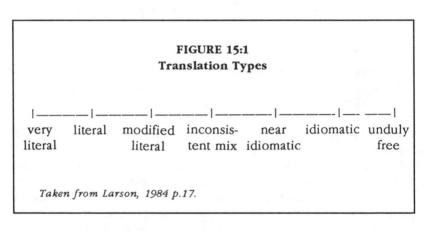

FIGURE 15:1
Translation Types

| —————— | —————— | —————— | —————— | —————— | —— —— |

very   literal   modified   inconsis-   near   idiomatic unduly
literal   literal   tent mix idiomatic   free

Taken from Larson, 1984 p.17.

Many communicators fail to realize that literal translation is not translation at all, because meaning is largely ignored. While not advocating 'unduly free' translations (the *Cotton Patch* Version should not be a model since it violates many key translation principles), it is essential that a translation communicate in the same style that people communicate. This is one reason for the proliferation of versions in English; they appeal to people from different dialects, socio-economic status, and levels of education.[1] Similarly, we should attempt to produce translations that utilize local styles and thus are recognizable to the people who use them. We must maintain the balance between historical and cultural fidelity to the source on one hand, and license in the use of receptor forms on the other. This is why the transfer of deep structure concepts (discussed in chapters 8 and 14) is so much more important than surface level forms. The receptor must be able to grasp the intent and meaning of the source, but that meaning can only be relevant as it is communicated within the receptor context: the language and culture of which people are a part.

Literal translations do not take culture into account. The cultural meaning of the source is seldom communicated to the receptor, perhaps because it is not understood by the translator. In fact, literal translations are much easier to produce because an equivalence of meaning is not sought. The translator simply works through a word for word translation that can go quite quickly, but meaning transfer may be minimal. Such translation often produces misunderstanding resulting from a wide variety of interpretation and diversity of opinion as to what the text means. A quick look at the history of problems associated with literal translations demonstrates this. Receptors can read their own meaning into them; they are open to interpretations that are not part of the intended meaning. Doctrinal disagreement stemming from the same proof text and misunderstanding of key terms such as 'baptism' are examples in English. Several so-called cargo cults in Melanesia and some African Independence Churches exemplify the problem in non-English speaking areas.

Because literal translations are essentially culture-free with respect to the receptor context, people are free to interpret them as they like. Therefore, a syncretistic church often results from literal translation. As already demonstrated, a people's worldview forces them to approach information from their frame of reference. When the words are understood but the meanings are not, the intentionality of those words is perceived in relation to a focal perspective and interpretive error is the natural (and expected) result. The translation then becomes the people's understanding of Scripture rather than God's Word.

This is not the case with idiomatic translations which force the receptor to deal with the meaning of the passage. In terms of meaning transfer, it allows for personal identification with the material, forcing people to evaluate their lifestyle and make decisions based on their understanding of what God is saying to them.

IMPLIED INFORMATION

As communicators relate their messages, there is much they assume along with their audience. This body of common knowledge allows them to allude to background information that everybody knows (prior reference), compress their speech in order to remove unnecessary redundancy (ellipses), and focus their communication in order not to bore an audience with unnecessary details (principle of dynamics). Much of communication depends on this implied information which, in turn, is largely cultural in nature. People in a particular context assume a great deal about what is correct behavior. Their worldview dictates a preconceived notion of what to expect. Hence they are able to concentrate on the concepts, logic, argument or story that requires their attention rather than on cultural matters that are assumed. Where cultural assumptions are shattered by uncultural behavior, attention is quickly drawn to those matters regardless of the intended message.

For translators, the focus on what is important creates a significant problem. What Biblical authors viewed as important are different than those things which the receptors now consider important. Implied information is very much a surface problem. When a message is transmitted from the deep structure meaning to the surface structure of the source, the cultural factors which impinge on a message were taken seriously by the communicator and the audience understood the message and acted upon it— some of the great Bible stories are about people's reaction to God's truth. When a translator communicates this same message in the modern context the only way to ensure it is not considered strange or irrelevant is to focus on the meaning of the message— not the original forms. However, because of cultural variance as well as time and space distinctions, the implications for today's receptors are different than for the original audience. Unless these issues are taken seriously, skewing will be the unfortunate, and often tragic, result.

This brings translators face to face with worldview clash. In order to avoid this type of clash (which by the very nature of culture is manifest at the surface level), the implications which were assumed by the original audience, but are not part of the receptor's context, must be supplied. Meaning is in focus here. Larson (1984:36ff) discusses three basic types of meaning within every text:

1. *Referential Meaning* - communication has "meaning because it refers to something that happened, or may happen, or is imagined as happening ... [It] is what the communication is about. It is the information content."

2. *Organizational Meaning* - communication is structured so that it "puts the referential information together into a coherent text... [It] is signaled by deictics, repetition, groupings, and by many other features in the grammatical structure of a text." For example, how is new information introduced, what organizational forms signal old information, and how is new and old information kept straight? These are organizational concerns which relate directly to the propositional studies discussed in chapter 14.

3. *Situational Meaning* - communication takes place within a specific context. "The relationship between the writer or speaker and the addressee will affect the communication." The circumstances of the communication and any background information known to all parties involved combine to result in situational meaning.

Within a text each type of meaning may be made obvious and clear (explicit) or left for the receptor to assume (implicit). However, what is clear and understood by one audience may not be so to another, especially if thousands of years separate the two. Implied information, despite its apparent absence, is very much part of the communication event.

> Some information, or meaning, is left implicit because of the structure of the source language; some because it has already been included elsewhere in the text, and some because of shared information in the communication situation. However, the implicit information is part of the meaning which is to be communicated by the translation because it is part of the meaning intended to be understood by the original writer (Larson 1984:38).

The critical question for the translator, then, is when and how to make implied information explicit and vice versa (explicit sometimes needs to be made implicit, see Larson 1969). Beekman and Callow (1974:57ff) suggest several well-known rules. Implicit material may be expressed explicitly when (1) "required by the receptor grammar", (2) "required by fidelity to the meaning", i.e. when fidelity to the original demands explication in order to avoid zero or wrong meaning and (3) it is "required by dynamic fidelity", i.e. when fidelity to the receptor demands structural or stylistic changes to ensure correct communication. Thus, "to correct wrong meaning that distorts the message of Scripture, the use of implicit information is always justified" (Beekman and Callow 1974:59).

I would like to add another principle that, though inferred above, needs to be made clear. The principle states: *implied information relevant to the source cultural context but not to the receptor, must be made explicit.* Whenever it is culturally necessary to provide information in order to maintain fidelity, either to the source or the receptor, translators must do so. This assumes that translators are aware of the cultural context of both and able to ensure that receptors sufficiently understand the source context in order to avoid miscommunication. The application of the cultural factors discussed in previous chapters now becomes obvious. It is imperative that translators be adequately aware of the total translation context in order to effectively communicate the message.

Referring again to the example of sackcloth and ashes (Mt.11:21), Jesus uses the phrase to show that the heathen of Tyre and Sidon, foreigners, would be more repentant than the Jews who knew so much about God. The idea of repentance and foreignness are both implied here but well understood by the people to whom Jesus was speaking. This was a real indictment on the 'unbelieving towns'. In order for the same message to be understood by modern receptors it may be necessary to make explicit the purpose for such behavior, as well as the cultural impact of indicating to the Jews that the 'heathen' were more receptive to God. Each receptor context will demand a different type of adjustment, but generally speaking the indication can be accomplished by adding a descriptive phrase such as: "in order to show repentance/remorse the heathen of Tyre and Sidon would have put on sackcloth and ashes." Another solution may be the substitution of a cultural practice that accomplishes the same purpose: "as you sit on the burial platform and wail in grief, so the foreigners of Tyre and Sidon would have put on sackcloth and ashes in grief for their sins."

The use of cultural substitutes, however, demands caution. Fidelity to the historical context of the source must not be violated. We should not provide absent information which the author may have considered irrelevant or unnecessary to the communication. Balance between adding information, i.e. turning the translation into a commentary, and supplying implicit information, is always difficult. The focus must be on the receptors and their understanding. Material is necessary to the extent that it provides understanding of what the source assumed. Beyond that it is not translation and separate resource materials should be produced to provide extra background and information. In the above example, the Jews would never have wailed on a burial platform as the Samo do. Therefore, this information in the translation of Jesus' words to the Jews is not acceptable—the implied information should be made clear and the cultural data communicated in a note or other culturally appropriate medium.

As translators we dare not use this principle to shift the focus of the message—sidetrack the receptors. The inclusion of implied information is legitimate only to maintain faithfulness to the message and ensure that it is understood. Implied information must be explicated when receptors can misinterpret if the assumed knowledge that was part of the original is not part of the receptor context. Culture is such a pervasive part of these concerns that without an understanding and application of it, the translator is severely handicapped.

FIGURES OF SPEECH

Figures of speech relate to words and their extended meanings. While the primary and secondary senses of words bear close resemblance to each other, by sharing a thread of meaning, figurative senses are based on association of some sort: meaning must be inferred or derived from the larger context. Again, culture plays an obvious role.

In a book designed to assist in Bible study, Clinton has organized figures of speech into broad classes based on the relationship between the primary and figurative sense of words and the reality they symbolize. A figure of speech "is the unusual use of a word or words differing from the normal [primary] use in order to draw special attention to some point of interest" (Clinton 1977:11). Figures of speech can be classed as 'figures of comparison', 'figures of substitution', 'figures of restatement', and 'figures of apparent deception'. Figure 15:2 diagrams and identifies the constituent types of figurative usage.

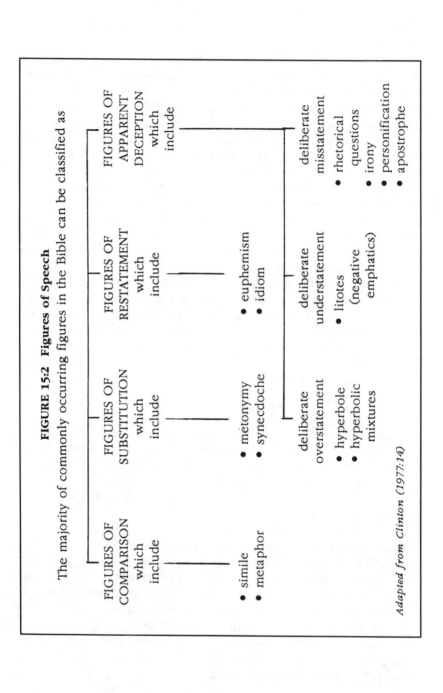

FIGURE 15:2 Figures of Speech

The majority of commonly occurring figures in the Bible can be classified as

FIGURES OF COMPARISON which include

- simile
- metaphor

FIGURES OF SUBSTITUTION which include

- metonymy
- synecdoche

FIGURES OF RESTATEMENT which include

- euphemism
- idiom

FIGURES OF APPARENT DECEPTION which include

- deliberate misstatement
- rhetorical questions
- irony
- personification
- apostrophe

deliberate overstatement

- hyperbole
- hyperbolic mixtures

deliberate understatement

- litotes (negative emphatics)

Adapted from Clinton (1977:14)

Focus on Meaning

In order to understand the meaning of these figures, Clinton introduces the idea of 'capture': (1) recognize the author's intended meaning, (2) replace the figurative language with non-figurative, (3) restate the figure with another or similar meaning or in a manner which reflects both the meaning and emphases of the figure in its context (1977:12).

Context is the critical word here. It is all the linguistic and cultural assumptions necessary to make up the totality of both the source and receptor environment. All languages reflect figurative usage, but the figures are specific to the context of people's experience; cultural meaning is reflected in speech forms. Translation lies not so much "in the linguistic code but in the context, which carries varying proportions of the meaning. Without context, the code is incomplete since it encompasses only part of the message" (Hall 1976:86). Thus analysis of the figures is essential in order to 'capture' the source meaning and transfer that to the receptor context.

Figures of Comparison. The topic and image of most figures of comparison are culturally based. So are the substitute items in figures of substitution. Assumptions about the qualities of items in a figure originate within the cultural base and must be effectively communicated through the translation. For example, Jesus told His disciples to go "tell that fox" (Herod), what He was doing (Lk. 13:32). What did He wish to communicate? What qualities did Herod and a fox share that would have triggered such a statement? Jesus may have been implying one or more of several qualities: cleverness, slyness, stealth and/or predatoriness. However, to the Cuicatecox of Mexico, the comparison indicated Herod was a homosexual. The Zapotecs of Villa Alta thought it meant that he cried a lot, and the Otomi were sure Jesus had called Herod a chicken thief (Beekman and Callow 1974:138). To the Maxakali of Brazil, Jesus was calling Herod a redhead, and to the Samo, who had never seen a fox, it meant nothing at all. It is not sufficient to use your own cultural assumptions about qualities being compared in the Bible. We need to research the assumptions of the source as well as those of the receptor with respect to the qualities of each metaphor or simile. We need to use an equivalent form to communicate the meaning or remove the figure and state the qualities the author intended.

Figures of Substitution. For figures of substitution, the figurative sense of words is based on association with the primary meaning of a lexical item. When the Apostle Paul refers to Christ as the "Head of the Church" (Eph. 1:22, Eph. 4:15, Col. 1:18) the analogy of the Church as Christ's body is obvious to English speakers and does not need explanation. While in English, it is natural to associate people with body parts in this way, it may not be so in other languages. In fact, it may be viewed as degrading to reduce a person (especially someone like the Lord) to a mere part of the body. Each culture has acceptable associations that are viewed as relevant, and when unacceptable associations are introduced the value of God's Word may be considerably reduced. Again the meaning of cultural attributes, features, and associations is necessary to effectively communicate the intentions of the author.

Figures of Restatement. These figures abound with cultural information unique to the context in which they are used. Idioms are highly language and culture-specific and can never be translated literally without total loss of original meaning. Euphemism alerts translators to taboo subjects in the culture or topics of embarrassment; e.g. body functions, death, spirits, and many more. The Jews avoided using God's name and Matthew, accommodating them, speaks of the "Kingdom of Heaven", and refers to Christ as the "Son of Man". Luke, on the other hand, eliminates the euphemistic expressions when communicating primarily to Gentiles, using "Kingdom of God" and "Son of God" to express the same ideas. Both authors desire to communicate the meaning clearly to their audience. To do so, one must use euphemism in order not to offend, while the other must be more direct in order to remain clear. Such examples from Scripture give insight to the way the Holy Spirit is aware of and utilizes cultural factors for more effective communication.

Figures of Apparent Deception. Hyperbole, irony, litotes and rhetorical questions are only 'deceptive' from an outsider's perspective. From the perspective of those who use them, these figures do not deceive, but rather provide style and variety to communication. While clarifying in one context, their transfer to another setting may be cause for confusion and miscommunication. Rhetorical questions, for example, are a favorite of the Apostle Paul. The Greek language allowed their usage in a way not entirely unfamiliar to speakers of English. For the Samo, however, rhetorical questions are restricted almost entirely to ridicule. Unless this was the implication of a particular passage, I had to rephrase a question as a positive statement which more correctly conveyed Paul's intended meaning.

Translating Figures of Speech

When translating figures of speech, translators should be able to identify the problem (this goes without saying for all the translation principles, not just figures of speech). They should then follow the process of 'capture' and relate that understanding to the receptor. Analysis of the propositions involved, their relationship to each other, the semantic features which share in the communication and the nature of the cultural context, all provide material for restatement into the receptor context.

At this point the figure is ready for translation. Unfortunately, most translators now ask, "What is the best way to translate this?". The more appropriate question is, "How might the author have written/said this if the receptor language was the language of communication?". This implies a series of related questions. What is the most accurate and natural way to communicate these concepts in order to maximize receptor comprehension? How does the receptor use the semantic features expressed in the source? When are they appropriate? What are the surface structure manifestations of deep structure semantic meaning? If, indeed, the author intended to be understood, then translators must communicate in a way that the same message is received by the new audience. If receptors are unable to supply the missing or implied information, or the extended senses assumed in the source text, then translators have failed to communicate the author's intended meaning and, therefore, have not really translated the text.

OTHER STRUCTURAL PROBLEMS

Many other problems lurk in the source text materials: pronominal referents, genitives, passives, quotations, order, and, of course, key terms. All of these have been covered in detail with respect to their linguistic qualities.

In all this discussion, however, there is little focus placed upon the context from which these difficulties emerge: the culture which spawns their usage on the one hand and their transfer and appropriation on the other. Cultural considerations strongly affect the interpretation of structural forms hence the need to understand and apply semantic analysis. Many forms vary their meaning with the context. It is crucial to match the proper forms with the intended meaning if that meaning is going to communicate.

Pronominal Reference

The Samo have a complex pronominal system which emphasizes person, including duality, focus on actor or action, exclusivity and possession. In all this, the Samo are interested in maintaining close identification of individuals involved since names are only used as introducers (K. Shaw 1983). Pronouns, then, are used to keep things and people, relationships and actions in focus. If the author of a source text uses a pronoun in a manner which may confuse the referents, i.e. by extending the primary usage in a particular way, the translator must clarify that usage and ensure that if maintained, it does not confuse the receptor audience. As with other lexical items, pronouns have a primary, secondary and extended or figurative usage that must be understood semantically before transferring it to the new context. Ultimately, pronouns, like all other lexical units, must be translated in such a way that the receptors understand what the source intended. Where culture plays a role in this complex of associations, it must be understood and utilized for maximum communication.

Order

Order often affects understanding. Some languages are more event oriented than others and this affects the way they process information chronologically. Order not only affects a time sequence but relates to logic which, by its very nature, is dictated by the genius of the language and culture. The source language has a logic that is different from that of the receptor, and translators need to handle both to ensure effective communication. This is why the relationships of a SSA are critical. The particular relationships between the words, phrases, paragraphs, and discourses of one system may be common to both the source and receptor, but the way they are manifest will probably be very different. This is another reason to pay close attention to meaning rather than surface forms.

For example, the way different languages introduce a story or new information varies considerably. This is particularly obvious in narrative texts, but pertains to all types. How does the source establish the setting, individuals involved, and then proceed to develop the story line or argument? It is quite likely that the receptor language does not follow this same sequencing. In Samo, the text is introduced by giving a one line overview of what is to come. The characters are then introduced and chronological order is strictly maintained. The conclusion is always an overview of the story or a summary of the intended moral. In order to maintain this combination of sequencing and logic, Scripture translation for the Samo often entails a considerable amount of restructuring. If the original order is maintained the message will not communicate within the Samo system of logic. Thus for Col. 1:12-17, the Samo translation actually orders the section backwards (beginning with the creative acts of God and concluding with the forgiveness of sin). The Samo conclusion: "Christ was truly first, having done all this for us; we must give thanks to God."

Such restructuring, of course, makes verse numbering in a printed edition difficult, as well as making it hard for outsiders to follow along. Of central importance, however, is how a translation communicates, not how verse numbers are printed. The specifics of the receptor language are different than Greek. If people are to understand the message it must be communicated with respect for their frame of reference. That frame of reference is, by its very nature, closely tied to their cultural expectations—the presuppositions which determine the way they will perceive and understand reality. Reality, as discussed at length in chapter 2, is created by God. However, the way reality is perceived is relative to a particular worldview. Thus a "Biblical relativism", to borrow a phrase from Nida (1954:52), is essential for successful translation. We must not be afraid to restructure the text in the surface forms of the receptor language, for that is the only way to communicate the meaning intended by the author who himself was forced to structure messages using the style and perspective of a specific language and culture (see Kraft 1979:116ff).

Use of Quotes

Quotations, quotations within quotations, and indirect quotations pose a severe problem (especially in an oral society unfamiliar with quotation marks). Styles of reference to what was said in the past, by whom and to whom, are highly culture specific. In a context where anything beyond remembered history is part of a murky heritage populated by nebulous ancestors, citations of the exact words spoken by individuals who lived thousands of years ago is suspicious at best. On the other hand, indirect quotes are unnatural in many Amerindian languages. Hence the precise quotes of Old Testament material are important despite their imprecise reference. The fact that they were used and are considered relevant by another author lends credibility to the message. This in itself could act as a strong incentive for Scripture translation—the preservation of God's Word for future generations, a validation of God's impact upon human beings.

Perhaps this reasoning affected many of the quotes New Testament writers used, despite their imprecise introductions: "it is written..." or "God says..." (II Cor. 4:13, Heb. 5:6, etc.). This may also indicate audience familiarity with Scripture, leaving the citation implied so as not to insult their intelligence. Regardless of the rationale, the cultural context of the source communication was very different from our academic concerns for literary devices essential to precision. Other modern cultures are more oral than literary and appreciate the use of background material (including quotes) to validate an argument. The form such validation takes, however, is often cultural in nature and implies the context in which it was used.

When translating for people who are often more oral than literary, we should be very much aware of these culturally based attitudes and relate to them in the translation. We need to carefully choose a style of communication that will not alienate all but the educated few (who may be products of their interaction with industrial nations). Our translations should utilize, to the extent possible, communication styles common to the group, for then they will identify with the message because the communication is not foreign. We now briefly consider this topic.

NON-VERBAL ASPECTS

Though not a traditional translation principle, Hall (1959 and 1976) makes clear that kinesics or non-verbal communication is culturally relative and critical to communication. It also has a significant effect on the translation process. Sperber and Wilson make a similar point when discussing relevance theory (1986:46ff). Scripture abounds with culturally specific gestures, actions which convey meaning to the audience. In every culture, certain actions are symbolic and it remains for translators to determine what that symbolism is and communicate it through appropriate gestures or meanings, recognizable to the receptors. When a phrase such as "wagging their heads" (Mt. 27:39 and Mk. 15:29) is used, it may have a very different meaning in the receptor culture than it did to the source. At the very least, an adjustment indicating the nature of the implied information is necessary, e.g. "they wagged their heads in ridicule". We must exercise caution to avoid obscenities when translating symbolic action. Appropriate gestures in one context are often inappropriate in others. We do not want Christ communicating obscenities in the translation; meaning must be the focus.

Smith (1971) has enumerated eleven symbol systems which interact to form total communication. These eleven channels of communication are: verbal, written, pictorial, audio, kinesic, tactile, spatial, temporal, artifactual, optical, and olfactory. The signals from styles early in the list are more explicit while those towards the end are more implicit. The further down the list one goes, the heavier the cultural load, i.e. the more culturally specific the information and the meaning it conveys.

People use these signals to varying degrees, often reflecting their culture type; those from Industrial cultures place heavier emphasis on the interaction of these channels with writing while much of the rest of the world develops these with verbal forms. In most cultures, non-verbal features convey much of the meaning of communication, and when the 'said' contradicts the 'unsaid', the audience puts more faith in the latter since it is unconscious and reflects more basic assumptions (Tyler 1978:461). In American English, for example, we place considerable emphasis on paralanguage phenomena: intonation, stress, length, pause, etc. Reading an unedited transcript of spoken forms can be frustrating—the gestures, voice quality, relevant feedback, etc. are all missing. The contrast between interactive, oral communication, and the exact same message in a literary format is considerable. The message remains the same, but the communicative value is entirely different (one reason why it is essential to heavily edit oral communication for publication). Thus oral and written style are very different forms—written translations and translation on cassette tape should not be the same.

In some Amerindian languages, onomatopoetic forms are used liberally in verbal communication. Failure to use them in dramatic stories, such as the fall of Jericho, results in an unnatural, uninteresting, artificial recitation of facts that have little feeling. We want our translations to feel right, to communicate emotively. In his book on the oral communication of Scripture, Klem addresses these issues with respect to the Nigerian context (Klem 1982:110ff). African languages are full of idiophones, proverbs, poetry, plays on words, and audience participation that make oral communication an art form. The tonal languages lend themselves to musical interplay that makes the distinction between oral and musical communication a fine line that is often irrelevant (King 1983). Communicators are skilled orators who know that their communication is far more than a matter of words, much less words on cold, non-interactive paper (King 1987). A friend from Ghana described his experience upon returning home after completing his Western education; "the elders took me aside to put proverbs back in my mouth". A Nigerian translator said at the completion of a course: "I must revise the translation to include local word-play and interactive styles. My translation is too stilted for my audience." Such examples come from around the world.

The communication styles that are so much a part of people's lives should become part of the translation in order to make sense. These styles give the gospel a quality that people can take seriously. When the local mythology presents a morality that is considered relevant, then Scripture must demonstrate applicability to the same points. When the proverbs a people use every day communicate the necessity for smooth interpersonal relationships, the translated Scriptures must communicate this just as dynamically. For Scripture—the holy Word of God—to be considered meaningful and worthy of attention, it must do so in forms people consider relevant. As communicators must earn the right to be there, to have a people's trust, so must the translation earn its own credibility in order for people to pay attention to it. The truth of the gospel must be clear. It should be presented in such a way that people consider it more powerful, more complete than their own wisdom tradition. Translators who overlook these styles may find people have little interest in their translations. Every effort should be made to remove translation from the "stimulus poor" category in contexts where "the expectations concerning the use of communicational stimuli are high" (Klem 1982:145).

IDIOMATIC TRANSLATIONS

Meeting people's cultural expectations within the translation process may revolutionize the whole concept of translation and the communication of the gospel in general. Traditional translators ministering out of a primarily industrial culture base have considered translation part of a literary tradition and strongly encouraged recipients to learn to read. By doing so they imply that non-readers are unable to understand God's Word. An elaborate educational system established by many missions in the 19th century became the basis of modern education in many nations around the world: monuments to the Western emphasis on writing skills and reading Scripture. Research now indicates the great importance people themselves place on their own traditions and communication styles. Therefore, rather than insisting that people adapt to industrial communication emphases and styles, the focus needs to shift to adapting Scripture within an oral communicational emphasis that more closely reflects kinship or peasant styles. We should attempt to know and use the richness of those traditions to transmit, "transculturate" to use Kraft's term (1979:276ff), Biblical concepts within the receptor's communicational framework.

TRANSCULTURATION

Transculturation is to the cultural and non-verbal aspects of communication what translation is to the verbal; both are essential for effective communication. A translation should communicate at all levels of human experience. Beekman and Callow recognize this principle when they focus on the clarity of communication so that the work "does not appear to be a translation at all" (Beekman and Callow 1974:32). Nida and Taber make the same point when they state: "each language covers the totality of experience with symbols" (Nida & Taber 1982:19). Kraft presents the concept well.

> The idea of transculturating the message is not new, though the label we use may be. There are, however, certain dimensions of the process . . . (1) Transculturation starts with the process that every faithful interpreter of the Scriptures goes through in seeking to *exegete* from these documents the *meanings* that the *original* authors sought to *communicate* to their hearers. (2) It then involves the would-be communicator in an attempt to *understand* the *relevance of these meanings* for his or her audience. (3) It involves the interpreter in the *communication of the message to the hearers* in a manner dynamically equivalent to the manner employed by the original participants . . . *Translation* aims to provide a faithful written record of the biblical events. *Transculturation* attempts to take both speaker and hearer behind that record into a recreation of equivalent events in today's cultural context (Kraft 1979:281). [emphasis added]

Figure 15:3 depicts the process. This very much resembles the SMR model presented by Nida and Taber (1982:22,23) and developed in chapter 2 of this book. It utilizes the translation context concept and focuses on the importance of each aspect of the process from exegesis to effective communication. If properly executed the result should be a life-changing response. The process, as Nida and Taber note, includes response with respect to the entire translation context: the source, the effect on the translator (both personally and in relation to understanding the source context and anticipating receptor reaction) and the receptor.

The importance of style and expression in the receptor context is further reinforced by Nida and Taber's "expressive factor":

> Dynamic equivalence in translation is far more than mere correct communication of information. In fact, one of the most essential, and yet often neglected, elements is the expressive factor, for people must also feel as well as understand what is said. The poetry of the Bible should read like poetry, not like a dull prose account. Similarly, the letters of Paul should reflect

FIGURE 15:3
The Process of Transculturation

SOURCE MEANING	TRANSLATOR UNDERSTANDING	RECEPTOR COMMUNICATION
Exegete source context including the forms and meanings used to effect response.	Understand original meaning with respect to the translator's context and the receptor's situation. Appreciate source response and anticipate receptor reaction.	Communicate/translate source meaning using receptor cultural and linguistic forms that effect a life-changing response.

THE TRANSLATION CONTEXT

The entire process is necessary for Transculturation

something of the freshness of a general letter, and not sound
like a theological dissertation (Nida and Taber 1982:25).

Through the years, translators, in large measure, have attempted to reproduce oral style in written form. While this may
have helped the communication to some extent, Klem, Kraft, and
others call for an application of these principles to a full
transculturation of the message. Receptors should have the privi-
lege of receiving the message in their context and making
decisions accordingly.

As national translators come into prominence and relate the
source message and style to their particular context, they should
be encouraged to explore all possibilities. Experimentation with
traditional forms (oral, musical, dance, and drama) may ultimately
communicate to the receptors how God understands them and
can incarnate in their context, even as He did among the Jews.
"Most religious ritual, the Christian as well, has its roots in
dramatic reenactment, in reliving sacred events so we can
participate in them. In the Eucharist we step by divine play into
the drama of redemption" (Kelsey 1984:96). The message of the
Bible must not be considered a strange religion developed by
people speaking strange tongues and living in far-off places long
ago. Rather it should be presented in ways that will be recognized
as relevant and life-changing. The message should communicate
in such a way that it becomes part of the context in which it is
presented, viewed as important and necessitating a response. This
is transculturation—true translation.

Dialect/Language Specificity

A word of caution is appropriate here. The more culture
specific the translation, i.e. the more acculturated or contextualized it is, the more limited will be the audience. Thus in a
complex socio-linguistic situation where several dialects intermin-
gle, the idiomatic appropriateness of a word, metaphor or gesture
may be misunderstood in a neighboring dialect. Though mutually
intelligible the focus may be different and the impact lost. For
example, Kenneth Taylor's widely distributed Living Bible is quite
specific to American English, making it less appropriate to other
English speakers. An Australian friend pointed out the distraction
of specific American forms such as "Saul went into a cave to go to

the bathroom" (I Sam. 24:3). Inasmuch as this was a euphemistic expression in Hebrew (Saul covered his feet), an English euphemism may have broadened the applicability of the translation (Saul relieved himself). If, however, translators want to be specific (as Taylor did) then such transculturation is appropriate and communicates at a level which helps receptors establish an identity with Scripture and the God who spoke in a way not possible through generalisms. Thus the Australian version should read, "Saul went to the toilet". Compromise on dialect specifics may be the key to a broader reception of a translation, but the cultural identity should be maintained for relevance and impact of communication.

Relevance

People act out their lives in real circumstances. The Scriptures must appear to be real as well. If the actors in Scripture do not appear real there will be more limited identification and the message will not be considered relevant. Therefore, individuals within a translation must not only talk right as has been the traditional emphasis, but they must also act right to be believable. As the Scriptures function in a dynamic way within a cultural context, the people will have a model to follow as they seek to apply its meaning to their lives. Christians must be able to act out their salvation if it is to have any meaning. Similarly, the actors in the Biblical case studies they read should appear real.

This is not to say that all cultural activities different from those of the receptors can be glossed over or changed to fit the context. Rather they must be communicated in such a way that the receptors view them as valid though different, happening in another time and place. History cannot be ignored nor passed over lightly. The Biblical peoples did things differently than modern people, especially if the modern receptors come from Industrial cultures. Those actions, however must be believable and the implied information relative to them communicated so that the receptors understand the deeper message—why those accounts were included in Scripture.

Ignoring cultural issues and their impact upon Biblical interpretation and the established principles of translation will dramatically affect the relevance of Scripture. Exegesis is essential to a correct understanding and appreciation for the source message

and context, the totality of meaning communicated through the
Word. The application of anthropological principles to traditional
translation principles allows for a transculturation of a message
within the context of very different times and places. The
principles provide a mechanism for transfer, the translation
process *per se,* while cultural considerations provide the mechanism for emotive and non-verbal transfer of information. This
allows modern receptors to respond to the same Word the
original receptors understood. They can then apply it in ways that
are unique to their situation and develop their lives accordingly:
God's Word in every language and culture.

Red and yellow, black and white,
All are precious in His sight.

Suggested Reading

Nida, Eugene. *Toward a Science of Translation.* Tavistock, 1964.
Nida, E. and C. Taber. *The Theory and Practice of Translation.* Brill,
1982.
Wilss, Wolfram. *The Science of Translation.* Gunter Narr Verlag, 1982.

Notes

1. Translations that are not idiomatic are hard to understand and are,
therefore, not used much. The apparent exception to this is the ever
popular King James Version in English. Though a reasonably good
translation, communicating well to the people of its day, three
centuries have passed and it has become the holy language Bible
appreciated by many for its literary or classical use of language
regardless of its incomprehensibility. When an individual wants to
really understand the message, a more popular version is consulted.
Unfortunately, the K.J.V. has affected our Christian language usage
and much of our speech is filled with 'God talk'—language peculiar
to the Church: 'justification', 'sanctification', 'thee' and 'thou', and
other spiritualisms that are unintelligible to non-Christians. The fact is
that many of these terms, so much a part of our evangelicalism, are
literalisms from the Greek and have become theological terms—'born
again', 'the world', 'the church', 'in the name of . . .', 'believe on . . .',
etc. I am not criticizing the terms themselves, but rather calling for an
idiomatic translation of them for our day. Christians in the American
culture need to learn how to talk to non-Christians in a language they

know and understand. New Christians need to know the meaning of the terminology, not simply repeat holy words in a magical formula that the Holy Spirit will somehow use in their lives. Unfortunately, all too many Christians do not stop to think about the meaning of these terms. They tend to accept them by faith as something that can only be spiritually discerned. This is the point of an idiomatic translation; it relates directly to the language usage which reflects the life experience of those who use it. Only an idiomatic translation effectively takes culture into account and relates the Heavenly message to it. Cohen (1987) very nicely points out this use of spiritual language and its effect upon those who don't understand—we must speak their language or dialect and relate to their culture, wherever that may be !

CHAPTER SIXTEEN
Translation, Evangelism and the Church

What is the end result of a translation project? How does it affect people's lives? How does the translator ensure the on-going use of Scripture in the life of the Church? We now face the larger missiological question of the church in the culture and how the translation relates to it. Here the translator and the missionary closely interact (or become one) to ensure that the communication of the gospel takes place. The translation acts within the total context of the church and its mission to reflect the needs and concerns of the culture. Within the church Scripture, however, is not primarily a medium for evangelism, but for "instruction for right living" (II Tim.3:16). Missionaries, whether involved in translation or not, should be as culturally sensitive and aware as translators who produce Scripture. To be meaningful, the church and the Scripture it uses cannot be divorced from the people it seeks to reach. It cannot extract the church members from their culture, nor should it intrude with an outside religion. Most of the principles and concerns expressed in this book for Bible translators and the translations they produce applies equally to missionaries and the church that results from the efforts of both.

Translation does not take place in a vacuum. It enters into a culture and a church in order to communicate the good news. It is "useful for teaching the truth, rebuking error, correcting faults, and giving instruction for right living" (II Tim. 3:16). No translation stands alone. The goal of a translation project is not a bound book on a shelf, but dirty Bibles used in homes and churches, studied to build faith, and referenced for truth, God's truth, when error is questioned. In short, the goal of a translation project is Scripture in use—the Bible applied to people's lives.

SCRIPTURES IN THE CHURCH

Part of the cultural context into which the Scriptures fit is the church within the cultural community. Whether the church is the result of a translator's efforts (believers responding to Scripture for the first time) or a long established church with a recognized position in the community, vernacular Scripture should be part of it. In a new chapter to his revised *Bible Translation Strategy,* Dye notes that 90% of all Bible translation around the world today takes place where an established church already exists. Many of these churches represent several denominations, and widely divergent Christian traditions. Moreover, many of these churches are now in local hands and missionaries have either left or are in advisory roles. Thus, if a translation is to be accepted by the church, translators must interact with all individuals involved and encourage participation in the translation project to the extent possible. Perhaps the church needs to take primary responsibility for the translation. If the church does not feel a part of the translation project, it can hardly be expected to wholeheartedly accept it when made available (Dye 1985:274 ff). We now turn to a discussion of issues that often impede acceptance of vernacular Scripture and the cultural implications they raise both for translators and the churches they serve.

Leadership Training

It goes without saying that a translation project includes a considerable amount of leadership training. The Apostle Paul strongly encouraged discipleship, as did his mentor, Jesus Christ. He best expresses this principle when writing to Timothy: "Take the teachings that you heard me proclaim in the presence of many witnesses, and entrust them to reliable people, who will be able to teach others" (II Tim. 2:2). Leadership is passing on what one knows to others who will do the same. The mechanism for accomplishing this will be specific to each culture, but the basic principles remain the same.

As translators closely interact within the community and relate to local leadership, so they must relate to the leadership within the church (however that may be defined). Translators may see translation as their primary responsibility, but what they produce needs to fit within the church context. This implies that while focusing on Bible translation, translators are actually working for the church which will use the materials they produce. If this is to happen, we should be closely involved with those who will be responsible for ensuring its use. Thus a close cooperation between translators and pastors is strongly encouraged.

Church leadership should form a translation committee (however the culture defines that). This committee could assist the translator by (1) providing personnel (hopefully assistants from each recognized denomination would be represented on the translation team), (2) discussing and approving key terms used in the translation, (3) suggesting the choice and order of materials to translate (this could be affected by a congregation's need for the "Sunday/weekly reading"), (4) serving as a checking committee or appointing one that is representative of the local churches, dialects, or other groupings, and (5) making the translation available to the community at large (determining price, methods of distribution, etc.). Committee members can act as innovators who bring Scripture to the people and encourage its use.

This committee can be a demonstration to the society as a whole that the entire church is part of this project. It makes the translation theirs and translators, whether expatriate or national, are only a part of the total effort (not the prime mover), an advocate not an innovator. It also relieves translators from making key decisions and appearing to be independent. Together they strive to produce the best results and educate the community.

Seminars focusing on principles of translation, dynamic equivalence, key terms, and the Biblical basis for vernacular Scriptures can be useful for educating the committee as well as the entire Christian community. If the church is well established and familiar with trade language Scriptures, the introduction of a new translation may be threatening to many, especially those in positions of leadership. Understanding the social structure and the prestige of the Christian leadership may be central to the successful introduction of vernacular Scripture. Seminars can assist in reducing some of the concerns of leadership and laity alike. By becoming familiar with exegetical issues, and the semantic meaning of Biblical terms, pastors may develop a greater appreciation for the source text and communicate this to their congregations. They need to feel that the translation will improve their ministry, rather than pose a threat to it.

Trade Language Versions versus Vernacular Translation

Sometimes pastors, familiar with trade language Scriptures, feel somewhat threatened by the introduction of a vernacular translation. This is especially the case if their sermons are basically an effort to translate and make the trade language version clear in the vernacular. Though an apparent contradiction, the fact is that many of these pastors feel they have little to say if the Scriptures are clear. Familiarity with trade language materials could cause pastors to have difficulty in using (and especially reading) the vernacular translation (particularly if the vernacular is not their mother tongue). Hence there is a need for transfer materials as well as vernacular based literacy.

This is an issue that pertains both to custom and to prestige. It may be that pastors or other church leaders were originally selected on the basis of their ability to use and/or read the trade language. This gave them a certain amount of prestige as well as an avenue to education. Within their community they are looked up to and sought after for matters far beyond their ecclesiastical expertise. They are considered both cultural and spiritual leaders. If Scriptures that anyone can understand become available, perhaps some of this prestige will be reduced and along with it a certain amount of cultural status.

In order to avoid this, translators need to model a Biblical lifestyle and assist these individuals in their use of vernacular Scriptures. In many areas of Papua New Guinea, pastors have been among the first to learn to use the vernacular orthography and were given literacy lessons designed to assist them in reading the vernacular. Thus they became the first readers and maintained their prestige by often becoming the best readers. If they have worked closely as part of the translation team, they realized they had nothing to fear and could promote rather than retard the use of Scripture; their honor has been maintained because the church now has their work to use for spiritual growth.

Because of widely divergent sound systems and grammatical structures vernacular Scriptures may appear very different from trade language versions. Reordering of verses, discourse structure, and the transliteration of names and places can make the vernacular materials appear quite dissimilar. While this may make people proud of their own language, it can serve to detract from the use of Scripture if pastors, and others who use it, have difficulty comparing the materials or finding their way through what was once familiar. The production of diglot versions, and the education of leaders on linguistic and cultural distinctions can be helpful solutions. Again, translators must work closely with those who will be most affected and seek their advice when making strategic decisions.

As we prepared to publish the *Mini New Testament* in Samo, I asked the church leaders what the cover of the book should look like. Without hesitation they emphasized the need for dark blue with white lettering. I was somewhat confused by this request until I reflected on their experience with trade language versions. Both the Tok-Pisin and the Hiri Motu translations, produced by the Bible Society, had dark blue covers with white lettering. When the boxes of Scripture came off the plane and were opened people immediately exclaimed, "It's our Bible". Even non-readers knew what a Bible should look like and recognized theirs when they saw it.

Working with the leadership of the church in this way may also mean that translators are not as free to make cultural adjustments. Names and places familiar in the trade language may look and sound quite different in the vernacular. For example, in Catholic areas, it may be better to use the Latinized 'Maria' rather than the Anglicized 'Mary' for the name of Jesus' mother. The translation of passages pertaining to baptism or the eucharist may require compromise. While this can frustrate translators who desire to produce the most idiomatic translation possible, it may result in Scriptures that are accepted and used. With the goal of translation in mind, some flexibility at this point may result in Scriptures that are widely dispersed versus books only sitting on shelves. Of central importance is that the translator did not make this decision alone, it was the result of committee consensus.

Finally church leaders should be encouraged to use vernacular Scripture for their own spiritual growth. Demonstrating its use in devotions and small groups can do much to break down resistance, whatever the reason. As the leadership sees Scripture bear fruit among their people they will be encouraged to sponsor its use throughout the community. The Samo church bought a large number of Scripture portions for pastors and lay leaders to take with them when they went to other communities. As part of their interaction in these communities, they would distribute the books and encourage Bible study. One elder became adept at teaching people to read and used Bible study as a motivation for his students.

Doctrinal Issues

It is particularly difficult in a multi-denominational context, to keep everyone happy in matters of doctrinal difference. Proof texts in a literal trade language version may not be so obvious in the vernacular. If these are difficult to find, or appear significantly different in content, the local translation may be rejected. This can be a delicate matter, especially if a translator's theological bias is evident in the translation. However, by faithfully following exegetical and translation principles as discussed in chapters 14 and 15, such bias can be largely eliminated. Translators should also maintain a non-partisan position—interact equally with all denominations to the extent possible. This does not mean they cannot have opinions and worship specifically as they feel led. Officially, however, they should attempt to be "all things to all people" (I Cor. 9:22). There is more to translation than the appropriation of principles and cultural factors. Bible translators need to be politically astute and do everything possible to ensure that the translation is faithful while at the same time acceptable.

The value of a committee on which all entities are represented is particularly valuable at this point. While an element of compromise may prevail, the end result, compatibility and acceptance of the finished product, is well worth the time and effort spent discussing these issues. Exegetical faithfulness and the translator's familiarity with the source is also crucial. The churches must understand that Scripture is first an instructional tool within the Christian community. The lifestyle of believers should evangelize unbelievers in the community, while Scripture instructs believers how to live so that others cannot speak against God (Titus 2:5,7,8,10).

In churches where Christianity has become nominal, vernacular Scriptures can serve as a key to revitalization. Unfortunately this frightens many of the leaders who may take issue with some of the manifestations of revival. Here, again, culture is crucial. How is revitalization manifest within the culture? How do people demonstrate dissatisfaction with the *status quo* and strive to bring about change? Wallace's discussion of nativistic movements and the process of revitalization is very helpful to communicators at this point (Wallace 1956).

Translators, then, should work in conjunction with church leaders, as well as any dissatisfied elements in the church, to effect renewal from within rather than developing separatist, or break away movements. For the latter to be the result of a translation project is unfortunate indeed. Renewal should be an expected result of the availability of God's Word, but that should come from the work of the Holy Spirit. Maintaining a non-partisan position is crucial to effective Bible translation. Translators need to understand the cultural factors and apply that knowledge to effective assistance in the life of the church, both through their own lives and through the translations they produce. Translators are "well advised to be as objective as possible about all the churches which in God's providence are actually present in the minority group" (Dye 1985:289).

Distribution of Scripture

Culture also affects Scripture distribution. The usual means of distributing Scripture assumes that it is in written form: a bound book. The form of the message becomes, to a large extent, the message itself. If an outside form, such as writing, is the only medium for Scripture, it may not be used by the people who most need it. The cultural ideal may demand other forms. Perhaps the best colporteur is a story teller, a poet, or a singer. These culturally defined roles help individuals communicate the gospel in forms which are accepted throughout the region. Once accepted, the Scriptures in written (outside) form may be accepted as well. If pastors are able to combine their theological training with their traditional communication styles, Christianity may be perceived as more meaningful, something worth paying attention to. Scripture should be used in ways familiar to the entire community. If pastors are not comfortable in this role, perhaps lay ministers or others in the community will be. On a recent visit to the Samo area, an elder told me they had put nearly 100 verses into the repetitive style of Samo song. These songs were being sung throughout the region by literate and non-literate alike. God's Word was in their hearts and on their tongues, reducing the drudgery of garden work and encouraging believers as they met together to share the Word.

This is not to say that Scripture should not be written down, or members of the society never taught to read. Literacy has its place, especially as modernity affects predominantly non-literate societies. Initial distribution, however, may be best when the most familiar forms are utilized. This approach will speak volumes about translators' attitudes toward local communication styles.

Scripture distribution, pertains to more than making the Word available. It relates to people's lives and their interaction with others of their society. As non-Christians see the effects of Scripture in the lives of Christian relatives, friends, and neighbors, they will be more inclined to appropriate it to their own lives. Translators should not wait for the day when published copies of Scripture arrive. The more Scripture in culturally recognized forms, as well as portions and pre-publication drafts, is used the more people will recognize its value, and be inclined to use it when The Book does arrive (Gould 1986). Each day in a translator's life is a chapter in the story of the Word. The final production is just part of that story, not the story itself. Availability and creativity are essential to effective distribution, whatever the form.

THE CHURCH IN THE CULTURE

As with the translation, the perceived relevance of the church with respect to the culture will be directly proportional to its interaction within that context—in the culture but not part of it, to paraphrase Jesus' words (Jn. 17:14-16). Church growth, then, will always be a cultural matter. Relevance is the critical factor. When the church and the Scriptures, which are the foundation upon which it is built, are perceived as meaningful and concerned with cultural issues and needs, the Christian message will more likely be accepted, i.e. evangelism will generally be successful because the evangelists are culturally real.

A translator's life style, as discussed in chapter 13, can act as a model for members of the culture as they interact with others. This can also provide another role for the translation committee. Cultural insiders are far better gospel communicators than outsiders! They know the cultural rules, where Scripture forces reflection and what they have done about it in their own lives. As these believers unite within a culturally relevant church their witness will be increasingly identified with that grouping. This may result in another social or religious entity within the culture, thereby effecting culture change. So long as local churches, as well as people in them, relate to and change with the culture, there is a good chance for on-going relevance.

TRANSLATION NEVER ENDS

When the translation is complete the work has just begun! Most translators do not realize this, with the result that the translation becomes a thing in itself, the embodiment of a person or team and their work, a task or goal oriented result. Instead, translation should be on-going, a part of the life of the church. In this way it maintains a vitality in keeping with culture change and the continuing influence of outside forces upon the minority group.

For this to happen, translators need to be involved in training those who can continue to revise and produce new translated material. As long as the language and culture are changing, there will be a need for continued translation and up-dating. Translators need to be aware of the importance of acquiring and training the right assistants who can become co-translators. Their interaction within the culture and the church combined with their willingness to train others is crucial to the continued influence of Scripture upon the community. Training is the key to all this. No one translator can possibly do all that is necessary, nor will translation continue, without competently trained co-workers.

Another matter of great concern is the availability of materials other than Scripture. For pastors to grow and understand the relevance of Scripture to the culture, they need extra-Biblical materials: commentaries, Bible dictionaries and materials about Biblical cultures. These materials should be in the vernacular and compliment the Scriptures. However, this is usually considered beyond the responsibility of translators who often view their job as complete when Scripture is in the hands of the people. Again, the church can take the lead here, requesting such materials from translators. Or, better yet, they can assign various members of the committee to work on providing materials that will enhance their understanding and improve their worship.

More than Biblical studies are necessary if people are to develop an appreciation, and see a need, for reading and writing. People need to be encouraged to develop their own literature, expressing in writing what has heretofore been available only in oral form. As the traditional cultures of the world are affected by rapid change that has been forced upon them by social, political, and ideological pressures from outside, they sense a need to preserve their own traditions. Unfortunately many of the rich cultural traditions of these people groups are dying with the older generation. Preservation is thus a major concern of many cultural leaders today. National writers should be encouraged to exper- iment with modernizations of traditional styles, using drama, dance, and music to enhance their literary work. Encouragement from expatriates can be a real assistance in the initial stages. In my experience, once writers begin to feel more confident and others catch their zeal, there is no turning back. In fact, when enthusiasm for such a developing literature catches on, the motivation for literacy is high and people become excited about reading and using their new literary skills. In those cases where the Scriptures are the only literature, however, literacy programs often fail (Shacklock 1967:100).

Translators often ask: when is the job complete? This question has little relevance if (1) the translation takes place within the rubric of the church within a culture, and (2) the primary translators are members of the community—not outsiders. This assumes considerable change in traditional translation projects. First, it demands that translators be part of a team, working with committees and churches to bring the gospel to the entire community. Second, such an approach becomes a movement within the society. Because of Christians within a culture, others are evangelized, churches are planted and the message contex- tualized. Christianity becomes a dynamic part of the culture because it demonstrates relevance. This, in turn, assists the society in its effort to survive in an ever-changing world.

To meet the challenge of change, revisions and new transla- tions should be produced along with an on-going literature. Ultimately members of the church may become burdened to share this good news with other societies and go to evangelize them. Beyond indigeneity and independence is mission—expansion of the church beyond its traditionally imposed borders (Tippett 1969:136).

This is the challenge of Bible translation and missions today. Reaching beyond one's borders to encompass those who, when properly trained and motivated, can do so much more for themselves. Expatriate translators can motivate and encourage, while enabling others to do more than they can accomplish on their own. Such an approach, a change of focus, raises many questions about the nature, purpose, and means of implementing on-going translation projects around the world today. Much more research is needed, many questions must be answered. In this broader context, however, translators should see themselves, not as responsible for a specific task within the church, but as part of the movement of the church acting on behalf of a living Christ. They are part of Christ's Body, the Church triumphant.

Suggested Reading

Aldrich, Joseph. *Life-Style Evangelism*. Multnomah Press, 1981.

Dye, Wayne. *The Bible Translation Strategy*. Wycliffe Bible Translators, 1985.

CHAPTER SEVENTEEN
Teamwork

This chapter is more than a conclusion to a book. It is really an introduction to the next era of Bible Translation. As with the rest of missions and the world in general, rapid change and world-wide conditions demand that we re-evaluate and determine priorities. As we review the past, we see the strategic role of Bible Translation in reaching the peoples of the world. As we anticipate the future, we look forward to an even greater impact as new programs are developed to meet the needs of an ever changing world.

We now enter an era of increased awareness. Much research has been done by the Summer Institute of Linguistics and the Bible Societies to determine translation needs. Now with some idea of what should be done, how do we go about accomplishing the task? It is clear that the methods of the past fifty years, while appropriate at the time, are no longer sufficient to insure the availability of Scripture to over three thousand languages currently without any portion of Scripture (Grimes 1985). We must devise ways to speed up the translation process, to encourage translators, and develop partnerships that will result in effective implementation of skills and expertise so that people who need and want it may have God's Word. I have attempted to bring what has often been an unconscious cultural awareness to the surface and make it a dynamic part of every translator's tool kit. It is necessary to understand the entire cultural context of a translation project and to apply that awareness, both to living with the people and communicating the meaning of God's revelation to them. This awareness however, has ramifications that must be explored, particularly as that relates to encouraging national translators. This chapter looks forward to that task, rather than backward to what may have been.[1]

The goal of this chapter is not to draw clear conclusions (these will vary with every situation), but rather to point the way to research that will provide better translations for future generations of receptors—for the church. I take the risk of raising more questions than I answer at this point, but I accept that risk in order to develop a base for research that relates culture to the translation task. All the answers are not in. Indeed, this is only an initial attempt to validate the cultural issue in the translation process—it is still very much an introductory effort.

IT TAKES A TEAM

There are many types of translation projects today. They range all the way from expatriate, other tongue translators (OTT) who take primary responsibility, to national mother tongue translators (MTT) who are primarily responsible (Figure 17:1). These are extremes on a continuum that allows for a wide variety of effective programs. Finding the right balance is important. Indeed, every translation program must be evaluated on its own merits and the appropriate means established to meet the needs of the people involved. In contexts where little or no outside education is available and people have no background to undertake a translation project, clearly an OTT type program (with the translators either expatriates or nationals working in a language other than their own) is a necessity. In other contexts, however, MTT can and should be encouraged to do the job themselves (Pasut 1983). This does not mean that expatriates walk away and leave the people on their own; it does mean they assume very different roles as we shall discuss shortly.

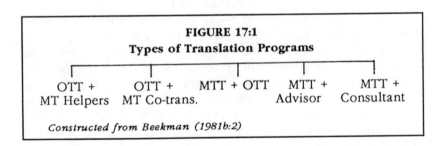

FIGURE 17:1
Types of Translation Programs

| OTT + MT Helpers | OTT + MT Co-trans. | MTT + OTT | MTT + Advisor | MTT + Consultant |

Constructed from Beekman (1981b:2)

Within the receptor community, people with varied abilities and interests should be incorporated into the program; a translation should become a community project. Some individuals will be skilled with words and give special "attention to the details of word structure", others are more "helpful in finding an equivalent for technical terms", and still others for "explaining the meaning of a verse ... [and giving] quick, and often times surprisingly spiritual, explanations of a passage". Others are able to "suggest many valuable syntactical changes as well as shifts in sentence order" while still others , the talkative and impetuous, may prove to be a "source of idiomatic expressions". All are critical to effective translation whether the primary translator be an expatriate or a national (Beekman 1952:24-25). The collective complementarity of abilities and strengths of a wide variety of people striving for a common goal produces the desired result, Scripture in the hands of the people.

The emphasis on teamwork goes far beyond the immediate project team (translators, helpers, church leaders, etc.) discussed in chapter 16. Consultants, at all levels, are essential for a successful translation. The more consultants become a part of the process, insuring balance and appropriateness of exegesis and language, fidelity and clarity, the more they will be viewed as assistants rather than hurdles. A tremendous psychological barrier results from the attitude that consultants are to be appeased and circumvented. Rather they should be incorporated with other team members in order to be viewed as the "skilled helpers" on the team (Egan 1986:4-55).

Another group that are very much a part of the team are the supporters, those who provide the expertise and funds necessary to get the job done. On the field are the artists, computer specialists, pilots, printers, and technicians of all types, not only doing their job but praying and encouraging local groups as best they can. In the so-called 'sending nations' are those who pray and provide financial assistance so that the work may go on. Just as the Church is a body and each member has a specific function (I Cor. 12:12-26) so the translation team works together, each with separate functions, producing the end result. Each has a specific ministry within the team and maximizing strengths while minimizing weaknesses together in love is part of the great commission (I Cor. 12:27-31).

THE CHANGING SCENE OF GLOBAL MISSION

As we look at the world, we see some significant changes in the last twenty years; increasing nationalism, space-age communication and technological advances have produced radical socio-cultural change. O'Collins notes three major stages in a progression from colonial to post-colonial.

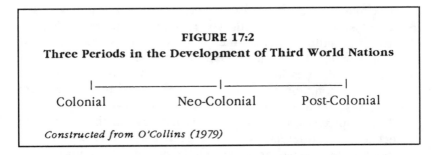

FIGURE 17:2
Three Periods in the Development of Third World Nations

Colonial   Neo-Colonial   Post-Colonial

Constructed from O'Collins (1979)

The colonial period can be characterized by outsiders imposing their ways on others. Imperialism and a desire to do things *for* people was the prevailing attitude. Finances largely came from outside the context but were often a product of export items used to benefit the colonizing nation. With respect to missions, personnel came to bring the gospel to poor benighted heathen who had no other way to know the truth. Education, medicine, and services of all types were provided in the hope that nationals would ultimately learn to do it for themselves. Many colonialists, religious and secular alike, meant well and genuinely wanted to help, but did so from their cultural perspective rather than that of the peoples they sought to usher into the modern world. As nationalism and freedom fires began to burn and independence became the order of the day, the colonial empires fell, but the prevailing attitudes changed little.

The neo-colonial era is characterized by nationals maintaining expatriate methodologies and attitudes. Though carried out by nationals, styles of government, education, medicine, and missions continued much as before; only the faces changed. I am always amused when I see a picture of my friend Chief Justice Sir Buri Kidu in his white powdered wig presiding over the Supreme court of Papua New Guinea. I smile when I hear parliamentarians discuss on which side of the aisle they are sitting. These traditions are not wrong, in fact, they help create an identity within a long tradition. They are, however, a part of colonialism rather than the indigenous context of the new nation. Within the church, the buildings, styles of worship, and presentations of the gospel message are still much as they were before independence and nationalization.

The post-colonial period is characterized by nationals doing things their own way. As Bernard Narokobi maintains, change is necessary for relevance, there need to be appropriate forms in order to elicit appropriate responses. People need to understand the "Melanesian way" and utilize Melanesian principles to rule their lives as well as their nation and their church (Narokobi 1981). Only as this happens will peoples and nations be free, able to develop their own identity and project an image that is distinctive in an ever-changing world. Basic worldview differences must be considered and taken seriously especially as expatriates work cross-culturally. The emphasis is on working *with* the people, so they may realize their God given potential.

E. Stanley Jones has drawn on the language of developmental psychology to discuss relationships between missionaries and the church in India. He uses the terms 'dependent', 'independent' and 'interdependent' to describe this progression away from colonialism. A post-colonial mission program should emphasize interdependence with the initiative coming from those who will benefit, i.e. the local church and individuals who need Scripture for the nourishment of their faith (Jones 1957:211-215).

FIGURE 17:3
A Comparison of Terms

O'Collins	*Jones*
COLONIAL	DEPENDENT
NEO-COLONIAL	INDEPENDENT
POST-COLONIAL	INTERDEPENDENT

Several recent books have influenced our understanding of world-wide changes. Alvin Toffler's *Third Wave* puts into perspective many current events. Recognizing that all cultures are in transition and knowing how these affect the various culture types as well as whole nations at different stages of development is helpful as we work in those contexts. John Naisbitt's *Megatrends* points to key changes that are shaping the world we all live in. Being aware of how these trends affect business, missions, and politics is crucial for the implementation of appropriate strategies for development and change. As Goodenough noted twenty five years ago, there must be "cooperation in change" (Goodenough 1963).

DEVELOPING NATIONAL TRAINING PROGRAMS

Despite the move away from colonialism, the need for idiomatic translations of Scripture has not diminished. Many people feel the need of Scripture in their own language. Too long they have struggled with a trade language Bible and found it inadequate. They hunger for an understanding of what God says to them, and they are often willing to work hard to obtain it. Not only must the gospel message be transculturated as discussed in chapter 15, but so must the process by which Scripture is made available (chapter 16).

A key post-colonial need paralleling the colonial era is for idiomatic translation of the Scriptures which can provide models for human interaction with God. The methods for the provision of vernacular Scripture, however, should parallel socio-political changes taking place throughout the world. Hence the entire process is now under review: translator training and roles, relationships with churches and local believers, and technical assistance of all types. Nationals must be encouraged to function in ways that will be most advantageous to their specific context and seek, from expatriates, assistance and perspective not available in that context. Of far greater importance than apparent 'independence,' is the 'interdependence' that comes from cooperation and mutual respect.

As churches and people groups have recognized the need for Scripture in their own language, so they also recognize the necessity of being involved in producing it. The Bible Societies and the Summer Institute of Linguistics have been, in recent years, besieged to assist in developing national training programs. Initially courses followed expatriate training models—emphasizing linguistic analysis and translation principles. Yet the people who were taking these courses planned to translate within their own language and culture (E_1). They knew the receptor context. What they severely lacked, was the very thing the training courses assumed, Biblical background. Hence, courses became increasingly focused on teaching about Biblical cultures, and giving instruction in Biblical languages and interpretation. The focus for the national translator is largely the reverse of an expatriate translator. As outsiders focus on understanding the receptor context, so those who are insiders need to understand and place an emphasis on the source context. Appreciating this difference is essential for an effective program of national training—developing skills with respect to the source which can combine with inside knowledge to effectively communicate within a particular language and culture.

Learning Styles

Communication and learning styles are critical when training nationals the concepts of Bible translation (or any other discipline). Western styles of learning are often quite distinct from those of other peoples. Learning by example, inductively, is different from a more direct, deductive, approach (Harris 1980). This implies that working through a passage and handling the problems as they develop may be a better teaching/learning technique than presenting all the problems in a categorized list complete with definitions, analytical procedures, and alternative solutions. It also suggests that passages selected for teaching translation principles should be carefully chosen for the problems they contain.

The particular principles needed to solve specific translation problems can be made the focus of a lesson or entire seminar / workshop. These principles combined with an experiential component (the actual translation of passages containing the problem in focus and reinforcement through translation in the field) provide a useful model (Barnwell 1981). Therefore, rather than teaching everything a translator needs to know in a few major courses, more specific courses for shorter periods may be necessary for people with experiential learning styles (Sanders 1983). This whole matter of how people learn and how to apply that knowledge to curriculum development is a crucial research concern. We need pedagogical ethnographies, documentation of existing programs, and experiments that integrate local styles. Sanders (1988:111-133) is an attempt in this direction.

Training Materials

If national training programs are going to be taken seriously, and they must, then an area of great concern is the development of materials that meet the needs of those being trained. As we have focused on receptor-oriented communication within the translation task, so we must also pay close attention to the receptors in training, i.e. the trainees. Materials made available in major languages of the world are a great need. At the moment, most materials are only available in English. Some original works are available in major European languages, and some materials have been translated into French for the peoples of West Africa, Portugeuse for students in Brazil and Spanish for the rest of Latin America. However, materials even in these languages are limited. If materials are lacking in these major languages of colonialism, how much greater is the problem for the major languages of the world. Virtually nothing exists in Swahili, Hindi, Chinese, or Neo-Melanesian (which unites people who speak over 1000 languages). Such an endeavor, of course, needs to be accomplished by speakers of these languages working closely with consultants who are familiar with the concepts and principles that need to be communicated. Each region of the world reflects specific styles, interests and concerns that should be reflected in training. This is a major challenge that calls for a considerable amount of effort in the immediate future. For national training to become effective and provide the personnel necessary to translate Scripture for the thousands of people groups that need it, there must be a major thrust to provide the materials necessary for that training.

Nearly all the translation agencies around the world are now becoming involved in the training of national translators. The Bible Societies and Living Bibles International have basic training syllabi for adaptation as necessary for specific training needs (Loewen 1981). Most of the training materials to date, however, have been produced in English by expatriates e.g. Loewen's materials for teaching translation principles in West Africa (Loewen 1973). In her work as a translation consultant for the Nigerian Bible Translation Trust, Barnwell has produced simplified Semantic Structural Analyses to help African translators solve exegetical problems (Barnwell 1984). Courses have been taught in Papua New Guinea since 1978 and extensive teaching materials have been developed for it (Patrick 1983). However, all these are only initial models that point the way for a broad development of materials for and in non-Western languages.

The day must soon come when nationals, familiar with local concerns, languages, and translation issues, will be producing their own materials. This implies a level of training that has prepared them to do this job. The School of World Mission at Fuller Theological Seminary has now established a graduate level Bible Translation program that is dedicated to training and research necessary to provide the background for understanding international concerns and implementing change in the methods and principles used. Many questions remain: How do local leadership styles relate to choosing Bible translators? How can the best people be encouraged to do translation in nations where money and political power are attractive alternatives to the painstaking tasks of a translation project? How do Bible translators fit back into their communities after a period of training? What is the relationship between the churches and Bible translators? These and other questions form the basis of research currently in progress.[2] We are on the verge of an explosion in understanding and appropriating Bible translation to the mission strategy of the Church; a strategy that will carry us into the next century. We need many more like Dr. Frank Oyungu, an African consultant for Living Bibles International, and Dr. Daniel Ajamiseba, teaching linguistics and anthropology to fellow Indonesians.

A group of national leaders from around the world met in the Cameroon in May, 1985. Their purpose was to establish an organization that would facilitate an exchange of information and ideas not previously possible; the National Bible Translation Organizations were born. Such a development points to the way in which Bible translation is changing. Because of increased levels of education and cross-cultural travel, there is a new sense of urgency among nationals who want their churches to grow. Among expatriates there is a conspicuous shift in approach. It is important that we all work together to accomplish this great task for the glory of God.

THE NATURE OF NATIONAL TRANSLATION PROGRAMS

Programs for which MTT are the primary translators may not initially appear much different from previous OTT programs. An expatriate or properly trained national desiring to encourage local translation should begin by carefully choosing an entry language based on socio-linguistic research in a region or language family. As they become involved in language and culture learning they will seek to establish close ties with secular and religious entities and encourage participation by individuals who desire to see vernacular Scripture made available.

The Local Level

As discussed in chapter 16, translators should try to encourage as much regional and local participation as possible. As the churches appoint or provide translators, local training programs and an assessment of skills and needs should be included in program development. Close interaction within a language family brings together people with common interests and concerns. Due to their geographical proximity the OTT who initiated the process can hold training seminars, and participating MTT can encourage each other in their various projects. To have such interaction, outsiders need some grasp of the linguistic features of the languages in a region, should be able to discuss translation problems in a language mutually intelligible to all within that region, and be available to help individual MTT when problems arise. Rather than working in-depth on one translation, they can thereby assist many MTT, consulting on a broad scale in several languages.

However, it must be clear, this is not a matter of outsiders moving up a translation hierarchy to be replaced by nationals at the local level. This is not vertical status climbing (advising/consulting is not better than translating), but horizontal diversification —building a broader translation base. It is a team effort, each member providing expertise necessary to produce a more effective final product. Just as OTT could not work without the assistance of local helpers, so MTT need the assistance of advisors and consultants who have access to a wider range of source materials. Outside translators should become servant consultants who work closely with inside translators. This is a significant role change in keeping with socio-political changes the world over. Figure 17:4 helps explain the interdependence of translators and consultants. At the local level, there is an increasing number of translators working in their own languages. While they may not have had extensive Western educational opportunities, they are committed Christians, members of local churches who are well respected within the society. Training programs (perhaps using a trade language) serve to develop their understanding of translation to a level that advisors are able to work with them to provide quality translations. Keeping our discussion of cultural distance in mind (chapter 12), these MTT are often the best ones to provide Scripture for their own people.[3]

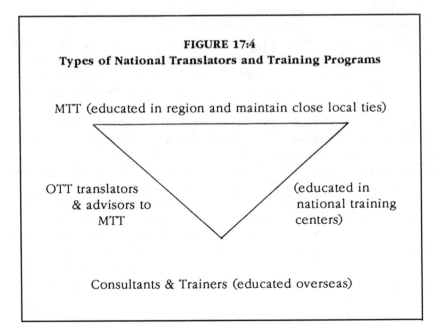

FIGURE 17:4
Types of National Translators and Training Programs

MTT (educated in region and maintain close local ties)

OTT translators
& advisors to
MTT

(educated in
national training
centers)

Consultants & Trainers (educated overseas)

The National Level

While a large number of MTT provide the village-based task force, other types of programs are also necessary. OTT who receive training in national seminaries or special courses designed to develop pastoral or translation skills should be encouraged to work closely with the MTT. In fact, there is an increasing demand for their services. Such training is now being provided under the auspices of institutions such as Union Biblical Seminary in India, the Philippine Normal College in Manila and the Associacao Linguistica Evangelica Missionaria in Brazil (to name only a few examples). Most of these trainees plan to work in languages other than their own, but in a similar context, i.e. in an E_2 environment. At the same time they can assist MTT in the region by providing Biblical background and exegetical help as well as expertise in translation principles.

The International Level

Beyond this small, but increasing, group of nationals translating in languages other than their own are individuals with special consultant, advisory and leadership skills who need training overseas. These selected few should train in contexts that will help them develop their skills. Keeping the particular needs of their nations in focus, they should research ways that will enhance translation in those contexts. Courses should be designed to assist them in acquiring cultural and linguistic awareness, Biblical background, leadership skills and translation methods, principles, and theory. These individuals will become the experts on the team, trained to train others, able to consult at all levels, and have the national perspective within which local programs can develop and flourish in a coordinated manner.

Led by the School of World Mission, courses are being offered at Biola University, Asbury Seminary, and several Bible Colleges in the U.S. and Europe. Through on-campus and extension courses, as well as in-service training, national leaders have an increasing opportunity to obtain the skills necessary to develop programs at all levels within their own nations or the regions in which they serve.

An Integrated Program

Grimes (1974) has adapted a marketing model that is helpful to us. He notes an optimal region within which distribution from a center is effective. Beyond a certain radius efficiency decreases and another center is necessary. He relates this to the linguistic similarity between dialects, but the principle applies to translation as well. In the model developed here, a large group of locally based translators supervised by less local, but understanding, advisors who, in turn, are assisted by highly trained consultants, maximizes the effectiveness of personnel and skills within a region. Their contiguity assists in the administration, technical support and mutual encouragement necessary to accomplish the job. The Bible Translation Association project in the Admiralty Islands of Papua New Guinea is one example of such a program. Four strategically placed OTT have the potential to reach 28 languages (Martin 1982).

Programs of this nature are beginning to appear in parts of Africa, Latin America, the Philippines and Papua New Guinea. Each national context will demand a shift in focus or a reorganization of the model to fit the particular needs and concerns of its situation. This is as it should be. Top level consultants, regardless of their national origin, should become sufficiently bonded to the region and be able to work with people from all sectors to establish the best possible way to make Scripture available.

Besides acting as resident "information specialist" (to borrow a term from Naisbitt) non-local translators/advisors can be of great encouragement and assistance in numerous ways. Developing cultural awareness and interacting within a community of languages, these assistants can encourage transculturation and incorporate the Christian message in relevant forms and styles so they apply to people's daily lives. Maintaining a sensitivity to both the source and receptor, these specialists can encourage local congregations to determine the manifestations of Scriptural meaning within their specific communities. They can encourage Bible study and assist in the technical process of producing an alphabet, printing Scripture, and making adjustments to the changing world. They can also encourage exploring the adaptation of Scripture into communication styles the audience best understands. To be sure, these are significant role changes from the traditional approach to Bible translation. But they are changes

necessitated by modernity and the recognition that interdependence is a more effective strategy than either dependence or
independence. Together we need to "love one another warmly as
Christian brothers, and be eager to show respect for one another"
(Rom. 12:10).

THE DYNAMIC WORD OF GOD

Translated Scripture that becomes a part of the local community gives people a clear choice as it brings God's Word through
meaningful thought forms. People must grapple with Scripture as
it confronts their worldview. Where there is contrast between
God's way and their way, people must determine who their
master will be—where they will place their allegiance. When the
Holy Spirit enables people to make those decisions, based on a
knowledge of Scripture and cultural patterns, the change that
results will be understood and more easily communicated to
others. Such change is far more meaningful than decisions based
on what an outsider has encouraged (Shaw 1981b).

Vernacular Scriptures act as the foundation upon which the
local church can grow. As long as individuals are dependent on
other people or languages for their knowledge about God,
Christian development will be less dynamic. People need to
develop a relationship with God based on understanding Him in
relation to themselves and their culturally determined needs. This
can happen much more effectively as Scripture is available for
every context of life. A reduction of syncretism and doctrinal error
should result. Out of this understanding comes a natural sharing
of the Word with others, often in a communal context that
demands consensus as discussed in chapter 5. Available Scriptures
help people more effectively communicate their faith to others
and the church begins to grow.

Scripture in the language of the people also alleviates the
present world-wide trend toward nominalism. As relevant translations are made available, people will see God in forms that are
familiar to them while understanding God's intended meaning.
Churches based on antiquated (or inadequate) trade language
translations tend to be formalized and without meaning to those
who worship. While those Scriptures may have been dynamic for
the original audience, the current generation reflects significant
socio-political change. To keep pace with these changes, people

must be encouraged to revise existing Scripture. Through revision, Scripture has a better chance of being the dynamic Word of God. Just as new versions proliferate in English, largely as a response to continuing scholarship and language change, so regular revisions are necessary for vernacular translations (Niyang 1987).

In this process the members of a vibrant church should be encouraged to develop their own theology—understand God and His word from their own cultural perspective. As pastors and laity develop a theology, it will reflect the issues that are of concern to the culture at large. As they sought answers through their ideology, so now they ask God to assist in their day to day concerns as they live their lives. I recently received a letter from a mission executive requesting information on a "cross cultural commentary". This at once demonstrates the confusion among Westerners and the need to develop post-translation materials for use within the local church. As chapters 14 and 15 demonstrate, the request for a "cross-cultural commentary" is a contradiction of terms. A commentary, by its very nature, relates to interpretation which is always a reflection of a specific worldview. A commentary, like a theology, should discuss cultural interests from God's perspective. Therefore, vernacular commentaries will most help Christians desiring to use a particular translation. This, of course, is a monumental task. Self-theologizing and developing vernacular commentaries can only be a product of people who share a worldview and vernacular Scripture. As this happens people mature in faith, conform to God's standards and the church grows.

CONCLUSION

The rapid growth of Third World cross-cultural missions (Keyes 1981, Pierson 1983) indicates an increasing need for Scriptures in the languages of the world's people. Bible translation methods and principles should be consistently integrated and developed to meet the challenge of an increasingly post-colonial, interdependent, world-wide church. This signals the beginning of an exciting period in which Bible Translation becomes the foundation of the national church in all its manifestations. It allows people the dignity of making decisions for themselves based on an understanding of God's Word.

Every effort should be made to ensure that Third World missions do not repeat their mentor's mistakes: perceiving the mission of the church through their own cultural bias. Pierson notes an unfortunate neo-colonialism in many of these new organizations—imitating those who taught them rather than recognizing the need to impact communities with a gospel that is linguistically and culturally relevant (Pierson 1987:291ff). Some national leaders cannot accept the fact that they too are biased. However, ethnocentrism is a human universal. The focus must be on those who receive the Word (with all its God intended meaning) in their context.

This is an exciting time in missions in general and Bible translation in particular. Those now entering the field have an open door to develop the concepts presented here and communicate them within an ever broadening, interdependent world. We must all cooperate to develop programs that will be of greatest benefit for the Kingdom. It is the great commission that we are about: implementing all possible means to spread the Word and bring all people into the light of the glorious gospel.

Bible translation is one means of spreading this gospel. Like all missionary efforts, however, it must be carried out with an awareness of and a deep sensitivity to the cultural issues involved. As human beings, affected by Adam's fall, we are all culture-bound. By understanding the cultural factors which are so much a part of the human condition, we free ourselves and our message (including Scripture) and thereby allow God to communicate His truth in any context.

It is to freedom of communication that this book is dedicated. It is transculturation we seek. We attempt to free God's Word from cultural bias to the extent that receptors can understand what He says to them within their own cultural bias. In this way the Holy Spirit can guide them into all truth and mold them into the image of the God who is their creator and sustainer. He is their source of power and the origin of their universe. It is to Him they must give honor and glory for ever and ever (Jude 24,25).

Suggested Reading

Nida, E. and W. Reyburn. *Meaning Across Cultures*. Maryknoll, 1981.

Notes

1. In no way is this book a lament for translations that did not take culture seriously. Many good translators have done what has been encouraged here, whether or not they did it consciously. An important part of learning a language is understanding the culture that language represents. By extended cultural immersion and close interpersonal relationships with people, many of the early missionaries and translators developed an awareness that became a natural part of the translation process.

2. Research projects at the SWM include emphasis on training models (Gela 1986), learning styles (Sanders 1988), translation principles (Lim 1986), cultural issues (Popovich 1988), missionary methods affecting Scripture use (Gould 1986 and Niyang 1987), and the impact of Scriptures on Muslims (Leano 1988). This research will provide the books that update this chapter; books that answer some of the questions.

3. This by no means implies that expatriate OTT will no longer be involved as primary translators. As the number of MTT grows, OTT will find themselves working with people in remote areas where the level of education is not sufficient to train people in independent translation skills. Nationals who can take training will, by definition, be from the more sophisticated regions of a nation—areas that have had longer exposure to the rest of the world. Because of their broader experience, they will be able to assist their own people in a way expatriates cannot. As they work in remote areas, expatriates should still encourage heavy local participation in the translation project and train people in that context to develop an on-going translation program within the church.

APPENDIX
Toward Discovering Semantic Structure

This Appendix is designed as a brief introduction to Semantic Structural Analysis (SSA). It is not intended to equip the reader to use the method, only to become aware of its basic features and develop an interest to pursue the subject in greater detail. This material is adapted from SIL materials and is used with the permission of their academic publications department.

THE UNITS OF SEMANTIC STRUCTURE

The Concept

The smallest semantic unit has been called the *concept*. A concept is a recognizable unit of meaning in any given language. Each language has its own unique inventory of concepts, because each culture with its own worldview has a different perception of reality (see discussion in chapter 2). With such diversity, how can concepts be identified?

The concept is often represented by a word but can be any meaningful element such as pluralization, gender, tone or even word order. Each concept is associated with a particular area of meaning which is distinct from that of other concepts in the language. This area of reference is identified more precisely by listing the components of meaning for concepts.

Four Classes of Concepts. It has been suggested that all concepts can be analyzed as belonging to one of four semantic classes (Barnwell 1980:142).

THINGS - This class includes all things or objects, whether tangible or intangible.

e.g. house, tree, man, dog, fire, air, angel, soul, unicorn, fairy, dragon

(This classification makes no judgement on reality or truth. It is nothing more than a conceptual classification.)

EVENTS - This class includes all actions, processes and happenings, including all movements, whether voluntary or involuntary, and also mental processes.

e.g. run, jump, fall, break, write, melt, freeze, know, think, rejoice

ATTRIBUTES - This class includes qualities or quantities of Things, Events or other Attributes.

e.g. red, white, long, cold, quickly, suddenly, twice, two, very, too

RELATIONS - Relational concepts show the meaningful relationships between Things, Events and Attributes. They can also relate larger semantic units. They typically show—

position: in, on, under, behind
direction: toward, away from
time: present, future, past
logical relations: because, if, in order that, etc.

This method of classifying concepts into four semantic classes is discussed by Beekman and Callow (1974:67-69), and by Nida and Taber (1982:37-55). It is further developed by Beekman et. al. (1981:41-52). Beekman and Callow point out that the theory probably first derived from George Campbell's, *The Philosophy of Rhetoric,* first published in 1776.

These semantic classes are regarded as *universal,* i.e. any concepts in all languages can be classified in this way. This is in contrast to grammatical classes which must be defined for each language individually, according to the particular grammatical patterns of that language: again the deep structure/surface structure principle applies.

The Relationship Between Semantic
Classes and Grammatical Classes

Although semantic classes are quite distinct from grammatical classes, there is some kind of fit between them. In the simplest, basic form of most languages:

THING concepts are expressed by NOUNS or PRONOUNS
EVENT concepts are expressed by VERBS
ATTRIBUTE concepts are expressed by ADJECTIVES or
    ADVERBS
RELATIONAL concepts are expressed by CONJUNCTIONS,
    PREPOSITIONS, ORDER, etc.

In most languages there is the possibility of considerable skewing between these semantic concepts and the surface level grammatical functions. Though events are usually expressed by verbs, in English they can also be represented in a nominalized form such as faith, hope and love. If these are recast to convey the event meaning, the author's intent often becomes clearer (Barnwell 1980:141-144).

e.g. James 4:9 Let your *laughter* be turned to *mourning* —>
              Don't laugh any more; instead, begin to mourn.

The Proposition

It is especially helpful to discover the underlying *event* concepts in a text because each *event* acts as the nucleus of a proposition. Furthermore, it is comparatively easier to identify the *event* concepts in a discourse. Because of the complexity of the semantic structure of languages, it is not easy to identify the concepts in a discourse, or to free one's mind of the surface forms in order to discern the deep structure, the semantic relations as distinct from the grammatical forms. Therefore, the identification of *event* concepts provides a useful starting point.

After identifying each concept in a text, pull out all the event concepts and list them with their respective participants and other material necessary to bring out the meaning (implied information, background material, emotive force, connotation, etc.). These events,with their attendant information, are the kernels or propositions that cluster to develop the discourse.

A proposition has been defined as the smallest unit of communication. In other words, it is the smallest unit of language which actually says something about something. Concepts have semantic meaning but it is only when they are brought into relationship with other concepts that meaningful communication occurs.

A proposition is a semantic unit that may be expressed by many different grammatical surface forms, for example:

the boy grows
the growing boy
the growth of the boy
the boy's growth.

These different forms all represent the same meaning and demonstrate the skewing effect of grammar (Barnwell 1980:159, 160).

Propositions fill two primary functions within a discourse: develop the story line, argument, etc. of the author or support it. As Beekman and Callow state:

> The semantic unit developed or supported may be a supported proposition within a paragraph, the theme of a paragraph, or the theme of a group of paragraphs. Propositions which develop a semantic unit are *developmental propositions* and are of equal rank semantically within the discourse.
>
> Support propositions sustain associative relations to the proposition they support. In this respect they differ from developmental propositions which are linked together by sharing the same relation. Also, a support proposition is considered to be of unequal rank relative to the [developmental] proposition [it supports].
>
> Support propositions may be classified on the basis of their semantic function in a discourse. There are three functions, as follows:

1. The support proposition *clarifies* another proposition by explaining or highlighting it.
2. The support proposition *argues* for another proposition by giving its logical antecedent or consequent.
3. The support proposition *orients* another proposition by giving its setting relative to time or space or other Events. *(Beekman and Callow 1974:288-290).*

THE ORGANIZATION OF SEMANTIC STRUCTURE

Relations Between Propositions

Propositions cluster together in a variety of relations to form larger units of communication. In a longer discourse, each cluster of propositions is further related to other clusters in a hierarchy of layered semantic groupings.

The term 'communication unit' is used to describe clusters at any level. The particular communication units needed to describe a discourse will depend on the nature of the individual discourse type the author used to communicate the message.

There is a limited number of relations between propositions and/or larger communication units. These relationships pertain to the type of propositional function (development or support) and the discourse type (chronological or non-chronological). About forty different relations have been distinguished and much research is now in progress in order to refine the classifications. Figure A:1 summarizes the organization of the most common relationships which serve to structure the propositions and larger semantic units within a discourse.

These relations are universal in the sense that every language has ways of expressing them. However, the particular grammatical forms by which the relations are signalled will, of course, vary widely from language to language (Barnwell 1980:177).

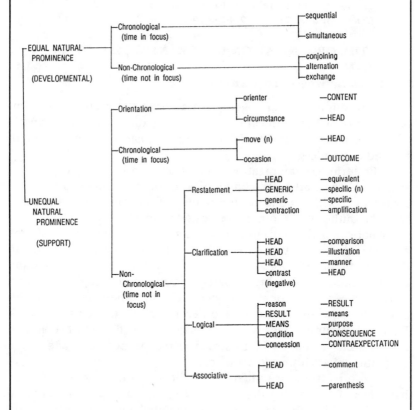

FIGURE A:1
Summary Chart of Semantic Relationships

Relations between propositions, or between larger communication units.

These relations are given in the usual order in which
they are most commonly found in New Testament Greek.

Adapted from Beekman, et. al., 1981:112

Rules for Propositional Displays

Inasmuch as semantic meaning must be conveyed via a linguistic structure, we cannot have a completely grammar-free semantic description. However, to the extent possible, we want to reduce the skewing between the deep structure and its surface manifestations. To do this, a list of rules has been developed.

1. Grammatical and Semantic classes must match
   Things/objects = nouns or pronouns
   Events = Verbs
   Attributes = adjectives or adverbs
   Relationals = conjunctions, prepositions, word order, case markers, etc.
2. Use the finite form of the verb.
3. The natural topic is placed in the subject position of the clause.
4. All obligatory roles for any event concept are stated.
5. State all the implied information such as point of similarity in similes and metaphors and unstated elements of figures of speech.
6. Use only primary senses of words used to verbalize a semantic notion, not secondary or figurative meanings.
7. All figures of speech should be expressed non-figuratively.

THE MEANING OF SEMANTIC STRUCTURE

How to Use the Semantic Relations Chart

1. Start at the left hand side of Figure A:1 and ask a series of questions of the propositions or text clusters that have been isolated.

   (a) Are these units of 'equal prominence' or does one 'support' the other? If equal move to that portion of the chart and ask the next question moving to the right.

   (b) Are these development propositions chronological or non-chronological in relation to each other? Having answered that question again move to the right and ask questions which follow.

(c) Are these units in a time sequence or simultaneous time relationship to each other (if chronological) or in a conjoining, alternation or exhange relationship (if non-chronological).

2. Continue this same process for propositions in a support relationship to developmental units. Determine if they serve to orient, or are chronological or non-chronological. Move to the appropriate position in the chart to determine the specific ways the proposition or cluster relates to those it supports, e.g. restating, clarifying, developing logic, or associating in some way (Shaw 1988:49,50).

Steps for Doing a Propositional Analysis

1. Identify the structural semantic elements - T.E.A.R.
2. Pull out the Events.
3. Fill in the Participants and other necessary information (implied information, figures of speech, etc.). Much of this material is cultural in nature.
4. State the Propositions and cluster them semantically.
5. Determine the relationships between the propositions.
6. Diagram the propositional relationships.
7. Restate with the Receptor language in mind—relate the meaning back into a living socio-linguistic context. This is called an *auxiliary translation.*

Following these steps, and thereby developing an exegetical process, will assist translators in handling a text first hand. It will also help them use a prepared SSA to further exegete a given passage. The use of this approach can make a significant difference in the way material is communicated within the translation context.

The process focuses on the source (except for the last step), eliminating (to the extent possible) the translator's biases. Everything up to the auxiliary translation is exegesis. The last step applies this understanding to the receptor context, providing a hermeneutic essential for communication. This is where transculturation takes place, affirming linguistic and cultural forms specific to the new audience while ensuring that meaning intended by the source is communicated. Most of the concerns raised in this book are designed to ensure this last step takes place—that receptors understand and appreciate source meaning while recognizing that those meanings require specific, cultural responses with respect to the ultimate source of the message: God.

BIBLIOGRAPHY

```
ABBREVIATIONS USED IN BIBLIOGRAPHY

FTS —    Fuller Theological Seminary. Pasadena, CA.
NOT —    Notes On Translation, A publication of Wycliffe
         Bible Translators.
PA —     Practical Anthropology
PNG —    Papua New Guinea
SIL —    Summer Institute of Linglustics, Dallas, TX.
SWM —    School of World Mission, at Fuller Theological
         Seminary, Pasadena, CA.
TBT —    The Bible Translator, A publication of the
         United Bible Society.
TNN —    Theology News and Notes. A Quarterly
         Publication of Fuller Theological Seminary.
UBS —    United Bible Society, Leiden, London, New York.
UTA —    University of Texas at Arlington, Arlington, TX.
WBT —    Wycliffe Bible Translators, Huntington Beach, CA.
```

Aldrich, Joseph C.
1981   *Life-Style Evangelism: crossing traditional boundaries
        to reach the unbelieving world.* Portland: Multnomah
        Press.

Allen, Roland.
1913   *Missionary Methods: St. Paul's or ours?* New York:
        Fleming H. Revell.

Anderson, Francis I.
1969   Isrealite Kinship Terminology and Social Structure *TBT*
        20:29-39.

Bailey, Kenneth E.
1983   *Poet and Peasant and Through Peasant Eyes: a litera-ry-cultural approach to the parables in Luke.* Grand Rapids: Eerdmans.

Bakke, Raymond and Vinay Samuel (eds.)
1985   *Evangelizing World Class Cities: ministries and models for leadership training.* Overseas Crusade.

Barnett. Homer G.
1953   *Innovation: the basics of culture change.* New York: McGraw-Hill.

Barnwell, Katharine
1980   *Introduction to Semantics and Translation.* Second Edition. Horsley's Green: SIL.

1981   *Translation Consultant Training Seminar.* Syllabus, Juba: SIL.

1984   *Translator's Notes for African Translators.* Unpublished Materials. Dallas: SIL.

Beekman, John
1952   The Value of Using Several Translation Helpers. *TBT* 3:24-25.

1965   General Procedures for Bible Translation Among Aboriginals. *Notes on Translation With Drills.* Santa Ana: SIL. pp. 11-38.

1981a   The Selection, Training, and Evaluation of Translation Consultants. *NOT* 84:2-15.

1981b   Different Working Relationships with a Mother-Tongue Speaker in a Translation Program. *NOT* 85:2-8

Beekman, John and John Callow.
1974   *Translating the Word of God.* Grand Rapids: Zondervan Publishing House.

Beekman, John, John Callow and Michael Kopesec
1981   *The Semantic Structure of Written Communication.* Dallas: SIL.

Bellah, Robert N. and Richard Madsen, William Sullivan, Ann Swidler, and Steven Tipton
1986   *Habits of the Heart: individualism and commitment in American life.* New York: Harper and Row.

Benedict, Ruth.
1934   *Patterns of Culture.* Boston: Houghton.

Bohannan, Paul J.
1971   Dyad Dominance and Household Maintenance. *Kinship and Culture.* Francis L. K. Hsu, (ed.). Chicago: Aldine. pp.42-65.

Bohannan, Paul and John Middleton (Eds.)
1968a   *Kinship and Social Organization.* Garden City: Natural History Press.

1968b   *Marriage, Family and Residence.* Garden City: Natural History Press.

Booth, Henry K.
1933   *The World of Jesus: a survey of the background of the Gospels.* New York: Charles Scribners Sons.

Brewster, E. Thomas and Elizabeth S.
1976   *Language Acquistion Made Practical: field methods for language learners (LAMP).* Colorado Springs: Lingua House.

1982   *Bonding and the Missionary Task.* Pasadena: Lingua House.

1983   *Language Exploration and Acquisition Resource Notebook.* Pasadena: Lingua House.

Brown, Dennis Edward, Ed.
1983   *Worldview and Worldview Change: a reader.* Pasadena: FTS.

Bush, Fredrick and James Butler
1985   *The Pentateuch.* Course Syllabus, Pasadena: FTS.

Cairns, David
1953   *The Image of God in Man.* New York: Philosophical Society.

Callow, Kathleen
1974   *Discourse Considerations in Translating the Word of God.* Grand Rapids : Zondervan Publishing House.

Campbell, George
1963   *The Philosophy of Rhetoric.* Reprint. Lloyd F. Bitzer (ed). Carbondale : Southern Illinois University Press. (First printing, 1776.)

Casagrande, Joseph B. and Kenneth L. Hale.
1967   Semantic Relationships in Papago Folk Definitions. *Studies in Southwestern Ethno-linguistics.* The Hague : Mouton and Co.

Chafe, Wallace L.
1970   *Meaning and the Structure of Language.* Chicago : University of Chicago Press.

Clinton, J. Robert
1977   *Interpreting the Scriptures : figures and idioms.* Pasadena : Barnabas Resources.

Cohen, Bob
1987   They Speak in Other Tongues. *People of Destiny,* Vol. 5, No. 3, pp. 24, 29.

Cohen, R and J. Middleton, (Eds.)
1967   *Comparative Political Systems.* Garden City : Natural History Press.

Conn, Harvie M.
1987   *A Clarified Vision for Urban Mission : dispelling the urban stereotypes.* Grand Rapids : Zondervan.

Cowan, George
1979   *The Word that Kindles : people and principles that fueled a worldwide translation movement.* Chappaqua : Christian Herald Books.

Daniel-Rops, Henry
1962   *Daily Life in Palestine at the Time of Christ.* Ann Arbor : Servant Books.

de Vaux, Roland
1961   *Ancient Israel.* New York : McGraw Hill, Two volumes.

Donovan, Vincent J.
1978　　*Christianity Rediscovered: an epistle from the Masai.* Maryknoll: Orbis Books.

Dundes, Alan
1965　　*The Study of Folklore.* Englewood Cliffs: Prentice-Hall.

Durkheim, Emile
1965　　*The Elementary Forms of the Religious Life.* New York: Free Press. (First edition, 1915.)

Dye, Sally F.
1974　　Decreasing Fatigue and Illness in Field-Work. *Missiology* 2:79-109.

1982　　*Strength for the Task: studies on managing stress and illness among missionaries.* M.A. Thesis. Pasadena: SWM.

Dye, T. Wayne
1976　　Toward a Cross-Cultural Definition of Sin. *Missiology* 4:27-41.

1980　　*The Bible Translation Strategy.* Dallas: WBT. (Second Edition, 1985.)

n.d.　　*Three Types of Cultural Systems.* Unpublished Mss. Pasadena: SWM.

Edersheim, Alfred
1976　　*Sketches of Jewish Social Life in the Days of Christ.* Grand Rapids: Eerdmans. Reprinted.

Egan, Gerard
1986　　*The Skilled Helper.* Third Edition. Monterey: Brooks / Cole.

Eliade, Mircea
1964　　*Shamanism: archaic techniques of ecstasy.* Willard R. Trask (trans.). Princeton: Princeton University Press

Fisher, Lawrence E. and Oswald Werner
1978　　Explaining Explanation: tension in American Anthropology. *Journal of Anthropological Research.* 34:194-218.

Foster, George M.
1973　　*Traditional Societies and Technological Change.* New York: Harper & Row. (First edition, 1962.)

Foxe, John
1926   *Fox's Book of Matryrs.* Chicago : The John Winston Co.

Frazer, James G.
1933   *The Fear of the Dead in Primitive Religion.* London :
        Macmillan.

Fry, Euan
1979   An Oral Approach to Translation. *TBT* 30 :214-217.

Geertz, Clifford
1973   *The Interpretation of Culture: selected essays.* New
        York : Basic Books.

Gela, David
1985   Cultural Factors Reaction Paper. Unpublished mss.
        SWM.

1986   *An Analytical Study of the National Translators and
        Literacy Training Program: Papua New Guinea.* M.A.
        Thesis. Pasadena: SWM.

Gibbs, Eddie
1982   *I Believe in Church Growth.* Grand Rapids : Eerdmans
        Publishing Company.

Gill, Jerry H.
1981   *On Knowing God: new directions for the future of
        theology.* Philadelphia : Westminister.

Gilliland, Dean S.
1984   *Pauline Theology and Mission Practice.* Grand Rapids :
        Baker Book House.

Glasser, Arthur F. and Donald A. McGavran
1983   *Contemporary Theologies of Mission.* Grand Rapids :
        Baker Book House.

Goodenough, Erwin R.
1953   *Jewish Symbols in the Greco-Roman Period.* Bolligen
        Series xxxvii. New York : Pantheon Books.

Goodenough, Ward H.
1956   Componential Analysis and the Study of Meaning.
        Language 32 :195-216.

1957   Cultural Anthropology and Linguistics. *Report of the Seventh Annual Round Table Meeting on Linguistics and Language Study.* Monograph Series on Languages and Linguistics, No. 9. Paul Garvin, (ed). Washington, D.C. : Georgetown University Press. pp. 167-173.

1963   *Cooperation in Change.* New York : Russell Sage Foundation.

1965   Rethinking 'Status' and 'Role'. *The Relevance of Models for Social Anthropology.* Association of Social Anthropology Monograph 1 London : Tavistock, pp.1-24.

1970   *Description and Comparison in Cultural Anthropology.* Chicago : Aldine.

Gottwald, N. K.
1979   *The Tribes of Yahweh: a sociology of the religion of liberated Israel, 1250-1050 BC.* Maryknoll : Orbis Books.

Gould, Sydney W.
1986   *Missionary Strategy and Scripture Reception: a case study among the Huli of Papua New Guinea.* M.A. Thesis. Pasadena: SWM.

Grimes, Barpara F. (ed.)
1984   *Ethnologue: languages of the world.* (tenth edition). Dallas : WBT.

Grimes, Joseph
1974   Dialects as optional communication networks. *Language.* 50 :260-269.

Grunlan, Stephen A. and Marvin K. Mayers
1979   *Cultural Anthropology: a Christian perspective.* Grand Rapids : Zondervan.

Guli, John
1984   The Book of Ruth in Higi. Unpublished mss. Pasadena: SWM.

Hadas, Moses
1959   *Hellenistic Cultures: fusion and diffusion.* New York : Norton.

Hagner, Donald A.
1973   *The Use of the Old and New Testaments in Clement of Rome.* Supplements to Novum Testamentum, Leiden: E.J. Brill.

Hall, Edward T.
1959   *The Silent Language.* New York: Doubleday and Company.
1976   *Beyond Culture.* Garden City: Anchor Press/Doubleday.

Hammond, Peter
1964   *Cultural and Social Anthropology: selected readings.* New York: Macmillan.

Harris, Marvin
1968   *The Rise of Anthropological Theory.* New York: Thomas Y. Crowell.

Harris, Stephen
1980   *Culture and Learning.* Darwin: Northern Territory Department of Education.

Headland, Thomas N.
1974   Anthropology and Bible Translation. *Missiology* 11:411-419.

Hengle, Martin
1974   *Judaism and Hellenism: the message, form and background of the Old Testament.* Grand Rapids: Eerdmans.

Hesselgrave, David J.
1978   *Communicating Christ Cross-Culturally.* Grand Rapids: Zondervan.

Hiebert, Paul G.
1982a   The Flaw of the Excluded Middle. *Missiology* 10:35-47.
1982b   The Bicultural Bridge. *Mission Focus* 10:1-6.
1983   *Cultural Anthropology.* Second Edition. Grand Rapids: Baker Book House.
1985   *Anthropological Insights for Missionaries.* Grand Rapids: Baker Book House.
1986   *Phenomenology and Institutions of Folk Religions.* Course Syllabus, Pasadena: SWM.

Hoebel, E.A.
1954   *The Law of Primitive Man: a study in comparative dynamics.* Cambridge : Harvard University Press.

Hogbin, Ian and C.H. Wedgwood
1953   Local Grouping in Melanesia. *Oceania* 23 :241-276; 24 :58-76.

Hsu, Francis L. K.
1971   Hypothesis on Kinship and Culture. *Kinship and Culture.* F.L.K. Hsu (ed.), Chicago : Aldine. pp. 3-29.

Johnson, Aubrey Rodway
1964   *The Vitality of the Individual in the Thought of Ancient Israel.* Cardiff : University of Wales Press.

Jones, E. Stanley
1957   Three Stages to Maturity. *Christian Maturity.* Nashville : Abingdon. pp.211-215.

Jordan, Clarence
1970   *The Cotton Patch Version . . .* New Century Publishers.

Kearney, Michael
1984   *World View.* Novate : Chandler & Sharp Publishers.

Keesing, Felix
1958   *Cultural Anthropology.* New York : Holt, Rinehart & Winston.

Keesing, Roger
1975   *Kin Groups and Social Structures.* New York : Holt, Rinehart and Winston.

Keirsey, David and Marilyn Bates
1978   *Please Understand Me: character and temperament types.* Del Mar : Prometheus Nemesis.
Kelsey, Morton T.
1984   *Companions on the Inner Way: the art of spiritual guidance.* New York : Crossroad.

Keyes, Lawrence
1981   The New Age of Missions: third world missions.
         *Perspectives on the World Christian Movement: a read-
         er.* R.D. Winter and S.C. Hawthorne (eds.). Pasadena:
         William Carey Library. pp.754-762.

Kiki, Albert Maori
1968   *Ten Thousand Years in a Lifetime: a New Guinea
         autobiography.* Brisbane: Cheshire.

King, Roberta
1983   The Nature of Tone and Tune in African Song. Unpub-
         lished mss., SWM.

1987   Say It was a Song. *Impact.* Vol. 44, No. 1. pp. 10, 11.

Kingston, Peter K.E.
1975   The Gospel of Mark: good news or confusion? *NOT*
         57:22-29.

Klem, Herbert V.
1982   *Oral Communication of the Scripture: insights from
         African oral art.* Pasadena: William Carey Library.

Kluchholn, Clyde
1965   *Mirror for Man.* New York: Fawcett World Library.
         (First edition, 1944.)

Kopesec, Michael F.
1980   *A Literary-Semantic Analysis of Titus.* Dallas :SIL.

Kraft, Charles H.
1979   *Christianity in Culture.* Maryknoll: Orbis Books.

1983   *Communication Theory for Christian Witness.* Nash-
         ville: Abingdon.

1986   *Worldview and Worldview Change.* Course Syllabus,
         SWM.

Kraft, Marguerite G.
1978   *Worldview and the Communication of the Gospel.* Pa-
         sadena: William Carey Library.

Kroeber, Alfred Louis
1909   Classificatory Systems of Relationship. *Journal of the Royal Anthropological Institute* 39 :77-84.

Kubo, Sakae and Walter F. Specht
1983   *So Many Versions: 20th century English versions of the Bible*. Grand Rapids: Zondervan.

LaSor, William S, David A. Hubbard and Frederick W. Bush
1982   *Old Testament Survey: the message, form and background of the Old Testament*. Grand Rapids: Eerdmans.

Larson, Mildred L.
1969   Making Explicit Information Implicit in Translation. *NOT*. 33 :15-20.

1975   *A Manual for Problem Solving in Bible Translation*. Grand Rapids: Zondervan.

1984   *Meaning-Based Translation: a guide to cross-language equivalence*. Lanham: University Press of America.

Leaño, Lealani
1987   Translating Names of God among the Kalagan Muslims. Unpublished Mss. Pasadena: SWM.

1988   *Animism Among the Kalagan: its implications for Bible translation*. M.A. Project. Pasadena: SWM.

Leclair and Schnider (eds.)
1968   *Economic Anthropology*. New York: Holt, Rinehart and Winston.

Lim, Guek Eng
1986   *Cognitive Processes and Linguistic Forms in Old Testament Hebrew and Chinese Cultures: implications for translation*. Ph.D. Dissertation. Pasadena: SWM.

Lingenfelter, Sherwood G. and Marvin K. Mayers
1986   *Ministering Cross-Culturally: an incarnational model for personal relationships*. Grand Rapids: Baker.

Loewen, Jacob A.
1964   Culture, Meaning, and Translation. *TBT* 15:189-194.

1971   Form and Meaning in Translation. *TBT* 22(4):169-174.

1973   *Handbook of diagrams for translator training.* Lusaka :
        UBS.

1981   *The Practice of Translating.* London : UBS.

1985   Translating the Names of God. *TBT* 36:201-207.

1986   Which God Do Missionaries Preach? *Missiology* 14 :3-19.

Loewen, Jacob A. and Anne Loewen
1967   The 'Missionary' Role. *PA* 14:193-208.

Macky, Peter W.
1981   Living in the Great Story. *TNN* 12/81:21 - 25.

Mair, Lucy
1965   *An Introduction to Social Anthropology.* London : Ox-
        ford University Press.

Malherbe, Abraham J.
1983   *Social Aspects of Early Christianity.* Philadelphia : For-
        tress Press.

Malina, Bruce J.
1981   *The New Testament World: Insights from Cultural
        Anthropology.* Atlanta : John Knox Press.

Malinowski, Bronislaw
1922   *Argonauts of the Western Pacific.* New York : Dutton.

1954   *Magic, Science, and Religion and other Essays.* Garden
        City : E. P. Dutton and Co.

Martin, William
1982a   Guidelines for National Translator Programs. Unpub-
        lished Mss. Ukarumpa : SIL.

1982b   Manus Bible Translation Strategy : a mutual apprentice-
        ship approach to mother tongue translation. Unpub-
        lished mss. Ukarumpa : SIL.

Mayers, Marvin K.
1987   *Christianity Confronts Culture: a strategy for cross-
        cultural evangelism.* Grand Rapids : Zondervan. (First
        edition, 1974.)

1982   *The Basic Values: a model of cognitive styles for analyz-
        ing human behavior.* La Mirada: Biola University.

McLuhan, Herbert Marshall and Quentin Fiore
1967   *The Medium is the Message.* New York : Bantam Books.

Meeks, Wayne A.
1983   *The First Urban Christians: the social world of the Apostle Paul.* New Haven : Yale University Press.

Meyers, Eric M. and James F. Strange
1981   *Archaeology, The Rabbis, and Early Christianity: the social and historical setting of Palestinian Judaism and Christianity.* Nashville : Abingdon.

Morgan, Lewis H.
1871   *Systems of Consanguinity and Affinity of the Human Family.* Washington D.C. : Smithsonian Contributions to Knowledge.

Murdock, George P.
1949   *Social Structure.* New York : Macmillan.

Murphy-O'Conner, Jerome
1982   *Becoming Human Together: the pastoral anthropology of St. Paul.* Wilmington : Michael Glazier, Inc.

Nadel, S.F.
1942a   *A Black Byzantium: the kingdom of Nupe in Nigeria.* London: Oxford University Press.
1942b   The Hill Tribes of Kadero. *Sudan Notes and Records* 25 :37-79.

Naisbitt, John
1982   *Megatrends: ten new directions transforming our lives.* Warner Communications Company.

Narokobi, Bernard
1981   *The Melanesian Way.* Pt. Moresby : Institute of Papua New Guinea Studies.

Nida, Eugene A.
1947   *Bible Translating.* London : UBS.
1954   *Customs and Cultures.* New York : Harper and Row.
1964   *Toward a Science of Translation.* London : Tavistock.
1984   *Signs, Sense and Translation.* Cape Town : Bible Society of South Africa.

Nida, Eugene A., J.P. Louw, A.H. Snyman and J. W. Cronje
1983   *Style and Discourse.* Cape Town : Bible Society of South
         Africa.

Nida, Eugene A. and William D. Reyburn
1981   *Meaning Across Cultures.* Maryknoll : Orbis Books.

Nida, Eugene A. and Charles R. Taber
1982   *The Theory and Practice of Translation.* Leiden : E.J.
         Brill. (First edition, 1969.)

Niyang, Stephen
1987   The Comparison of Two Translations : literal vs. idioma-
         tic translations in Nigeria. Unpublished mss. Pasadena :
         SWM.

1988   *Factors Affecting the Use of Translations in Northern
         Nigeria.* Th.M Thesis. Pasadena: SWM.

O'Collins, Mave
1979   Social Justice and Neo-Colonialism : implications for
         education and research at the University of Papua New
         Guinea. Inaugural Lecture. Pt. Moresby : University of
         Papua New Guinea.

Olson, Bruce
1978   *Bruchko.* Carol Stream : Creation House.

Opler, Morris F.
1945   Themes as Dynamic Forces in Culture. *American Jour-
         nal of Sociology* 53 :198-206.

Parshall, Phillip
1980   *New Paths in Muslim Evangelism : evangelical ap-
         proaches to contextualization.* Grand Rapids : Baker
         Book House.

Patrick, Heather
1983   The Development of Mother-Tongue Bible Translator
         Training in Papua New Guinea. *NOT* 95 :38-46.

Pasut, Ursula
1983   Working Relationships in Bible Translation. Unpub-
         lished Mss. Pasadena: SWM.

Pierson, Paul E.
1983   *Historical Development of the Christian Movement.*
        Course Syllabus, Pasadena : SWM.

Pike, Kenneth L.
1967   *Language in Relation to a Unified Theory of the
        Structure of Human Behavior.* The Hague : Mouton &
        Co.

1979   Christianity and Culture: incarnation in a culture.
        Journal of the American Scientific Affiliation 31 :92-96.

Pippert, Rebecca M.
1979   *Out of the Salt Shaker and into the World.* Downers
        Grove : InterVarsity Press.

Popovich, Francis B.
1980   *Social Organization of the Maxakali.* M.A. Thesis, UTA.

1988   *Social and Ritual Power in Maxa Kali Society.* Ph.D.
        Dissertation. Pasadena: SWM.

Prost, Gil
1986   A Pauline view of Culture? Unpublished mss. SIL.

Radcliffe-Brown, A. R.
1931   Social Organization of Australian Tribes. *Oceania* 1 :429.

1965   Primitive Law. *Structure and Function in Primitive
        Society.* New York : Free Press. pp.212-219. (First edi-
        tion, 1933.)

Redfield, Robert
1963   *The Primitive World and Its Transformations.* Ithaca :
        Cornell University Press.

Reyburn, William D.
1960   Identification in the Missionary Task. *PA* 7 :1-15.

Richardson, Don
1974   *Peace Child.* Glendale : G.L. Regal Books.

1977   *Richardson - McDonald Discussion.* Unpublished Mss.

1981   *Eternity in Their Hearts.* Ventura : Regal Books.

Rivers, W.H.R.
1914   *The History of Melanesian Society.* Cambridge : Cam-
        bridge University Press.

Robinson, Wheeler
1980   *Corporate Personality in Ancient Israel*. Philadelphia :
         Fortress Press.

Rogerson, John Williams
1979   *Anthropology and the Old Testament*. Atlanta : John
         Knox Press.

Rosman, Abraham and Paula G. Rubel
1978   *Your Own Pigs You May Not Eat : a comparative study
         of New Guinea societies*. Chicago : University of Chica-
         go Press.

Sahlins, Marshall D.
1968   *Tribesmen*. Englewood Cliffs : Prentice-Hall.

Sahlins, Marshall and Elman Service, Eds.
1960   *Evolution and Culture*. Ann Arbor : University of Michi-
         gan Press.

Sanders, Arden G.
1983a   Training Mother-Tongue Translators : designing a begin-
         ning translation course in Melanesia. Unpublished Mss.
         Pasadena: SWM.

1988   *Learning Styles in Melanesia: toward the use and
         implications of Kolb's model for national translator
         training*. Ph.D. Dissertation. Pasadena: SWM.

Scheffler, Harold W. and Floyd G. Lounsbury
1971   *A Study in Structural Semantics : the Siriono kinship
         system*. Englewood Cliffs : Prentice-Hall.

Schieffelin, Edward L.
1971   The Influence of Contact on the Agricultural System of
         the Great Papuan Plateau. Mimio. Bronx : Fordham
         University.

1976   *Sorrow of the Lonely and Burning of the Dancers*. New
         York : St. Martin's Press.

Schusky, Ernest L.
1972   *Manual for Kinship Analysis*. Second Edition. New
         York : Holt, Rinehart & Winston.

Service, Elman R.
1962   *Primitive Social Organization*. New York: Random House.

1968   *Peasants*. Englewood Cliffs: Prentice-Hall.

Sevenster, Jan N.
1968   *Do You Know Greek? How Much Greek Could the First Jewish Christians Have Known?* Leiden: E.J. Brill.

Shacklock, Floyd
1967   *World Literacy Manual*. New York: Committee on World Literacy and Christian Literature.

Shaw, Karen A.
1983   *Samo Grammar Notes*. mss. Ukarumpa: SIL.

Shaw, R. Daniel
1972   The Structure of Myth and Bible Translation. *PA* 19 :129-132.

1973   A Tentative Classification of Languages in the Mt. Bosavi Region. *The Linguistic Situation in the Gulf District and Adjacent Areas, Papua New Guinea*. K. Franklin (ed). Pacific Linguistics, Series C, No. 26. Canberra: Australian National University, pp. 189 - 215.

1974a   Samo Sibling Terminology. *Oceania* 44 :233-239.

1974b   The Geographical Distribution of Samo Relationship Terms. *Kinship Studies in Papua New Guinea*. R.D. Shaw (ed). Ukarumpa: SIL. pp.223-246.

1976   *Samo Social Structure: a socio-linguistic approach to understanding interpersonal relationships*. Pt. Moresby: University of PNG.

1981a   The Good, the Bad, and the Human: Samo spirit cosmology. Paper Delivered. Adelaide: Australian Association for the Study of Religions.

1981b   Every Person a Shaman. *Missiology* 9 :159-165.

1986a   Ethnohistory, Strategy, and Bible Translation: the case of Wycliffe and the cause of world mission. *Missiology* 14 :47-54.

1986b   *Methods and Principles in Translation*. Course Syllabus, MB521. Pasadena: SWM.

n.d.   *Kandila: ceremonialism and interpersonal relation-
          ships among the Samo.* Forthcoming.

Shaw, R. Daniel and Charles H. Kraft
1983   Can Any Good Come out of a Condensed Bible?
          Eternity 34 :2 :28-29.

Shaw, R. Daniel and Karen Shaw
1973   Location: a linguistic and cultural focus in Samo.
          Kivung 6 :158-172.

1977   Samo Phonemes: distribution, interpretation and result-
          ing orthography. *Workpapers in Papua New Guinea
          Linguistics* 19 :97-135.

Schusky, Earnest L.
1965   *Manual For Kinship Analysis.* New York: Holt, Rinehart
          and Winston.

Smith, Donald K.
1971   Your Hands are Deceiving Me. Duplicated. Nairobi:
          Daystar Communications.

Sperber, Dan and Dierdre Wilson
1986   *Relevance: communication and cognition.* Cambridge:
          Harvard University Press.

Spindler, George and Louise (eds.)
—   *Case Studies in Cultural Anthropology.* New York:
          Holt, Rinehart and Winston. Individual ethnographies
          from cultures all over the world written by anthropolo-
          gists who have done research in the featured society.

Spradley, James P.
1979   *Ethnographic Interview.* New York: Holt, Rinehart and
          Winston.

1980   *Participant Observation.* New York: Holt, Rinehart and
          Winston.

Stott, John R., Ed.
1979   *The Gospel and Culture.* Pasadena: William Carey Libra-
          ry.

Strelan, John
1977   *Search for Salvation.* Adelaide: Lutheran House.

Tarn, W.W.
1952   *Hellenistic Civilization*. New York : New Horizon Library.

Taylor, John
1963   *The Primal Vision*. London: SGM Press.

Thielicke, Helmut
1984   *Being Human, Becoming Human: an essay in Christian anthropology*. Trans. by G. W. Bromiley. New York : Doubleday.

Tidball, Derek
1984   *The Social Context of the New Testament: a sociological analysis*. Grand Rapids : Zondervan.

Tippett, Alan Richard
1967   *Solomon Islands Christianity*. London : Lutterworth Press.

1969   *Verdict Theology in Missionary Theory*. Lincoln: Lincoln Christian College Press.

Titiev, Mischa
1960   A Fresh Approach to the Problem of Magic and Religion. *Southwest Journal of Anthropology* 16 :3 :292-298.

Toffler, Alvin
1980   *The Third Wave*. New York : William Morrow and Company.

Tyler, Stephen
1978   *The Said and the Unsaid: mind, meaning and culture*. New York : Academic Press.

Tylor, Sir Edward B.
1891   *Primitive Culture: researches into the development of mythology, philosophy, religion, language, art, and custom*. London : J. Murray.

van Gennep, Arnold
1960   *The Rites of Passage*. M.B. Visedom and G.L. Caffee, translators. Chicago : University of Chicago Press.

Wagner, C. Peter
1983   *On the Crest of the Wave.* Glendale : Regal Books.

Wallace, Anthony F.C.
1956   Revitalization Movements. *American Anthropologist*
        58 :264-281.

Walsh, Brian and J. Richard Middleton
1984   *The Transforming Vision: shaping a Christian world
        view.* Downers Grove: InterVarsity Press.

Werner, Oswald and Martin Topper
1976   On the Theoretical Unity of Ethnoscience Lexicography
        and Ethnoscience Ethnographies. *Semantics: Theory
        and Applications.* Proceedings of the Georgetown Uni-
        versity Round Table on Languages and Linguistics. C.
        Rameh (ed). Washington D.C. : Georgetown University.
        pp. 111-144.

Weymouth, Ross Malcolm
1978   *The Gogodala Society of Papua New Guinea and the
        Unevangelized Fields Mission.* Thesis. Adelaide, South
        Australia : Flinders University.

Whorf, Benjamin L.
1964   *Language, Thought and Reality: selected writings of
        Benjamin L. Whorf.* J.B. Carrol (ed), Cambridge : Massa-
        chusetts Institute of Technology Press.

Wilss, Wolfram
1981   *The Science of Translation: problems and methods.*
        Tubingen : Gunter Narr Verlag.

Wilson, Robert R.
1977   *Genealogy and History in the Biblical World.* New
        Haven : Yale University Press.

1984   *Sociological Approaches to the Old Testament.* Philadel-
        phia : Fortress Press.

Winter, Ralph
1975   The Highest Priority: cross-cultural evangelism. *Let the
        Earth Hear His Voice.* J.D. Douglas (ed). Minneapolis :
        World Wide Publications. pp.213-225.

Winter, Ralph and S.C. Hawthorn, Eds.
1981   *Perspectives on the World Christian Movement: a reader.* Pasadena : William Carey Library.

Wolff, Hans Walter
1981   *Anthropology of the Old Testament.* Philadelphia : Fortress Press.

GENERAL INDEX

AUTHOR INDEX

SCRIPTURE REFERENCE INDEX